teach® yourself

Hinduism
v. p. (hemant) kanitkar
and w. owen cole

For over 60 years, more than
40 million people have learnt over
750 subjects the **teach yourself**
way, with impressive results.

be where you want to be
with **teach yourself**

For UK order enquiries: please contact Bookpoint Ltd, 130 Milton Park, Abingdon, Oxon OX14 4SB. Telephone: +44 (0) 1235 827720. Fax: +44 (0) 1235 400454. Lines are open from 09.00–18.00, Monday to Saturday, with a 24-hour message answering service. Details about our titles and how to order are available at www.teachyourself.co.uk

For USA order enquiries: please contact McGraw-Hill Customer Services, PO Box 545, Blacklick, OH 43004-0545, USA. Telephone: 1-800-722-4726. Fax: 1-614-755-5645.

For Canada order enquiries: please contact McGraw-Hill Ryerson Ltd, 300 Water St, Whitby, Ontario L1N 9B6, Canada. Telephone: 905 430 5000. Fax: 905 430 5020.

Long renowned as the authoritative source for self-guided learning – with more than 30 million copies sold worldwide – the *Teach Yourself* series includes over 300 titles in the fields of languages, crafts, hobbies, business, computing and education.

British Library Cataloguing in Publication Data: a catalogue record for this title is available from The British Library.

Library of Congress Catalog Card Number: on file.

First published in UK 1995 by Hodder Headline, 338 Euston Road, London NW1 3BH.

First published in US 1995 by Contemporary Books, a division of The McGraw-Hill Companies, 1 Prudential Plaza, 130 East Randolph Street, Chicago, IL 60601, USA

The 'Teach Yourself' name is a registered trade mark of Hodder & Stoughton Ltd.

Typeset by Transet Limited, Coventry, England.
Printed in Great Britain for Hodder & Stoughton Educational, a division of Hodder Headline Ltd, 338 Euston Road, London NW1 3BH by Cox & Wyman Ltd, Reading, Berkshire.

Hodder Headline's policy is to use papers that are natural, renewable and recyclable products and made from wood grown in sustainable forests. The logging and manufacturing processes are expected to conform to the environmental regulations of the country of origin.

Impression number   10 9 8 7 6 5 4
Year   2009 2008 2007 2006 2005 2004

contents

acknowledgements

The authors wish to thank Predrag (Prem) Zivkovic for help in typing much of the manuscript, and Dr Helen Kanitkar and Gwynneth Cole, our wives, for their constant support at every stage of writing the book. Mel Thompson, Sue Hart and Sarah Mitchell of Hodder & Stoughton Educational have been very patient and always ready to provide advice when asked. We are grateful to them for their kindness, which exceeded the limits of professionalism.

The friendship of many Hindus in several countries has increased our own understanding of beliefs and practices, which are far too diverse to be encompassed in one book. Nevertheless, we hope that we have not failed them but given the reader helpful and interesting insights into what it means to be a Hindu.

For the new edition

Thanks are due to Mr Tilak Suriya for help in typing much material needed for the updating of the book.

Helen Hart, Katie Roden and Sue Hart have been very patient and ready to discuss the extra material for the new edition.

The authors appreciate all the help received.

Material concerning the Hindu Diaspora is added at the end of Chapter 17, and the bibliography is updated. The new chapter on global Hinduism, which includes latest facts and figures from the Internet, makes this book invaluable for the 21st century.

Photographs

All photographs are reproduced with kind permission of V. P. (Hemant) Kanitkar.

authors' introduction

Hinduism is still a developing, living tradition, one which maintains a capacity to adapt and modify itself according to the needs of its believers and its perceived relevancies to the socio-religious environments in which it functions. Without such adaptability it would have rapidly deteriorated into a cracked, decaying monolith, silent and ineffective, which could have no positive communication with twentieth-century seekers after truth.

In this book we have tried to show the life of Hinduism. This life has its roots in a varied scriptural tradition, encompassing images of God in the *Rig-veda*; the philosophy of rebirth and liberation in the *Upanishads*; the tales of gods and heroes illustrating dharma in the *Mahabharata* and the *Ramayana*; the development of the personal deity in the *Bhagavad-Gita*; and the ideas of worship in the *Puranas*. It nevertheless leaves room for individual and sectarian interpretations, ways of devotion, and recognitions of the Godhead in the forms of Vishnu, Shiva, or Shakti, the Mother Goddess.

The Banyan tree of Hinduism draws from its varied doctrinal roots the energy to nourish the spreading boughs of expression and practice, under the shade of which the varied definitions and experiences of the faith may thrive. It has been suggested that there are as many ideas of Hinduism as there are Hindus, and Hinduism does offer the individual considerable freedom of understanding and worship; but the roots of the *Sanatana Dharma*, the universal rule, or duty, hold firm for all, and secure the life of the faith.

It is this life that we try to show here; we hope that readers will be encouraged to seek out individual Hindus and talk to them about their beliefs and practices; those who do so will not be overwhelmed by variety but enriched by the different experiences that are living Hinduism.

V. P. (Hemant) Kanitkar and W. Owen Cole   June 1995

01

diversity and unity

In this chapter you will learn:
- about a British Hindu boy's sacred thread ceremony
- about the Gayatri Verse used in morning prayers
- about the importance of pilgrimage
- about priests
- about bathing in the Ganges.

'My name is Raj Mohan Joshi and my father's name is Mohan Ganesh Joshi. So my second name is my father's first name, and his second name is my grandfather's first name. Our family name is Joshi, which suggests that one of my ancestors probably worked as a priest in the village in western India from which our family comes.

Hindus in different parts of India follow varied systems of naming individuals.

In northern India, a person's name very often has two parts; the first is his/her personal name, the second is the family name. For example, Ramesh Chatterji, Hemchandra Goswami, Savitri Yadav, Uma Sharma.

In western India a person has three names. The first one identifies the individual, the second one is the father's name and the third is the family name. For example, Saguna Baburao Patil, Ratan Maganlal Shah.

In the south a person has four names. The first initial denotes the village of origin, the second is the father's name, the third is the person's given name and the fourth signifies caste. A famous southern Indian was Sir C. P. Ramaswami Aiyar, Chief Minister of Travancore.

'I was born in north London. My sister Meena was born when I was about four. My sister and I went to the local primary and secondary schools, wore European clothes and spoke English. At home my parents spoke Marathi and I picked up a few sentences, but because of the school work and constant contact with other pupils, we never learned to read and write Marathi. I am now studying for my A levels and hope to do computer science later on. My sister wants to be a doctor if she can get the necessary A levels in science and get admission to a medical college. I was born in Britain and my first language is English, but my skin is brown. When I was seven years old I became the target of name-calling in my school. Many pink-skinned boys and girls used to call me 'you bloody Paki' and say, 'you Paki go home'. When I said, 'I was born here', they used to call me 'a curry-smelling liar'. That experience put me off 'spiced food', so mum prepared sausages and beans for Meena and me, while Mum and Dad ate rice, chapattis and vegetable curry. Sometimes mum prepared chicken curry for dad, sausages or omelette for Meena and me, but she always ate only vegetable dishes.

'Since I was about five or six I have seen Mum doing a *puja* after bathing in the morning. She used to stand before a little shrine which is on a shelf in our kitchen. She would wash little metal statues and dry them, then offer a couple of flowers to the statues. She would light a small lamp and wave it about along with an *agarbatti* (Westeners often call it a joss stick), which had a strong smell. While she was doing puja she said prayers in Marathi that I could not understand. She used to ask me to stand before the statues, joining my hands in front of me, and say, 'Devaa viddya day' (God grant me learning). Then she would give me a sugar crystal from the metal bowl in front of the statues. I didn't really understand how the little statues would give me learning. I was in my primary school where the teacher was helping me to learn to read, write and do sums.

'The name-calling I had suffered at school made me want to find out more about my Indian family and what they believed in. All of us used to visit a temple every Saturday afternoon. My parents used to take some fruit to place before the statue there, put some coins in the gift box and say prayers in Marathi, a language spoken in western India. Meena and I always did our *namaskar* by joining our palms together in front of us and bowing low before the statue.

'Sometimes we visited another temple where there were many statues that looked like men and women, but two statues particularly amused me. One looked like a powerful monkey holding a club and the other was half man-half elephant, sitting on a chair and wearing a golden crown. Dad told me the names of the different statues, but it took me many visits to the temple before I remembered them all. He told me that these statues showed how different people imagined God to be.

'Once we visited a third temple where people said their prayers in a language that Mum and Dad did not understand. Dad said that the language was called Tamil, which was spoken in southern India. (When we got back home I looked at the map of India in the atlas and found the words Tamil Nadu towards the pointed end of the map.) The priest in that temple applied a little ash to my forehead in blessing, but when we visited the temple with many statues (I later learned that they were called Murtis) the *Pandit* there applied a little red powder to my forehead. Dad assured me that God's blessing was the same; only the colour of the powder was different.

'In our school there were boys and girls whose parents had come from India or east Africa. Their parents spoke Gujarati and regularly visited a temple which had a different murti. They said they were also Hindus but went to a temple where the grown-ups spoke Gujarati and the prayers were in Gujarati. There were two boys whose parents spoke Punjabi but one was a Hindu and the other was a Sikh. At that age I found it all very confusing but I accepted my father's assurance that I was a Hindu like all those people who spoke Punjabi, Gujarati or Tamil and went to different temples.

A sacred thread ceremony

'A few months before my eighth birthday dad received a letter from my grandfather who had retired from his teaching job and lived in Pune. The letter said:

> Raj will soon be eight years old; his sacred thread ceremony has to be performed during his eighth year. It would be a good idea if you all came to India for a short break so that our family priest can do the ceremony in our family house, where your younger brother Prakash now lives with his wife and children. Write and tell me in detail what you think of this idea and whether you four can make the journey when the time comes.

'Mum and Dad talked about the letter and the thread ceremony for weeks. Dad spoke to the Pandit in the temple about it.

"Does the ceremony have to be performed only during the eighth year?" he asked the Pandit.

"Strictly speaking, yes, Mr Joshi, but if the circumstances are not favourable, the sacred thread can be performed up to the age of twelve. In any case it should be done before marriage. You see, Mr Joshi", the Pandit went on, "the *upanayana*, which is the ceremony's correct name, is an educational sacrament, and it should be celebrated when the boy reaches an age of understanding. He should be able to learn the Sanskrit mantras when he has reached his eighth year. That is about the time he is beginning to find his school work interesting. If you leave it too late, Raj will have considerable difficulty in learning and reciting the Sanskrit mantras."

"But Panditji," argued my dad, "Raj was born in this country and his first language is English. He is going to be trained in the

English educational system. He doesn't need to learn Sanskrit mantras."

"That is true, Mr Joshi," said the Pandit, "but by experiencing the *upanayana*, Raj will be initiated into the duties and responsibilities of an adult Hindu. Without the sacred thread ceremony, he will be a Hindu in name only, since he was born of Hindu parents."

'Mum and Dad talked some more and decided that my sacred thread would have to wait until I had finished my primary school education. I would still be younger than 12 and my Dad would have time to save money for our trip to India. Then Dad wrote and explained everything to grandfather.

'Three years passed. My last term in primary school came to an end. I was to start secondary school six weeks later. During the summer holidays all four of us had arranged to visit India for my thread ceremony. Dad had booked our flight to Bombay, and because we had British Passports our visas were also arranged in good time. Meena and I were looking forward to our first air journey. We would meet grandfather and grandma for the first time. We were asked to address them as Ajoba and Aji when we met them. We also looked forward to meeting Uncle Prakash – Prakash-kaka, Auntie Leela – Leela-kaku, our cousins Vasant and Gauri, Dad's sister Asha-attya, her husband and their son, Arun. Mum and Dad bought saris, shirts, dresses, earrings, two watches and perfume sprays, so that everyone in our family in India would get a present.

'When all the passengers were in their seats the captain announced that we would take off in ten minutes. Mum and Dad said a prayer to the god Ganesha for a safe journey to Bombay.

'There were many Indian families on the plane, but I could not tell whether they were all Hindus.

'Our plane landed in Bombay at midday. It had rained that morning but as we got off the plane the air was hot and humid. Passport check, security and customs formalities took nearly an hour. Prakash-kaka and Leela-kaku met us outside the airport. Dad and Prakash hugged each other. We went by taxi to Leela-kaku's brother's place at Dadar, a little suburb of Bombay, where we all freshened up. Leela-kaku then lighted a little ghee lamp, put a dab of red powder on our foreheads and waved the lamp in front of us to welcome us and ward off evil spirits. We all made our namaskars to Ganesha and other gods in the shrine in the kitchen before having a late lunch.

'The next day we travelled by train to Pune. It was very sultry in Bombay and the noise of car horns never seemed to stop. As the train left Dadar station and travelled towards Pune, the noise and the crowds of Bombay vanished. I enjoyed the journey through the mountains; it was less dusty and we passed through 22 tunnels. Soon we reached Pune and met Ajoba and Aji. My grandparents cried as they hugged Meena and me. Dad and Mum bowed low before them and touched their feet. Prakash-kaka and my auntie did the same.

'Ajoba and Aji lived in a flat with two large rooms, a kitchen with a dining table and folding metal chairs, a toilet with white tiles and a pan sunk in the floor and a bathing room. At night, all the men slept in one room and all the women in the other room. During the day, the bedding was rolled up and the rooms became sitting-rooms. We stayed in Pune for three weeks. Ajoba took Meena and me to see various temples. I liked the Ganesha temple, which was about 30 years old and the Devi temple on the hill, which was over 200 years old. At the Ganesha temple I saw two holy men, which was a new experience for me. Outside the Rama temple there was a cow standing in the middle of the road, quietly eating some grass. No one tried to move the animal and many people respectfully touched its back as they passed it. Ajoba said that different Hindus see the One God in different murtis, and believe that trees and animals also have the spirit of God in them. A cow is considered holy.

'A few days after our arrival in Pune, our family priest – whom we always called Guruji – came and discussed the arrangements for my sacred thread ceremony. It was decided to hold the ceremony in Ajoba's flat. All our relations and some very close friends of Ajoba and Prakash-kaka attended the ceremony. I will always remember the important rituals.

'On the day of the ceremony we all bathed before sunrise. Mum and I ate a meal together. My head was shaved by a barber, leaving only a top-knot. Then I had to have another bath. Dad gave me white cotton shorts to wear and a soft cotton cloth to cover my upper body. A piece of deerskin on a cotton thread was placed round my neck like a garland. Dad and I offered puja and prayers to our family gods. Guruji lit a fire in a metal container, and Dad and I offered ghee to the fire while Guruji chanted the mantras in Sanskrit, which I did not understand. Guruji prepared the sacred thread, which was placed round my left shoulder and under my right hand. Dad touched my heart and I touched his feet. We sat before each other. A shawl covered us both. Dad said the Gayatri mantra, one word at a time, and I repeated it. Then I offered puja to a three-foot-long (1 m) staff of palasha, a medicinal plant, which is believed to stimulate intelligence. Guruji and the guests sang some verses of blessing and showered us with rice grains. Guruji then asked me to be respectful to my parents and teachers, to study hard and not to eat or drink anything that would be harmful to me.

ॐ भूर्भुवः स्वः । ॐ तत्सवितुर्वरेण्यं भर्गो देवस्य धीमहि । धियो यो नः प्रचोदयात्

Gayatri mantra

Transliteration
Om bhur bhuvah swahah. Om tat savitur varenyam bhargo devasya dhimahi. Dhiyo yo nah prachodayat.

Translation
We concentrate our minds upon the most radiant light of the Sun god, who sustains the Earth, the Interspace and the Heavens. May the Sun god activate our thoughts.
(*Rig-Veda*: III.62.10; transliteration and translation by Hemant Kanitkar)

Varansai

'In the distant past, Hindu boys would go and live at their Guru's home for their religious education, but nowadays boys only pretend to leave home and go on pilgrimage, often to the holy city of Varanasi, so I did this. My grandparents and parents gave me food and fruit for the journey. After the ceremony I received many rupees as presents and we had a ceremonial lunch.

'Grandfather told me that I was now allowed to study the Hindu holy books. Throughout my childhood in London I had not been quite sure whether I was a Hindu. After the sacred thread ceremony in Pune I was no longer in doubt: I was a Hindu.'

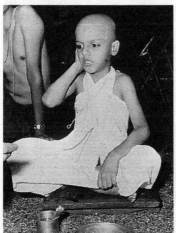

a Hindu boy after upanayana, carefully listens to the Gayatri verse at the morning prayers

Raj was given a surprise treat after his thread ceremony. He fully expected to return home to England, but his parents had planned otherwise. 'No point in seeing only Bombay and Pune,' his father had told his mother. 'Let's give him an experience he will never forget.' Little did Raj know that when he made as if to go to Varanasi at the end of the upanayana ceremony, he would actually be there in a few days' time. They travelled by plane to save time, even though his uncle said that the only way to see India is to go by train – second class! Once they had reached Varanasi they used scooter taxis. Taxis get stuck in the crowds, his dad explained; and the scooters were exciting enough.

When Raj became accustomed to the crowded streets, he started to pick out individuals. One was a solitary ascetic. Once he had noticed him, he realized that he was one of many. Varanasi is famous for them. Some were young men striding out purposefully, obviously going somewhere – probably to another place of pilgrimage. He also saw an old man shuffling along the road. All were wearing russet brown robes made of a single piece of cloth, and some wore sandals, though he noticed that some were barefoot. Each carried a staff, a water pot and a gunny bag; no other possessions. They are *sannyasis*, he was told, holy men who have quit the world to devote themselves to the spiritual quest. Religious people everywhere are aware of a tension between the everyday life which they have to lead, and the wish to concentrate their minds on eternity. Some resolve it by embarking upon a religious life in which they leave the world behind. Sannyasis do this, and most Hindus, though not all, recognize the value of their choice.

Pilgrims

Raj also met a family that was on a pilgrimage, and spent the day visiting temples with them. He wondered what the difference was between his tourist visit and their journey. He discovered that they were all going – husband and wife, his mother and their two children – to Vrindaban, the birthplace of Krishna. The husband's father had died recently, and he had taken some time off work to accompany his mother to important centres of pilgrimage for those who regard Vishnu as the supreme manifestation of God. Even though Varanasi is particularly sacred to the deity Shiva, there are associations with Vishnu. Most Hindus will find holiness in every temple or sacred place they encounter, no matter which deity they may especially worship. The old lady, the widow, was fasting, eating only vegetables and no milk products. Of course, meat had never touched her lips throughout her life. For the children, aged about seven and six, it was a holiday, a sightseeing tour, but they were picking up the spiritual significance of pilgrimage from their elders. Indian employers generally recognize the importance of domestic obligations. The man's job would still be there when he returned home after three months, and no questions would be asked if it took four, other than an enquiry about whether his mother had found the comfort of soul which she sought. She would find it. She was going to deposit her husband's ashes in the river Ganges at Varanasi. They hired a boat which rowed them into the middle of the river one morning at dawn.

Priests

Sitting at the entrance of many of the small shrines that Raj visited, and inside the others, were men robed in white – the priests. People came singly or in groups, as Raj's family did, bringing gifts of a few coins or fruit, which the priest offered on their behalf to the deity whose image was housed in the temple. The priest belonged to the *Brahmin varna*; his ritual purity set him apart from other Hindus and enabled him to represent them to God. His task is to make offerings and perform ceremonies, not to teach or give guidance. For that, Raj was told, the Hindu turns to a *Guru*. When Raj had made the family's offerings the priest gave them some nuts and fruit, *prasad*, the symbol of God's grace. Raj had seen priests before, of course – after all, his family was of the Brahmin varna – but never so many in one place.

Bathing in the Ganges

Each morning that he was in Varanasi Raj and his family joined hundreds of other Hindus to bathe in the Ganges, just before the sun rose across the holy river.

By the time Raj returned to Pune, and then to London, he realized that Hinduism is much more varied than he had expected. He still felt that he was a Hindu, but he hoped no one would ask him what he actually meant when he described himself as one.

'When we returned to London I noticed the dustfree atmosphere and the orderly traffic. In my new school, when the other boys and girls saw my shaved head they began to call me Hare-Krishna, but the teasing did not last long. My hair soon grew, and the experience of the thread ceremony gave me a new sense of belonging.'

After reading the experiences of a young British Hindu, you will have some inkling of the diversity and unity of Hinduism.

02

the temple

In this chapter you will learn:
- about a Christian GCSE pupil's visit to a temple in London
- about a Hindu businessman's visit to a temple on a festival day
- about Puja, Arati Verses of praise for different deities
- about temples in Britain and India
- about the parts of a temple
- about locations and styles of temples
- about the consecration of a murti.

The temple is the home of the *murtis* (images or statues), the material representatives of the divine spirit. Brahman, the Supreme Spirit, is believed to pervade the land, the oceans, rivers and air, all the creatures in the universe, vegetation, the planets and stars. A part of the creative force must be seen, and remain, in the creation. For this reason the murtis representing different aspects of Brahman (God) can be male or female; human, animal or bird; or a combination of these.

A Hindu temple is here described by Jane, a GCSE pupil, who is Christian.

A Christian school pupil visits a Hindu temple

I had to visit a Hindu temple and write a report as a part of my project for the GCSE Hinduism course. The temple is situated in a busy road in east London. The building is of solid, red-brick construction of British design, and gave no obvious indication that it might be a Hindu temple. However, there was some decorative oriental design in plaster above the entrance and a signboard which read 'Laxmi-Narayan Temple'. The door was closed, so I operated the push button of the electric bell and waited. The door was opened by a man in his late thirties. He was wearing Western clothes but had a red spot on his forehead. It is called *tilak* or *tika* and is a sign of spiritual purification. I explained my purpose and pointed out that I was not a Hindu.

'No problem, miss,' the man said, 'you are welcome, as long as you respect the way we worship God.' As I entered the temple, he closed the door. 'We have to be careful and keep the vandals out,' he explained. Just near the door there were shelves where visitors left their shoes before going into the entrance hall.

'Why do we have to remove our shoes?' I asked.

'Because leather is spiritually impure; all visitors to a Hindu temple enter barefoot.' I removed my shoes and went into the entrance hall.

As I stood in the entrance hall I noticed a small shrine behind me facing the main shrine, where the murtis of the god Vishnu and his wife Lakshmi were installed. The small shrine contained a murti of an eagle which I was told was Garuda, the vehicle of Vishnu. A brass bell hung from the ceiling near the Garuda shrine. The man who had welcomed me was the priest at the temple. He explained that the worshippers ring the bell to announce their presence before they approach the main shrine. The assembly area was 30 ft by 15 ft (9m by 4.5 m), and fully carpeted. The main shrine was in the form of a temple with an ornate spire. There was a marble platform in front and a marble floor round it so that the worshippers could walk around – circumambulate – it.

On the left hand side of the assembly area there were two small shrines set against the wall. The first one contained a murti of god Ganesha, and the second that of god Hanuman. While I was there some women came into the temple, rang the bell and offered flowers to the Garuda, Ganesha and Hanuman, before standing in front of the main shrine with their hands joined together and bowing. After offering this *namaskara* greeting and saying a prayer they walked round the Vishnu shrine, put some coins in the offering box, and sat on a carpet in the assembly area facing the main shrine.

The priest had left me to look at the temple and had gone to get ready for the midday worship. When he emerged from his room in the basement, he wore a white *dhoti*, a necklace of sandalwood beads and the sacred thread, leaving his upper body quite bare. I left the temple, hoping to return soon to witness the evening puja and the *arati* ceremony.

As mentioned above, consecrated murtis of gods and goddesses live in a temple; it is their home, and the priests are their servants who take care of them and treat them as if they were human. In large temples in India, the deities are awakened, bathed, dressed, garlanded and offered puja and food in the morning. After the midday puja the doors to the inner shrine are closed so the deities may rest. The evening puja and arati ceremony are well attended by the worshippers. At night the deities are put to sleep in a bed chamber. Worship in Hinduism usually takes place at home, and attendance at the temple is optional. The worshippers visit the temple as guests of the deities and ring the bell at the entrance to announce their presence. On festival days the deities visit the worshippers; replicas of the murtis are carried through the town or village in a procession, so that the people can pay homage and offer light, flowers and fruit to the murtis.

Here a Hindu businessman describes his visit to another temple at festival time.

The temple on a festival day

The temple I attend every Saturday is housed in a large hall. It is off the main road and there is a large parking area. After the hall was purchased a temple management committee was elected.

The existing stage was removed and in its place murtis were installed. It was decided that the temple should have murtis of Krishna and Radha at the centre of the altar, with Ambaji, the mother Goddess, on the left and Shiva and Parvati on the right. This arrangement of having Vishnu (Krishna), Shiva and Shakti in the same temple was approved by all. Two small shrines on either side of, but separate from, the main altar were built to install Ganesha and Hanuman murtis. When the main altar was built sufficient room was left round it for circumambulation. The assembly area is large and capable of seating about 500 people facing the altar, which is roped off from the worshippers. The temple is registered as a religious charity, and all expenses are met through donations from the worshippers.

Last year when we celebrated the annual birth festival of god Krishna, many Hindus from outside London attended the function and the assembly hall was packed to capacity. Normally the various Hindu festivals in Britain are celebrated on the Saturday nearest to the actual date of the festival, to enable people to take part. The evening began at about 9.00 pm with a discourse on the Bhagavad Gita, one of the most popular Hindu scriptures, by a guest speaker who explained god Krishna's message about each person's *dharma*, or moral and social duty. After the discourse a group of about 20 men and women led the singing of *bhajans* – devotional songs – in which the entire congregation joined. Two local musicians played a harmonium and a sitar (a stringed instrument), while the tabla drums and small brass cymbals provided the beat. Women and men sat separately on the carpeted floor and everyone, including the musicians, faced the altar. The singing of the bhajans went on until 11.30 pm.

The priest read the story of god Krishna's birth from the scriptures. At midnight, when Krishna is believed to have been born, everyone stood up and offered namaskara to the murtis in homage. There followed the arati ceremony, during which nine metal trays with ghee lamps and tablets of camphor oil were used. As the lights were waved in a vertical circle before the murtis, the priest and the men and women holding the trays sang verses in praise of the deities. The trays were then taken among the congregation for people to receive the warmth and blessing of the deities. Milk sweets were first offered to god Krishna and other deities and then distributed among the congregation as prasad, the blessed offering. The celebrations ended in the early hours of the morning. The next day a prasad lunch was provided for everyone.

Temples in Britain

A Hindu temple in Britain, unless it is in a private house, is a public building and as such is subject to fire and sanitary regulations. There are many temples in cities such as London, Southampton, Leicester, Coventry, Birmingham, Manchester, Leeds, Bradford and Luton. Many have kitchens, where *prasad* meals are cooked for the worshippers. There is a large temple in north London where upwards of 1,000 prasad meals are served every Saturday and Sunday. Mostly women, but some men, do the cooking and the food is vegetarian. Rules about spiritual purity and cleanliness are strictly observed (see Chapter 6 for these rules).

Worship in Hinduism takes place mainly on an individual basis. Each person offers flowers, rice, grains and prayers to murtis at the family shrine after the main puja is performed by the senior male or female. But in sectarian practice, worship becomes congregational; the priest performs the puja while the devotees closely observe the various rituals, and the whole group says the prayers together. In a non-sectarian temple in India, for example, where people gather together to celebrate a festival, at the end of a puja the arati ceremony becomes a congregational act, with the whole group joining in the singing of verse-prayers. Worship in Hindu temples in Britain is becoming more and more congregational, since a large number of people visit the temples and participate in puja, prayer and arati as a group. The arati ceremony involves the singing of prayers and the receiving of spiritual purification and the deity's blessing, as people pass their hands over the lights and touch their eyes and head. Young Hindus experience the spirituality of the tradition more through participation in the ceremony than through distant observation of a puja or through listening to the stories from mythology.

The arati ceremony

Two ideas are prominent behind the performance of the arati ceremony. The first is that of *darshan* – the viewing of the murti and receiving grace through sight of the deity. The second is that of *mukti* or *moksha* (liberation). The verse-prayers figure the word *mukti*, and seek God's help so that the worshipper may be able to break the chain of rebirths and achieve spiritual liberation.

Here are some arati verses in translation taken from three different hymns praising the Gods Ganesha and Vishnu, and the Goddess Durga.

Ganesha

Maker of happiness, remover of miseries, whose grace extends love to us, and does not leave a trace of any obstacle remaining, you have a layer of red lead around your whole body and a necklace of pearls shines brightly around your neck.

Victory to you, victory to you o god of auspicious form. At your sight [*darshan*] all desires of the mind are fulfilled.

(From Paul B. Courtright, *Ganesha*, Oxford University Press, 1985 p.165)

Vishnu

Om, victory to you god Vishnu, Lord of the Universe, o master, victory to you god Vishnu, Lord of the Universe. Dispel the difficulties of your devotees in an instant.

Victory to you god Vishnu, Lord of the Universe.

(Translation: Hemant Kanitkar)

Durga

O goddess Durga, without your blessing this life's path is hard to traverse. O Amba, the protector of the helpless, spread over us the mantle of your compassion. I am caught up in this long cycle of birth, death and re-birth. Release me [o Mother] from this calamity. Victory to you, o goddess, the destroyer of the demon Mahisha, the bestower of boons and the protector of all the gods [and humans].

(Translation: Hemant Kanitkar)

This is a translation of an arati hymn which is very widely used by Hindus in Britain:

> Victory to you O Vishnu, Lord of the Universe and Master of all. Accept our Homage, O Hari.*
>
> You remove the difficulties of your devotees in an instant. Victory to you O Hari. (Verse 1)
>
> You reward those who sing your praises and remove their Sorrow, O Master. Through your grace, happiness and prosperity become ours; and pain disappears. Victory to you O Hari. (Verse 2)
>
> O Lord, you are my Mother, Father and only refuge. There is no one but you; I desire no other refuge. Victory to you O Hari. (Verse 3)
>
> O Master! You dwell in all beings; you are perfect, all pervading, all powerful, and all seeing. Victory to you O Hari. (Verse 4)
>
> You are indeed the ocean of compassion protecting all. O Lord help and save me from my ignorance and lust. Victory to you O Hari. (Verse 5)
>
> You are the Life in all life, yet you are invisible to human eye. O Merciful Master, how can I find you with this burden of ignorance? Victory to you O Hari. (Verse 6)
>
> You are the support of the weak and the remover of pain and suffering. Protect me and bless me with your compassionate hand as I surrender myself to your will. Victory to you O Hari. (Verse 7)
>
> Cleanse me, O God, of my passion, suffering and sin. With your grace grant me firm faith, divine love and a spirit of service. Victory to you O Master Hari. (Verse 8)
>
> (Translation: Hemant Kanitkar)
>
> * 'Hari' is a commonly used epithet of the god Vishnu.

A temple in India mainly fulfils the religious needs of the community. A Hindu visits a temple mainly to view (*darshan*) the murti. Since visiting a temple is optional, a Hindu may go to the nearby temple every day, once a week or only at festival times. In Britain a temple has many social functions in addition to the religious one. By and large, Hindu families are scattered in different areas of Britain, although in some districts in London Hindus live in large numbers. Temples are not always conveniently situated for many people, and visiting a temple at the weekend may involve travelling 20–30 miles (30–50 kilometres). The temple therefore becomes a meeting place for distant families, who may phone each other and arrange to visit the temple on the same afternoon. Meeting friends, exchanging news about relatives in India and renewing friendships are very important social aspects enjoyed on temple visits.

Hindu families do not always do an elaborate puja at the home shrine, so full ritual in a temple, performed by a priest chanting the appropriate mantras, sacred phrases and verses from the scriptures, is very significant in instructing children in the religious tradition. Many temples hold three pujas every day, but the evening pujas and arati ceremonies at the weekends are attended by many worshippers, as they are free to do the necessary travelling. Various Hindu festivals are enthusiastically celebrated in the temples.

British-born Hindus speak English as their first language, and only a few are equally familiar with the language that their parents speak at home, such as Gujarati, Hindi or Bengali. Even fewer youngsters can read and write their parents' language. This language barrier often hampers everyday communication between parents and children, and also prevents the younger generation from fully understanding the sacred phrases and prayers, which are in one of the Indian languages. Many temples are remedying this situation by conducting language classes, where children are able to learn their parents' language.

Some temples hold music classes, where children can learn to play an Indian musical instrument, a sitar or a harmonium, for example. Other temples are fortunate enough to find qualified dance instructors to enable girls to learn classical Indian dance. Facilities for table tennis are possible at temples with larger premises. Hindu weddings or sacred thread ceremonies are performed at some temples.

A temple in Britain is not only a place of worship but also a community centre; as such, it plays a large part in the social life of Hindus of all ages.

Temples in India

In India, temples vary enormously in size. A shrine dedicated to some minor deity and situated near a winding mountain road is no larger than a medium-sized fridge. It is constructed with roughly-hewn stone slabs, and an egg-shaped stone covered with red lead symbolizes the deity. As it is believed to protect travellers, drivers of bullock-carts and heavy lorries stop to make offerings of food or small coins.

A temple in a village could be as large as a double garage and dedicated to Hanuman or a local version of Shiva. It is usually brick-built, with a short spire above the murti. Inside there is just enough room for three or four worshippers to make offerings and circumambulate the murti, always in a clockwise direction, taking God's grace in their right hands.

In a prosperous village, a temple dedicated to the patron goddess of the place could be twice as large as the Hanuman temple described above. The shrine housing the murti of the goddess is perhaps stone-built with a spire, while the assembly area in front of the shrine (capable of seating 50 people) has a corrugated iron roof. All newborn babies from Hindu families in the village are brought to the temple on their first outing.

In many small towns near rivers all over India, there are stone built temples above the steps leading down to the river. They are dedicated to Shiva, Vishnu or the Mother Goddess and given the local names of these deities. Some temples are situated in high mountains; others are on the sea shore. Some well-known Shiva temples are Kedarnath in the Himalayas, Somnath in Gujarat, Vishveshwer at Varanasi, Trimbak near Nasik in western India, and Rameshwer at the southern tip of India.

Popular pilgrimage sites are Vishnu temples at Badrinath in the Himalayas, Jagannath at Puri in Orissa, Venkateshwer at Tirupathi and Padmanabh at Trivandram. Famous temples dedicated to the Mother Goddess are Kali at Calcutta, Vishalakshi at Varanasi, Mahalakshmi at Kolhapur and Meenakshi at Madurai. In Mathura and the Vrindaban area, south of Delhi, there are many temples of varying sizes visited by a vast number of pilgrims. When a British pilgrim to Mathura asked his guide about the number of temples there, he was told that there were perhaps 500, perhaps 5,000! The guide was pointing out that Hindu homes are temples since they have home shrines where consecrated murtis are worshipped.

Parts of a temple

Hindu temples are built according to a plan, and each of the various parts of the structure has a special significance. A temple, or *mandir*, is a dwelling place for a god or a goddess, whose consecrated murti is installed in the inner sanctum, called the *garbha-griha* (literally, 'womb-house'). Directly above the inner sanctum is built a tapering tower or spire called the *shikhara*. The whole shrine containing the *garbha-griha* is called the *vimana*, which refers to the heavenly chariots of the deities mentioned in mythology. The *shikhara* symbolizes the sanctity of the *vimana*. The development of the temple as it is seen today was gradual, and the various parts were added to the initial essential element. The devotees who came to worship stood in front of the shrine. The space in front was cleared, and raised to form a platform, and an assembly area with a roof and pillars was built, evolving into the pillared hall called the *mandapa*.

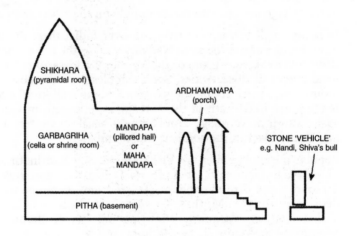

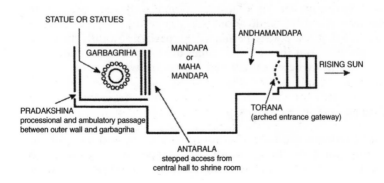

diagram of a Hindu temple

The *mandapa* was detached from the *vimana* at first so that there were two separate buildings, one for the deity and the other for the devotees. These two buildings were joined by a covered interspace, while at the front end of the *mandapa* was added a covered porch, a half-mandapa with steps leading down from the temple.

There are parts of the temple complex set apart from the main structure which are used for subsidiary functions, such as the preparation of food for the deity and the devotees, the chanting of the mantras, and the storing of the utensils.

the Lakshmi-
Narayan temple
in Delhi

In large temples there are separate buildings serving as the dancing hall for the temple dancers, the hall of offerings, and shrines for the consort of the main deity, as well as Hanuman and Ganesha. A separate shrine in front of the porch houses the vehicle of the deity. This is an animal or a bird on which the deity rides; for example, Nandi, the bull, for Shiva, and Garuda, the eagle, for Vishnu. Since going round the murti in reverence is part of the worship, many temples have a circular path round the inner sanctum so that the worshippers can circumambulate the deity. This type of temple structure is most commonly seen in north India.

In the south the temple plan is different. There may be three or four concentric squares covering the temple complex, the main shrine being in the innermost square. Between each square there is an open courtyard called the *prakaram*. Various small shrines dedicated to associated deities are set against the boundary walls of the squares. Each of the four walls of the outer squares has a tower built in the centre, those in the outermost walls being the tallest. The spire above the main shrine is very short; it may even be a dome. The towers in the outer walls are called *gopurams*. Some southern Indian temples, such as the Meenakshi temple at Madurai, or the Shriranga temple near Trichanapally, have very tall and highly sculpted *gopurams;* some are 150 ft (50 m) tall. The typical *gopuram* is rectangular in plan and tapers on all sides as it rises. The top is flat and holds six or seven small *shikharas* in a line.

The tallest structure in a northern Indian temple is the spire above the inner sanctum, but in the south, the tallest structure is the *gopuram* in the centre of the outermost wall of a temple complex.

Consecration of a murti

The procedure for consecrating a murti in a new temple is given in a Purana text. The statue is fully immersed in cold water. It is dried and the top of its head, eyes, ears, nose, mouth, chest, back, navel, arms and legs are touched with a piece of thin gold wire which is dipped in ghee and honey. It is then sprinkled with a mixture of milk, yogurt, ghee, sugar and honey, while mantras are recited. Afterwards it is bathed with cold water, dried, fixed on a pedestal in the inner shrine and offered an elaborate puja. After these rituals, the spirit of God is believed to enter the statue, which then becomes a murti to be worshipped as a symbol of the Divine Spirit. Four guardian spirits are invoked and established (although not in material form) at the four corners of the courtyard around the temple. Puja and offerings of cooked food and fruit to the guardian spirits make the plot of land and the temple sacred. These guardian spirits are believed to protect the temple from evil influences.

03 murtis and mythology

In this chapter you will learn:
- about three streams of worship
- about representations of Vishnu, Lakshmi, Shiva, Durga, Ganesha and Hanuman
- different names for the major deities of Hinduism.

The previous chapter shows how a statue of a deity can change in significance and become the home of the spirit of God, a murti. Hindus use murtis to represent the supreme spirit Brahman in worship, either at the home shrine or in temples. Murtis in most temples are made of stone or some metal alloy. Large wooden replicas of murtis in some temples are used for procession through the town at the time of the deity's annual festival. Many Hindus install consecrated clay murtis of deities such as Ganesha or Durga in their homes for the duration of the annual festival. These symbols of the divine are carried in procession through towns and villages and put in the local river at the end of the festival.

Broadly speaking, Hindus may be classified into three groups with reference to worship: those who worship Vishnu and Lakshmi, or Vishnu's important incarnations, Rama, Krishna and Narasimha; those who worship: Shiva in the form of the lingam or Nataraja, the cosmic dancer; and those who worship the Mother Goddess, Shakti, variously termed Parvati, Mahalakshmi, Ambaji, Durga or Kali.

There are many temple complexes in India that have murtis of Shiva and Parvati, Vishnu and Lakshmi as well as Ganesha and Hanuman, representing all three patterns of mainstream worship. Some temples in Britain also have similar arrangements, except that they have Krishna and Radha instead of Vishnu and Lakshmi.

The design of these temple complexes in India follows a square plan, where a large Shiva and Parvati temple is built at the inter-section of the diagonals. If a visitor stands facing the Shiva temple, a smaller shrine of Surya, the Sun, is seen at the front left hand corner of the Square, and a Vishnu shrine at the front right hand corner. Two shrines dedicated to Ganesha and Kartikeya, the sons of Shiva and Parvati, are seen respectively at the left and right hand corners of the square behind the Shiva temple. A shrine dedicated to Hanuman is not included in the square plan, but situated near a side entrance to the temple complex. A shrine of Nandi, the bull, who is Shiva's *vahana* (vehicle) is situated between the Surya and the Vishnu shrines, and faces the Shiva temple. All shrines can be circumambulated without any difficulty.

The mythologies of these higher gods and goddesses of Hinduism are given in sacred texts called the *Puranas*. There follow the mythologies of some important deities.

Vishnu

Vishnu was a minor deity of light in the vedic pantheon, but in modern Hinduism he represents the Preserver aspect of Brahman. He is spoken of as the luckiest of the gods in early scriptures. His worshippers consider him the greatest among the gods. He is referred to as Narayana, the ever-present and all-pervading. Vishnu is associated with primeval waters and is often depicted reposing on a lotus or upon the coils of the serpent Shesha. Vishnu, along with Brahma, the creator, and Shiva, the destroyer and regenerator, form the *trimurti*, the image of the three great gods of Hinduism.

The *Rig-veda*, the oldest scripture, describes in the hymn to Vishnu the legend in which the god of light covered the earth, atmosphere and sky in the 'three great strides', perhaps referring to the rising, zenith and the setting of the sun. Vishnu preserves and protects the universe and he is believed to have appeared on earth in his *avatars*, or 'descents', to save humankind from natural disasters or from cruel tyrants. The *Bhagavata Purana* mentions 22 avatars, but the best known and accepted avatars are given below:

- **Matsya** As a giant fish he saved the seventh Manu from the great flood.
- **Kurma** He took the form of a tortoise during the 'churning of the ocean'.
- **Varaha** In the form of a boar he destroyed the demon Hiranyaksha.
- **Narasimha** As a half-man, half-lion, he killed the demon Hiranyakashipu.
- **Vamana** As a dwarf he tricked the demon king Bali. The story in the *Purana* incorporates the 'three strides' legend mentioned in the *Rig-veda*. (Bali was a demon king who was renowned for his harshness as well as his virtue. He was generous to a fault, and never allowed any supplicant to go empty-handed. Through his penance he became invincible and ruled over the three worlds, heaven, earth and the netherworld. Indra, the king of heaven, appealed to god Vishnu to restrain Bali. Vishnu appeared as Vamana, a dwarf, in his fifth avatar, to protect the world from the tyrant. Vamana went to Bali and asked for just enough land for him to step over in three paces. Bali looked at the dwarf and was amused by the small request. Without any hesitation, Bali granted Vamana's modest wish. Immediately, Vamana

(Vishnu) assumed his cosmic form. He covered the heaven with one stride, the earth with another and, placing his foot on Bali's head, pushed him into the netherworld, where he was allowed to rule.)

- **Parashurama**   Rama of the Axe protected the Brahmins from the tyranny of the Kshattriyas.
- **Rama**   Rama's deeds of valour in his struggle against Ravana, the king of Lanka, are described in the epic Ramayana.
- **Krishna**   As Krishna he destroyed the wicked, protected the righteous and established a new order (dharma).
- **Buddha**   The founder of Buddhism.
- **Kalki**   The last avatar of Vishnu that is yet to come, at the end of the present 'Age of Darkness'. He is expected to appear as a rider on a white horse.

Vishnu is represented in sculpture and painting in human form, with a dark bluish complexion. In his four hands he holds a *padma* (lotus), a *gada* (mace), a *shankha* (conch) and a *chakra* (discus) which, when used as a weapon, returns to his hand after hitting the target. He wears a precious jewel round his neck. His *vahana* (vehicle) is Garuda, the eagle. Of his many titles, Keshava, Narayana, Madhava and Govinda are recited at the start of a puja.

Vishnu

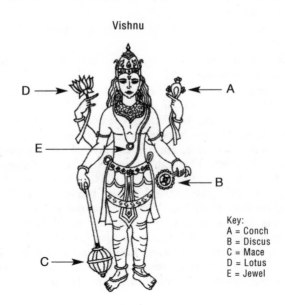

Key:
A = Conch
B = Discus
C = Mace
D = Lotus
E = Jewel

Lakshmi

The word Lakshmi is often used applied to define a fortunate woman. In one ancient story from mythology Lakshmi is the daughter of a great sage, Bhrigu. Once, being displeased with the gods, Bhrigu pronounced a curse on all celestial beings, which included his daughter. To escape from the curse, Lakshmi took refuge in the primeval ocean. When the gods and the demons churned the ocean to obtain the drink of immortality, Lakshmi appeared from the waters as a beautiful woman in a lotus flower; hence she is also known as Padma or Kamala, meaning lotus.

In a later story she is the wife of Vishnu. In her many incarnations she appears as the wife of the Vishnu avatars. When Vishnu came as Vamana, Lakshmi was Padma; when Vishnu became Rama, she was Sita; and when he came as Krishna, Lakshmi was Rukmini.

She is shown as a beautiful woman with four hands, rising from a lotus. In two hands she holds lotus flowers, with the third she bestows wealth in the form of gold coins and with the fourth she blesses the worshipper. As the goddess of wealth and good fortune, she is offered special worship on the Lakshmi-puja day during the Diwali festival.

Lakshmi

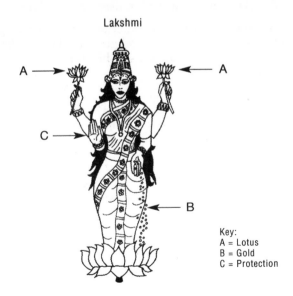

Key:
A = Lotus
B = Gold
C = Protection

Shiva

Long before the Aryan migration into northwest India, the people in the Indus valley worshipped a male deity whose picture is found on a seal. He is seen sitting cross-legged in a yoga posture, surrounded by animals. Rudra, 'the terrible', was a chief of the storm deities in the vedic pantheon, who possessed destructive as well as healing powers. Most scholars believe that god Shiva, the destroyer and regenerator aspect of Brahman in modern Hinduism, was the result of metamorphosis of the pre-Aryan and vedic deities mentioned above. Shiva worship combines many contradictory elements; fear, uncertainty of the unknown, regeneration, powers of death and destruction, mystic forces of human psyche and malignant aspects of nature. He is called Mahadeva, great god and Bhava, existence.

As Nataraja, the Lord of the Dance, he controls the ordered movement of the universe and as such he is the god of destruction. He is also the god of regeneration and sexuality, and in this aspect he and his shakti (female energy) are worshipped in the form of the linga and yoni, the male and female organs of generation.

He is called Mahayogi since he is the god of asceticism, and in this aspect he is represented as a naked man with matted hair, his body smeared with ash, sitting on a tiger skin, wearing a skull garland and absorbed in deep contemplation.

He is associated with evil and cruel spirits, ghosts, goblins, and vampires, which haunt funeral grounds. He is believed to have a third eye in the middle of his forehead, with which he destroyed the god of love.

As Nataraja, he is represented with one face and four arms. The two upper hands hold a *damaru*, a small hand-drum controlling the rhythm of creation, and a flame of the fire of destruction. He offers *abhaya*, protection, with his lower right hand and indicates salvation with the left hand. He dances on the demon of ignorance with his right foot, while the left foot is raised. His whole body is surrounded by a *torana*, an arch of flames. Shiva as the consort of the goddess Meenakshi is called Sundareshwar. The Sundareshwar murti in the Meenakshi Temple at Madurai depicts Shiva performing the Cosmic Dance with his left foot on the demon of ignorance while the right foot is raised. This pose is reversed in the representation of Nataraja Shiva at Chidambaram.

Shiva's abode is Mount Kailasa in the Himalayas. His wives are Parvati and other representations of *Shakti* (the Mother Goddess). His sons are Ganesha and Kartikeya. Some of Shiva's 1008 names are Bhairava (Terrible), Chandra-Shekhara (Moon-crested), Gangadhara (Ganges-bearing), Kedarnath (Mountain Lord), Mahakala (Dissolver of Time), Pashupati (Animal Lord) and Vishvanath (Universal Lord).

Nataraja

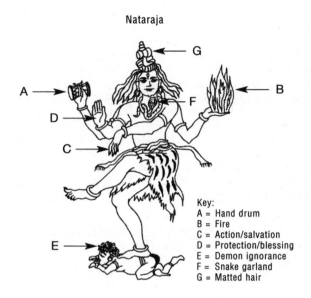

Key:
A = Hand drum
B = Fire
C = Action/salvation
D = Protection/blessing
E = Demon ignorance
F = Snake garland
G = Matted hair

Durga

The Mother Goddess, the female principle in creation, also known as Shakti, is worshipped in her own right and not merely as a consort of a male deity. Since Shiva is the god of regeneration, his consort Parvati, and her other forms, receive veneration as mother. Although all female deities, including Mahasarasvati and Mahalakshmi, are worshipped as Shakti, it is Parvati, Amba, Durga and Kali who are the main recipients of the title Mother.

Durga means 'inaccessible' or 'fort'; she is the warrior form of Parvati and closely identified with Kali. The story of Durga's origin is given in an episode called the *Durga Mahatmya* (or

Devi Mahatmya) in the *Markandeya Purana*. The *Devi* episode dates from 700 CE (i.e. of the Common Era, equivalent to AD). Historically she seems to belong to the non-Aryan tribal culture, but she is now among the higher deities of Hinduism.

A demon named Mahisha performed long penance and obtained a boon that 'he would be invincible to all enemies except a woman'. He defeated the gods in battle. The gods were angry at Mahisha's victory, and through anger gave out their energies, which combined to form a beautiful woman. Each god gave her his weapon so that she was armed with Shiva's trident, Vishnu's chakra, the wind god's bow and arrows, and a sword and shield from another god. She then confronted the demon and killed him. She appeared again and again to destroy the demons and protect the world. She was the creation of the male gods, yet she did not get any help from them when she faced and killed the male demons. Durga is described as the mother of the world, who produces food crops through her blessing.

She rides a lion and lives in the Vidhya forests. She holds many weapons. In sculpture she is shown standing over the demon Mahisha as she kills him. Her prominent breasts declare her 'Mother' status.

Her important epithets are Simhavahini (lion-riding); Vindhya-Vasini (Vindhya-dwelling), Shakambhari (Provider of food crops) and Jagat-dhatri (Support of the world). The Durga-puja festival is celebrated each year to honour her.

Durga

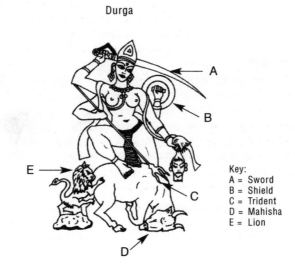

Key:
A = Sword
B = Shield
C = Trident
D = Mahisha
E = Lion

Ganesha

The Ganesha mythology is given in many *Puranas* (mythological texts). Here are two stories from it.

> Once, Shiva's wife Parvati made a statue of a little boy and threw it in the river Ganges. As it came in contact with the river goddess, the boy came to life. Both goddesses claimed him as their son, since Parvati had given him his body and Ganga gave him life.

> Once, Parvati, using the scurf of her body, made the figure of a boy and breathed life into him. She asked the boy to guard the house while she bathed. Shiva was absent at this point. When he returned, the boy barred the way and in anger Shiva cut off his head. When Parvati emerged from her bathing and saw the corpse, she said that she considered the boy her son. Shiva promised to replace the head and sent his attendants to bring the head of anyone found sleeping with their head pointing north. The attendants found a baby elephant in that position, and brought its head, which Shiva attached to the torso, bringing the boy back to life.

Shiva made their new son the leader of his *ganas*, semi-divine attendants, which is how the boy with the elephant's head came to be called Ganesha (Isha means lord or leader) or Ganapati. From the early Middle Ages, Ganesha came to be considered and widely worshipped as a god of good luck, a remover of difficulties and obstacles, a god of wisdom and a patron of learning. There is a widely-held belief that the sage Vyasa dictated the epic *Mahabharata* to Ganesha, who wrote it down. Prayers are offered to Ganesha at the beginning of a puja (prayer ceremony), as well as at the life-cycle rituals of the sacred thread and marriage, before leaving and after entering a house, at the start of a battle, or when faced with life's problems.

The Ganesha murti shows him with a large human body of pink complexion and an elephant's head with one tusk. He is riding on or attended by a rat. He has four hands, three of which hold a goad and axe, a snare, and modaka sweetmeats; with the fourth he offers protection and blessing to his devotees.

A ten-day annual festival is celebrated in his honour in western India.

Ganesha

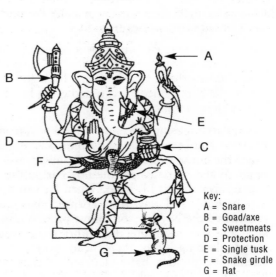

Key:
A = Snare
B = Goad/axe
C = Sweetmeats
D = Protection
E = Single tusk
F = Snake girdle
G = Rat

Hanuman

Hanuman, the monkey-chief, is the son of the wind-god Vayu or Marut and a semi-divine female called Anjana, who was married to a monkey, Kesari. Hanuman is renowned for his heroic feats as a helper of Rama and these exploits are described in the epic *Ramayana*.

There are many legends which idealize his qualities. He is regarded as almost divine and possessed supernatural physical strength. He was able to change his shape at will and, by leaping high, to cover great distances through the air. He had a very long tail of considerable strength, about which there are many stories.

Once Bhima, who was also the son of the wind-god Vayu, and so half-brother to Hanuman, came to see him. Hanuman pretended to be ill, his tail lying across the visitor's path. Bhima was proud of his physical strength and decided to move Hanuman's tail out of his way without disturbing its owner. Bhima failed even to lift it, let alone move it out of his path, and felt somewhat humbled when he realized that he was not so strong after all!

In the *Ramayana* there is an amusing tale of Hanuman's tail. Ravana, the king of Lanka (Ceylon) abducted Rama's wife, Sita, in the forest, and carried her off to Lanka where she was kept under guard in the palace garden. Hanuman was asked to search for Sita. He went to Mahendra mountain, leapt high and flew over the straits, landing near Ravana's palace. Assuming the form of a cat he wandered through the palace. After a long search Hanuman found Sita in the palace garden, gave her Rama's ring in token of recognition, and reassured her that she would be rescued soon. He was captured and brought before Ravana, who was seated on his throne. Hanuman made a seat of his coiled tail and sat on it at a higher level. Each time Ravana raised his throne, Hanuman raised his seat. Ravana's son suggested that Hanuman should be humbled and disgraced. Rags were tied to Hanuman's tail and set on fire. Hanuman lengthened his tail and, leaping from house to house, caused enormous fire damage to Ravana's capital. He returned quite unharmed and told Rama that Sita was alive and safe.

During the battle against Ravana, Rama's brother, Lakshmana, and other warriors, were wounded. The physician needed medicinal herbs to revive the wounded, but the herbs could only be found on a distant mountain called Gandhamadana. Hanuman was sent to get the herbs, but when he got there, he could not identify the plants, so he lifted the mountain and brought it to the battlefield. After the physician had got what he wanted, the mountain was returned to its original site.

When Rama had defeated and destroyed Ravana, and rescued Sita, he returned to his kingdom from his long exile. Hanuman went with Rama, Sita and Lakshmana to Ayodhya. In recognition of Hanuman's invaluable help and faithful service, Rama rewarded him with long life and everlasting youth. In many temples worshippers first take Hanuman's darshan and offer him puja before going to the main shrine. Devout Hindus believe that Hanuman is a living deity, and thousands of villages have shrines dedicated to him.

He is the deity of physical strength particularly honoured by wrestlers, and is depicted as a strong monkey with human hands and feet, holding an Indian club.

Hanuman

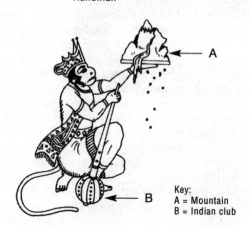

A

B

Key:
A = Mountain
B = Indian club

04 gods and priests

In this chapter you will learn:
- about prominent vedic deities
- about Brahman, saguna Brahman and Shakti, the Mother Goddess
- about major deities, godlings and grama devatas
- about the vastness of God in Hinduism – 330 million gods, One God or none at all?
- about the importance of rituals
- about the function of priests.

Prominent vedic deities

The concept of the Divine in some form or other occurs in most Indian (Hindu) philosophical systems. The samkhya systems of Hinduism and Buddhism, however, do not accept the existence of a Divine Being. The vedic Aryans showed reverence for the controlling spirits of the forces of nature. Natural phenomena were thought to be beyond human control, and brought danger to humans. The deities that presided over these phenomena were propitiated to gain favour and protection. They were praised and flattered through the hymns of the *Rig-veda*. They were propitiated through offerings made at the fire rituals. The chieftains and the householders performed sacrifices with the assistance of the priests. The offerings of oblations – ghee, grain and sacred woods – were made to Agni, the god of fire. It was believed that Agni would convey the offerings to the various deities. Agni is therefore called *Havyavahana*, the conveyor of oblations. The deities were invoked through the hymns and given oblations with the help of Agni.

Many deities are praised in the *Rig-veda*, the chief among them being: Aditi, the mother, and the Adityas, the deities of light (including Vishnu); Agni, God of fire; Aryaman, God of ancestors; Dyaus, God of the sky; Maruts, the storm deities, Rudra being the chief among them; Mitra and Surya (the Sun), deities of light; Parjanya, God of rain; Prithvi, Goddess of earth; Ushas, Goddess of the dawn; Varuna, God of water; Vayu, the wind God; and Yama, God of death. In successive periods of the evolution of religious thought among the Aryans, the predominant god varied. Dyaus symbolized nature worship; Varuna, the moral and ethical concept of *Rta* (cosmic order); Indra, conquest and domination; and Prajapati, ritual worship. Brahma, the creator God of later Hinduism, evolved from Prajapati. Vishnu became prominent along with Shiva, who evolved from Rudra. During the vedic period, the goddesses such as Aditi, Ushas and Prithvi were of secondary importance.

Although the Aryans revered many deities with diverse names and functions, the vedic sages had formed the idea that the various deities were really different aspects of one supreme power. They called it Truth. This concept is expressed in book one of the *Rig-veda*:

The One and the Many
Truth is One; the sages call it by different names such as Indra, Mitra, Varuna, Agni, Yama, Garutman or Matarishvan
(*Rig-Veda*: 1–164.46)

Brahman

You will often come across three similar words:

Brahman – the name often given to the One Supreme Reality, God.

Brahmin – the priestly *varna* or caste; sometimes used to describe the priest himself.

Brahma – Hindu creator god.

In some books the first two words are spelt the same. To remove this confusion we spell the word for the priestly caste with an 'i': brahmin.

This idea of One Truth in the *Rig-veda* was expanded and elaborated towards the end of the vedic period in the texts called the *Upanishads*, which were believed to have been composed in their present form between 400 and 200 BCE (BCE is the exact equivalent of BC, standing for 'Before the Common Era'). The *Upanishads* are discussions between teachers and pupils about the meaning of life. They form the basis of Vedanta philosophy, which is further discussed in Chapter 08. The One Truth of the earlier scriptures is termed Brahman in the *Upanishads*, to convey the abstract concept of the Divine; God as the Ultimate Reality beyond all description. Brahman is without attributes, unmanifest, eternal, all-knowing, all-powerful and all-pervading.

The *Isha Upanishad* says that 'this whole universe is pervaded by God, i.e. Brahman, Ishwara'. The *Brihad Aranyaka Upanishad* describes it as 'with form and without form, that which perishes and that which does not, the static and the dynamic, things that are seen as well as things which are beyond comprehension'.

Gradually, 'that Ultimate Reality, beyond all description' began to be described in terms more meaningful to ordinary men and women. The transcendent Brahman was said to have 'qualities', since the whole universe was filled with them. Phrases with three words were employed to express these qualities: truth, knowledge, infinity; truth, goodness, beauty; or being, awareness and bliss. Brahman was further described as the Supreme Soul, *Parama-atman*. This idea of the world-soul indicated a relationship between Brahman and the *jiva-atman*, the soul of an individual living being.

Worship of the formless Brahman was possible through prayer, and during yoga meditation the Supreme Soul is the object on which the mind is concentrated, in order that the atman may finally be one with the Absolute. In the early stage God was an abstract idea, the Absolute Reality quite independent of this world; however, later on it was thought of as shining forth, apparent and active. The One became the many through its act of will and brought into existence the visible world, sustaining it and finally taking it back into itself.

The *Chandogya Upanishad* says that the world is born from Brahman, is vitalized by it and ultimately returns to it. However, the first concept of Brahman as the Absolute Reality is maintained and emphasized by saying that the manifest world is mere sport, a diversion of Brahman brought about by its power of *Maya* (creating an illusion). In fact the world itself is unreal, and only Brahman is real.

The theory that Brahman created the world as a sportive diversion is not acceptable to the Samkhya doctrine, which suggests that the universe evolved through two self-existing principles, the Purusa, or cosmic spirit, and Prakriti, the cosmic substance. If Brahman is not the maker of the world, then how did it come into existence? It was put forward that Brahman, through its power or by a process of emergence, brought into existence agents who are responsible for the creation, the preservation and destruction of the world. This theory combined the 'one and the many' idea in the *Rig-veda* and the 'beginning, the middle and the end' concept of the *Chandogya Upanishad*.

Saguna Brahman

Brahman as the universal consciousness is too abstract a concept for ordinary men and women to comprehend. For them God needs to be something materially recognizable in order to be meaningful. Thus the agents or aspects of Brahman emerge as the major deities of Hinduism. Brahman is still thought of as *nirakara*, without form, and *nirguna*, without attributes, but to link the major deities to Brahman, it is described also as *sakara*, with form and *saguna*, with attributes. The many manifestations of God, worshipped in physical manifestations, are the diverse appearances under different names of the saguna Brahman.

In the *Chandogya Upanishad* the nirguna Brahman is in the neuter, as shown by the formula *Tat tvam asi*, 'you are it also'. If, however, Brahman is described as saguna, with attributes, might it not be human, animal, bird, male or female? Once the saguna concept was accepted, such varied representations of Brahman were inevitable.

Shakti, the Mother Goddess

It is believed that the vedic Aryans adopted the idea of the Mother Goddess from the Indus valley people, and in the post-vedic period the goddesses began to receive homage equal to that offered to the male deities. In the later sacred texts, called the *Puranas*, God is not only male but also female. The goddesses began to be worshipped in their own right, and not merely as consorts of the gods. The Mother Goddess in her many manifestations is termed Shakti, the female energy in creation, and worshipped as the supreme female aspect of Brahman. The Vaishnavites consider Vishnu as the supreme god, the Shaivites worship Shiva as the great god, Mahadeva; in the same way, the Shaktas worship Shakti as the Supreme Mother and look upon her as the creator, protector and defender of the world. The wife of god is referred to as Shakti, she who manifests her power. The god and the goddess together represent the power of the godhead. In many cases the female consort is inactive, for example, Indrani, wife of Indra, or Rudrani, wife of Rudra, and plays no significant part in the active life of the god. In some cases the consort of the male deity was considered more active and important, and when such divine couples were named, the female name was placed first, for example, Sita-Rama, Lakshmi-Narayana, Radha-Krishna, or Uma-Mahesha.

The epithet Shakti is applied primarily to the consort of the God Shiva. She is looked upon as One, combining the universal male and female, and is the central object of worship. Shakti is worshipped under different names, stressing her various aspects, such as the Mother Goddess or Mother. In this form she is represented with prominent breasts and swelling hips to emphasize her maternal qualities (see the line drawing of Durga in Chapter 03). Shakti as the tender and loving wife of Shiva is represented by Parvati or Sati. There are lesser goddesses called *matrikas* (mothers), and dozens of female deities worshipped in villages are also minor aspects of Shakti. Shiva is described by 1008 epithets, and Shakti by the female counterpart of each of these names. The terrible aspect of Shakti displaying terror, destruction and bloodshed is represented by Kali, Durga and Bhavani.

Hindus look upon god as all-powerful, all-knowing and all-pervading. Every possible aspect of the creation has some divine spark in it. These aspects or attributes of divinity are described in the *Bhagavad-Gita*. In Chapter 10 God Krishna says to Arjuna that 'the best of everything in the world is a part of me'. In the eleventh chapter, Arjuna sees the entire world in Krishna, as the deity shows his cosmic form. The representations of the Saguna Brahma are so diverse and numerous that the Hindu concept of the divine appears to be polytheistic, the gods and goddesses being worshipped as murtis (statues), pictures or symbols. The following table shows that Hindus have worshipped, and continue to worship, many aspects of the divine in the heavens, on Earth and in the sea.

In the heavens
Of the many vedic deities mentioned at the beginning of this chapter, Agni, Vishnu, Rudra and Shiva are worshipped in modern Hinduism.

Surya, Savita, Mitra	the Sun
Indu, Chandra	the Moon
Mangala	Mars
Budha	Mercury
Guru	Jupiter
Shukra	Venus
Shani	Saturn
Rahu and Ketu	a demon cut into two parts by Vishnu at the time of the churning of the ocean
Dhruva	the Pole star
Nakshatras	asterisms, constellations, some being considered inauspicious

All major gods and goddesses are believed to reside in their special abodes in different parts of the Heavens, but they are worshipped at special places of pilgrimage in India; some of these are mentioned in Chapter 02 of this book.

On Earth
Major deities

Brahma	The creator aspect of Brahman, worshipped only at two temples in India. His murti shows him with four

heads and four arms, holding a drinking vessel, a bow, a sceptre and a book. His vahana is a swan.

Saraswati The wife of Brahma, the goddess of wisdom and the arts. She is white in colour, shown as a graceful woman with two arms, holding a stringed musical instrument, the *veena*, and riding a peacock.

Vishnu The preserver aspect of Brahman. (see Chapter 03)

Lakshmi The wife of Vishnu. (see Chapter 03)

Shiva The destroyer/regenerator aspect of Brahman. (see Chapter 03)

Durga The wife of Shiva. Also known as Parvati, Amba, Kali, Bhavani and Uma, and by many epithets meaning mother. (see Chapter 03)

Ganesha The elephant-headed god of wisdom. The remover of obstacles (see Chapter 03)

Hanuman A hero mentioned in the Ramayana, considered almost divine. He is the patron of physical culture. (see Chapter 03)

Kartikeya The son of Shiva and Parvati. God of war and ruler of planet Mars. He killed the demon Taraka. He is depicted with six faces and six arms, holding many weapons in his hands. His vahana is a peacock. In western India married women rarely enter a Kartikeya temple. His other names are Skanda, Kumara; as Murugan he is widely worshipped in south India.

Rivers The goddesses as personifications of the river deities are offered homage and worship on the annual festival days. Many places along the banks of the sacred rivers are considered as *tirthas*, holy bathing places, where Hindus go to bathe; it is believed the rivers will wash away their sins. The seven sacred rivers are Sindhu, Yamuna, Ganga, Sarasvati, Narmada, Godavari and Kaveri. Haradwara, Prayag (Allahabad) and Varanasi are some of the well-known tirthas.

Lakes Lake Pushkara near Ajmere and Laka Manasa in the Himalayas are considered sacred.

Trees The Indian fig trees, namely banyan, pippal and udumbara; palasha (Butea Frondosa) and mango are considered sacred and are offered worship. Their wood is offered as oblation to Agni, god of fire, at

Hindu weddings and the sacred thread ceremony.

Animals The cow is considered sacred for its usefulness to humans. Nandi, the bull, and Mushaka, the rat, are sacred because they are the vehicles of Shiva and Ganesha respectively.

Birds Garuda, the divine eagle, is Vishnu's vehicle. The swan is the vehicle of Brahma. Saraswati and Kartikeya ride a peacock.

Flowers The lotus is the favourite seat of Lakshmi.

Other objects revered on earth are snakes, especially the cobra; implements of trade at Dasara; statues of famous men and women; tombs of Hindu and Muslim saints and departed ancestors at the annual remembrance. Sacred designs called *mandalas*, and the symbols *om* and *swastika* are used in worship.

In the sea

Bathing in the ocean is considered an act of religious merit. The conch shell is sacred and is sounded in large temples before the worship of the deity.

Some Hindus see the murtis and other symbols of the divine as aids to worship; to many others they became the objects of worship. It depends on the faith and the understanding of the worshipper.

A Hindu often chooses from the pantheon a particular god or goddess as his/her *ishta-devata* (personal deity) and offers special prayers and worship to the deity, yet without excluding other deities from the worship. This is well illustrated at the arati ceremony in a temple when verses praising many deities are sung. The higher gods of Brahminical Hinduism are called *deva*; the goddesses are termed *devi*. The minor deities and spirits are called devata, while the deities worshipped in villages are known as the *grama-devata*.

Devatas

These are the lesser manifestations (godlings) and spirits of the Divine, mentioned in various major scriptures and minor texts of Hindu mythology. They are usually associated with a major deity and cause no harm to humans.

Grama-devatas

The three male deities in the trimurti along with their respective consorts, Shakti (the mother in her various appearances), Ganesha, Kartikeya and Hanuman are sometimes called the higher gods and goddesses of Hinduism. Yet they reveal only half the story of the Hindu concept of the divine. Most of the large temples at the various places of pilgrimage in India are dedicated to these higher deities, but there are literally hundreds of small shrines in the villages which are dedicated to deities of local importance. The higher gods and goddesses are too remote for the Hindus living in the villages. The local deity in the village shrine is the real godhead for them, to whom they offer prayers and gifts in thanksgiving and in times of distress.

These lesser deities and spirits play an important part in the lives of millions of Hindus. They are called the grama-devatas, village gods and goddesses. Although in some villages the local deity is a male form of Shiva, most of the grama-devatas are female, and are considered guardians of the villages. These goddesses are looked upon as a mother and called by a local name meaning mother, such as Amma, Ma, Amba, Mata. A goddess named Maha-amma, 'Great Mother', or Mahamba was worshipped widely in western India. The patron goddess of Mumbai (Bombay) is known as Mumba-devi, which is believed to be a corruption of Mahamba. A goddess called Ellamma, another aspect of the Mother Goddess, is widely worshipped in south India.

The patron goddess of a village fulfils many functions. She is the deity of fertility and a woman wishing to have a child will pray to her and promise a gift, such as a sari or a chicken, after the child is born. She is the provider of food and the bringer of a good harvest, and as such she is referred to as *amma-purna* or *anna-purna*, the mother of plenty. All new-born babies are taken to receive her blessing.

If a child suddenly becomes ill, its parents visit the shrine of the guardian goddess with an offering of a coconut in order to please her, and pray to the 'mother' to protect their child. Prayers are offered to her whatever the difficulty, in the sincere belief that she will find a remedy. There are smaller shrines near the boundary of the village dedicated to spirits that bring disease and sickness. These spirits are believed to control diseases in that they cause the sickness when displeased and remove it when propitiated. As a result regular offerings of foods or a piece of red cloth are made to these evil spirits to ward off disease. Most of these spirits are female and preside over matters that are potentially dangerous, childbirth or pregnancy, for example. Shashthi is a goddess believed to injure babies on the sixth day after birth, so special gifts and prayers are offered to her on that day to protect the baby.

In rural Bengal, Manasa is propitiated against danger from serpents. There are poison deities and tiger deities who protect from those dangers when propitiated. The goddess Sitala is worshipped in many parts of north and western India for she is believed to control smallpox. In south India Sitala is known as Jyeshtha. Maraki or Mariaee is propitiated when there is a cholera epidemic. There are a number of spirits who are believed to reside in old trees or at the crossroads in the village who are made offerings of food to keep them pleased. These grama-devatas are approachable and are believed to understand the problems faced by the people in the village. The Kshetrapalas are the field guardians who protect and guard the crops.

In many villages the annual festival and fair of the guardian goddess is a joyous occasion attended by people from the neighbouring villages. In spite of the variety of grama-devatas a farmer would explain that these are different forms of the same Bhagavan; in the same way, a scholar might say that the higher deities of Hinduism are different aspects of the Saguna Brahman, the Absolute Reality.

How many gods?

You will have realized by now that God in Hinduism is not restricted to a particular place or limited by gender, appearance or name. The vastness of the concept of the Divine, the variety of forms and places of worship, and the multiplicity of murtis, icons and symbols as constant reminders of the sacred, have given rise to a misleading statement that Hindus have 330 million gods. Sometimes the number is increased to 330,000,003.

The *Rig-veda* refers to 33 gods, which is thought to mean that there are 11 gods in the heavens, 11 in the atmosphere and 11 on earth. But more than 33 are mentioned by name in the *Rig-veda*. Another vedic text also mentions 33 gods, which some scholars have decided include eight Vasus, the guardians of the directions, 11 Rudras, the deities of storms, 12 Adityas, the deities of light, Dyaus, the sky god and Prithvi, the earth goddess. In another interpretation, Indra, the god of conquest or the king of the heavens, and Prajapati, the Lord of creatures, are included, instead of Dyaus and Prithvi. Although 31 deities are put into three groups and called eight Vasus, 11 Rudras and 12 Adityas, each individual deity in each group had a separate identity, name and function; and when the two single deities are added to the list, there are 33 distinct gods. To explain the phrase '33 *Koti* devas', actually meaning '33 different kinds of gods', the word Koti appears to have been mistranslated. Because the word Koti means 'kind or type', as well as the number 10,000,000, use of the alternative meaning of the word Koti has given rise to the statement that Hindus have 330 million gods. At least, this appears to be the most logical explanation. Without going into arithmetical acrobatics, it can sensibly be said that Hindus have One Divinity, which is worshipped in various appearances and under different names.

330 million gods, One God, or – none at all?

Some Hindus do not believe in even One God, but in an impersonal cosmic principle – *Rta*. The term Rta signifies the cosmic order, or the regularity of the cosmic processes, such as day and night, the seasons, springtime and harvest; and the intrinsic justice, moral law and order underlying all things. The god Varuna of the Rig-vedic pantheon is the guardian of Rta.

Priests

There is no centrally trained and ordained priesthood in Hinduism. The efficiency and scholarship of a priest is largely determined by the scholarship of the teacher. Many men who have the ability to learn Sanskrit, the classical language of Hinduism, undertake a long course of study under the guidance of a local scholar and study the various scriptures. The scriptures include the *Vedas* and certain branches of post-vedic studies considered essential to the understanding of the *Vedas*, such as the texts giving the mantras and the order of actions in various religious rituals, performed in the home by the householders. They further include the study of the *dharma shastras*, the law books, phonetics, grammar and the metres of the *Vedas*. Some knowledge of Hindu philosophy, the epics (i.e. the *Ramayana* and the *Mahabharata*) and the *Puranas*, is also necessary.

The religious rituals performed to mark the growth and development of children are called *samskaras*. The mantras used in the sacred thread and marriage ceremonies are taken from the vedic scriptures, while the puja mantras are mainly taken from the *Puranas*.

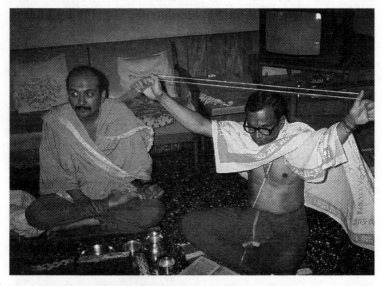

a family priest showing the consecrated thread to the Sun God at an upanayana ceremony in Mumbai (Bombay)

After completing a course of study, including wide knowledge of the theory and practice of Hinduism, these men function in various priestly capacities depending upon their inclination, scholarship and effectiveness. Some prefer to teach, some conduct rituals and ceremonies for their patrons, while others become religious mendicants seeking their salvation through asceticism and meditation.

Ritual

The theory of Hinduism is contained in its scriptures and in the various texts dealing with theology, philosophy, religious law, mythology and literature. The procedures and the mantras for the performance of rituals and ceremonies are contained, in codified form, in the texts called the *Grihya-sutras*. A balance between the understanding of knowledge and the correct observance of rites, rituals and ceremonies makes Hinduism a way of life.

The early scriptures, called the *Brahmanas*, which give the theory behind the rituals, maintain that the performance of ritual actions, *Kriya*, control the forces of nature. It is through these rituals that the spiritual forces are directed. Another scripture on philosophy says that knowledge and good deeds cannot produce human happiness without the accompanying rituals.

The chanting of the vedic or puranic mantras used in puja, the thread ceremony and marriage, without the appropriate ritual actions, will not, by themselves, enable the participants to experience the spirituality of the ceremonies. The physical actions necessary to make the various offerings to a murti in a puja; the actual wearing of the sacred thread, and learning the gayatri mantra in a thread ceremony; and making the offerings to the god of fire, exchanging garlands and taking the seven steps together at a marriage service, are all essential rituals which complete the ceremonies.

Ritual is important in the celebration of festivals. The actual travel and physical hardship, as well as the puja and *darshan* (viewing the murti) after the ritual bathing, make a pilgrimage more meaningful. Special ritual actions are performed in the ceremony of initiation into various Hindu sects. Recitation of the mantras by the participants is essential in all ceremonies. Knowledge of the theory and philosophy, with the accompanying breathing exercises and postures, are indispensable to the practice of yoga.

Putting the theory into practice by performing the correct rituals is known as *the path of rites*, which is believed to increase the participant's spirituality and therefore lead to ultimate liberation.

Many specialist priests take part during the performance of the vedic sacrifice, and their services are necessary if such a fire ritual is undertaken in modern Hinduism.

The vedic priests

Ritvij   The chief officiating priest who supervises the whole procedure.
Hotri   The priest who recites the *Rig-veda* hymns.
Adhvaryu   The priest who recites the hymns of the *Yajur-veda*.
Udgatri   The priest who sings the hymns of the *Sama-veda*.
Brahmin   The priest of the *Atharva-veda*.

The teachers who perform priestly functions

Acharya   A scholar. A spiritual or religious teacher and guide. An authority on the correct observance of *dharma*, religious conduct. He initiates and instructs pupils in the *Vedas*.
Guru   A teacher and spiritual guide.
Swami   A spiritual teacher and holy man, usually a *sannyasin* belonging to some order of Hindu monks.
Bhatta   A man of great wisdom, often a religious teacher.
Pandit   A scholar who interprets the Dharma Shastras, the law books, and philosophy.
Shastri   A man learned in the scriptures.
Pauranika   A man learned in the Puranas.

The priests who conduct the performance of rituals

Brahmin   A name applied to a number of priestly castes. Many priests are Brahmins, but not all persons belonging to the Brahmin *varna* are priests.
Purohita   A family priest who conducts religious rituals and ceremonies for a number of families. Sometimes he is addressed as *upadhyaya* or *Guruji*.
Jangama   A priest of the *Lingayat* sect. Different castes have their own priests.
Pandya   A Hindu temple priest and guide who also conducts rituals for the pilgrims at holy places. He keeps a record of families who worship at his temple.
Pujari   One who conducts puja at a temple or a shrine, concerned mainly with ritual procedure.

05

the family

In this chapter you will learn:
- about the joint or extended Hindu family
- about the hierarchical position of different family members
- about the changed position of women
- about the four stages of life and life cycle rituals
- about Hindus and their home in Britain
- about vegetarianism
- how different young Hindus follow their faith.

The joint or extended family

Before we consider what constitutes the Hindu family, try to answer the following questions. Who comes to mind when you think of 'family'? Write down their names, and the kinship term you would use to describe each one. Have you got your parents, brothers, sisters and cousins on your list? Did you include your aunts and uncles? All these relatives are members of the same family, but they do not all live in the same household. When a Christmas card is sent to Mr and Mrs Smith and family, it is meant for parents and their children living in that household. Gone are the days of large households. In Britain nowadays families are largely nuclear. Hindus who have settled abroad in the countries of their dispersion often tend to have a nuclear family unit, but in some Hindu households a paternal grandparent exercises a gentle cultural influence.

Until the middle of the 20th century many Hindu households in villages and towns in India had three or four generations living under one roof, pooling their incomes and having one kitchen where the women of the household prepared food for everyone. The decisions about how the family's money was spent were taken by the older men, with the informal advice of the senior women. There might be the expenses of a boy's education, or a granddaughter's marriage. Although the payment of a dowry has been made illegal by the Indian Parliament, the tradition continues to burden many Hindu fathers. Insufficient dowry payment to the bridegroom's family often results in ill-treatment of the new daughter-in-law.

This type of family structure has been described by sociologists as joint or extended; it applies to Hindu families as well as others. Both males and females had their places of authority and respect within the family hierarchy. Each member played a role in rituals. Men exercised a great deal of authority and had their meals before women and children. The hierarchical positions of different members of the 'extended' Hindu family still continue to indicate the authority of, and respect due to, individuals, through the kinship terms used to describe various persons. These positions come into play when a religious ritual, such as marriage, is celebrated in a British Hindu family, or when the younger British-born members travel to India to meet relatives living there. Hierarchy in Hindu families is important, and children will learn the correct kinship term and the behaviour that is expected when dealing with each relative. For example, many relatives attend a marriage and after the ceremony give their blessing to the newlyweds in hierarchical order. The newlyweds offer namaskar (greeting with hands together) to the family deities first, and then to their grandparents, the elder brother of the bridegroom's father and his wife, the bridegroom's parents, the younger brother of the bridegroom's father and his wife, then the mother's relations. The bride and bridegroom will bow before the elder relatives and touch the floor with their hands.

In English the word 'aunt' describes four different persons, namely, father's sister, mother's sister, father's brother's wife and mother's brother's wife. In Indian languages four different words are used to describe the precise relationship. For example, in Gujarati, an aunt might be called:

- **massi** mother's sister
- **faeeba** father's sister
- **mami** mother's brother's wife
- **kaki** father's brother's wife.

An elder brother is called *dada* in Marathi, and *anna* in Tamil. An elder sister is called *tai* in Marathi, and *akka* in Tamil. Indian languages have many kinship terms used by Hindus in various regions of India.

In the 1990s, through industrialization and urbanization, the traditional extended families are breaking up. Young men leave home for education or jobs and live in towns and cities. When they marry they have little spare space in their small flats for relatives to stay permanently. Modern Hindu women have the same rights to inherit property as their brothers, as a result of secular legislation. For example, I know of elderly parents who continue to live in the family house in a small town, with their younger son, his wife and their children. One elder son is in Bombay with his wife and children, another in Britain with his wife and daughter. Although these people do not now live under one roof, they still continue to think of themselves as members of a joint or extended family, in social, economic and ritual relationship. Decisions about the marriages of younger men and women will be taken by the father and his elder sons; contact with the parents will be maintained through visits, and the expenses of ceremonies and religious rituals will be shared by the father and his three sons.

an extended Hindu family, consisting of various nuclear units living in flats in Mumbai (Bombay), assembled here to celebrate a Hindu festival

The achievements of its members increase the prestige of a family. The bad conduct of any member affects the honour of the family. Males are the permanent members of the family; women move in or out of the family through marriage. A young bride will have a lot of work in the house and very little authority in her new family when she first marries. But after having children, especially sons, and with greater experience of life, she begins to exercise considerable influence.

The four stages of life

Hindu tradition holds that a man passes through four stages as he goes through life towards the final goal of spiritual liberation, or *moksha*. These four stages, called the *ashramas*, are of unequal length. Men, and some women, belonging to the Brahmin, Kshatriya and Vaisha varnas pass through the first three stages. The fourth stage is optional and only a few men enter it. Women are discouraged from entering the final renunciation stage.

The first stage is *brahmacharya*, when some boys embark upon a long course of study of the Vedas and other scriptures. In modern India boys and girls have equal opportunity for education, and many pass through primary and secondary school. But they still remain the privileged few. vedic study for boys begins after the sacred thread ceremony, called the *upanayana*.

The second stage is that of a married householder, *grihastha*. After completing either a vedic or Western type of education and obtaining employment, a young man marries and becomes a *grihastha*. In the Hindu family structure, he does not necessarily become the head of the household, since his father and even his grandfather may still be living.

The third stage is the retirement stage called *vanaprastha*. A man does not, in practice, leave home to live in a forest to meditate and study scriptures. He nevertheless hands over most of his responsibilities to his eldest son, and exercises his influence over major family decisions, such as marriage, as an interested bystander. Traditionally this stage is reached when a man sees the first son of his son; he is happy that the family will continue, and his son can take over a householder's duties.

The fourth stage is called *sannyasa*, an optional renunciation stage which a man may enter only after all his family duties are done. He then gives up his worldly possessions – even his name – and devotes his remaining life to pilgrimage, meditation and study of the scriptures, wandering from place to place, begging for food, journeying towards *moksha*. When he dies, he is buried, since he has no known male relatives to perform the cremation rites. His family, in fact, make *shraddha* (memorial) offerings in his name annually from the time he becomes a sannyasin, for, in theory, he has then abandoned worldly interests.

The householder stage is considered the most important, and in order to be of some service to society, a man has a religious duty to marry and have children who will continue the family name and traditions. We have already mentioned that in a large Hindu household women cook for all the family, the most senior woman setting the standards of cleanliness and ritual purity which the younger helpers follow. If a new daughter-in-law is to fit in with the established pattern of her new home, she needs to have had training under similar rules of ritual purity. That is one of the reasons why many Indian, including Hindu, marriages are arranged by the parents. The family, and particularly the householder, stage is considered the sustainer of other ashramas.

A Hindu lawgiver, Manu says:

> The four ashramas, brahmacharya, grihastha, vanaprastha and sannyasa all came into being from the householder stage.
>
> As great and small rivers finally find shelter in the ocean, so men of all ashramas find protection with householders.
>
> (Manu: 6.87, 90)

The head of a Hindu joint family is the senior male and the family property passes down the male line, but now, as a result of secular legislation, daughters inherit equally with their brothers. Many Hindus do not think it fair that a daughter takes wealth to her new family, as it can make a farm uneconomical when part of the land goes out of the family. The head of the family has a duty to ensure that the needs of all members are provided for, such as the children's education, marriages of the daughters and granddaughters, and the care of the elderly.

A householder supports the students, the retired folk and, through giving, the sannyasins, the religious mendicants. Thus the extended family is indeed the support for many persons. In India, generally, the group, such as the caste association or the family, is the unit to be reckoned with. The individual members owe loyalty to the group and, in return, other members of the group provide social, economic and moral support to the individual.

Women in Hindu families

Next let us consider how women fare in a Hindu family. All domestic decisions, like the performance of religious rituals, cooking, and buying clothes for women and girls, are in the hands of the senior woman in a large household in a village. The same responsibility befalls the wife in a small household in a city flat. Girls in well-off families are likely to receive a good education, but those in poor families in rural areas may not even reach the secondary school; they are probably needed to work in the fields or tend the cattle. Educated young women in cities can hold jobs in various offices and schools and are likely to keep them after marriage as they supplement the family finances. The father of an educated girl with a job may have to pay very little dowry when she gets married, but the dowry burden will be high for the family of a young woman who has little education and practically no prospect of a job. This old

Indian tradition seems to ignore the dowry prohibitions of modern lawmakers. Newspaper reports relate how the modern scientific technique of amniocentesis is misused to abort female foetuses, although the clinics in large cities charge up to 500 rupees to determine the sex of the foetus. Parents are prepared to spend that amount before the girl is born, rather than spend thousands at her marriage. Yet there are families who rejoice at the birth of a girl and do not neglect her in any way. Friendship across the sexes is practically non-existent, even when young men and women may be attending the same college or working in the same office. In this situation an arranged marriage is the safest way of finding a life-partner. Sometimes it is the only one!

A Hindu woman can now have a separate bank account, earn a salary, and own land and other property, in addition to enjoying the gold jewellery she is given as a bride. A wife can share in the performance of religious rituals with her husband, but women hardly ever have a priestly function, even in minor rituals.

Traditionally, property – especially land – belonging to a Hindu family passed to the next generation through the male line. This patrilineal succession enabled Hindus to keep the land in the family, provided they had sons to inherit. Many Hindu couples, even if they do not own land, wish for male offspring. The birth of a child is welcomed with joy, but that joy is greater when a son is born. A daughter is considered another's property for she will leave the natal family when she marries. A son will be a permanent member of the family; continue the family name and traditions; look after the parents, it is hoped, when they become old; and, when the father dies, perform the cremation rites. In many cases a son is the main financial support for the father in old age. The life-cycle rituals, called the *samskaras*, are performed for sons and daughters. These childhood sacraments mark the growth and development of children, and are occasions when members of the extended family gather together to celebrate them. It must be said, however, that these ceremonies, such as naming a child or taking it on its first outing, are more elaborate for sons than for daughters.

Ritual cleanliness, purity and pollution

In general religious terms, the concept of pollution marks out what is dangerous or threatening to the deity, the devotees, the faith and the rituals through which it is understood and expressed, and the whole community within which the religion is practised. Hinduism, as a 'way-of-life philosophy', takes its perceptions of ritual pollution into the secular sphere of daily interaction, so that avoidances of material objects, foods, or people (sometimes permanently, sometimes temporarily) may be enforced through scriptural teachings or popular myth. *Dalits*, or untouchables, are polluting to higher castes to varying degrees; their pollution is derived from the occupations they follow or the substances they handle, e.g. soiled clothes, leather, dead animals. In many religions worldwide, blood is a threatening substance: its uncontrolled loss can result in death, and death constitutes a threat to a community. The risk associated with menstruation and childbirth is linked with this belief. Where ideas of pollution operate so ubiquitously, in both religious and secular life, as in Hinduism, ritual means of purification must also be prominent.

A form of ritual purification, commonly performed at the beginning of a puja and other ceremonial acts of worship, is known as *achamana*. Water is taken in the hollow of the right hand, sipped and swallowed. Before the sipping of water Vishnu's name is uttered. These actions are done three times. Afterwards the name of the god Vishnu is spoken a fourth time, and water from the right hand is allowed to trickle into the copper dish before the worshipper. It is believed that evil vapours are formed in the mouth as a result of impure acts or thoughts, leaving the saliva and the mouth ritually unclean. This ritual cleansing of the mouth is essential before chanting the sacred mantras. Orthodox Brahmin priests not only clean the body with water after performing natural functions but also rinse the mouth thoroughly. Mourners always rinse the mouth after attending a cremation.

Bathing and external cleansing of the body is done before all religious rituals and cooking. Many Indians use a *neem* (lime) twig to clean their teeth. The kitchen is the area of ritual purity, and women bathe before the preparation and cooking of food. Footwear and soiled clothing are ritually impure; these are not allowed in the kitchen. For the entire cooking process only the right hand is used to touch the food, when preparing the dough for making chapattis, for example. When tasting a curry or dal to determine the level of seasoning, a small quantity is taken out of the pot and tasted. Of course, the spoon which has touched a human mouth is not used for stirring food.

In orthodox households menstruating women are not allowed to cook; they are even forbidden to enter the kitchen. When there is a death in the family, all adult blood relations and boys wearing the sacred thread are in a state of ritual pollution for up to ten days. Cooking is done by young, unmarried girls or neighbours. Food cooked by Brahmins is acceptable to all sections in Hindu society.

Rules about purity and pollution also govern the serving of cooked food and its consumption. The senior woman supervizes the cooking and serving of food. Each member of the family is served helpings of the different dishes on a metal plate called a *thali*. The right hand is used to convey solid foods, such as rice, vegetables and chapattis, to the mouth. A small spoon may be used for liquid foods. In a traditional household men eat first. Usually people sit on the floor, placing the thali in front of them, taking care not to touch it with their feet.

Westernized families in large cities like Bombay or Birmingham all sit together at a table for their meals, using china plates and spoons. Separate metal beakers are used to drink water at meal times. Some people do not touch the rim of the beaker with their lips but carefully pour water into the upturned mouth, which is rinsed carefully before and after meals.

Hindus in Britain

There are an estimated 380,000 Hindus in Britain who have come from India, east Africa, Sri Lanka, Trinidad and Mauritius. Nearly half that number are British born. The first generation Hindus from India brought with them many regional forms of the faith, and these variations are reflected in their food, in the language they speak at home and the way they worship. Seventy per cent originate from Gujarat and have come via east Africa. Fifteen per cent come from the Punjab in north west India. The remaining 15 per cent include those from Bengal, western India, southern India, Sri Lanka and other countries. Important Indian languages spoken in British Hindu homes are Gujarati, Punjabi, Hindi, Bengali, Marathi and Tamil. In spite of this variety, there are some features that are common to most Hindu families.

Visiting a Hindu home in Britain

If you have Hindu friends and are invited to visit their home, you will notice certain things not normally seen in other British homes. In the entrance hall there may be a framed picture of the Hindu god Ganesha. He is the remover of obstacles from human affairs, and most members of the family will offer namaskar (greeting with hands together) to him before leaving the house to seek blessings for a trouble-free journey. Ganesha will be paid similar homage when the person returns home in thanks for a successful day. You will also notice a decorative pelmet above the door to the main living room, depicting pictures of Lakshmi, the goddess of good fortune, and some auspicious religious symbols, such as a swastika and a vessel with a coconut on it. Major family affairs are probably discussed in the main sitting room, and divine guidance is sought through the symbols on the pelmet above the door.

All outdoor footwear, especially leather shoes and sandals, is removed on entering the house and kept in a cupboard or on a shoe-tidy near the front door. Some Hindus will insist that all visitors remove their shoes, others may be more tolerant and will excuse the visitors from the normal household practice. Leather is considered a polluting substance, and the reason why shoes are removed is because there is probably a household shrine, either in the kitchen or in the parent's bedroom.

If you are invited to have a meal, it is best to remain in the dining area. Your offer of help in clearing the table after the meal and with the washing up will be politely refused since the kitchen is the place of greatest ritual purity where visitors are not normally allowed, especially if the family shrine is located in the kitchen. Health visitors, social workers and the police need to be sensitive to these matters. Reluctance to allow a stranger, such as a police officer or social worker, into the main bedroom, implies neither secrecy nor guilt, but simply indicates that this room is their main place of worship, or houses the household shrine.

Hindu families in Britain experience tensions between parents and their British-born children over many factors. Some of these differences of opinion can be resolved through compromise; others may not be so easy to deal with. Food is a factor that can create tension in a Hindu family.

Vegetarianism

Vegetarianism amongst Hindus was not universal. Three thousand years ago the early Aryans ate meat and enjoyed intoxicating drinks. A vegetarian diet gradually became popular, as it was more suitable for a hot climate. Orthodox Brahmins generally prefer to remain vegetarian, and avoid onion and garlic during a four-month period from July to October, owing to the cooler weather of the monsoons and the need to officiate at the numerous votive rituals that occur during that period. A young Brahmin professional in cosmopolitan cities like Bombay or Delhi is not averse to eating eggs, fish or poultry, and sampling Indian-made beer or spirits. Even these 'rebels' will not knowingly eat beef. Meat is considered spiritually polluting and Hindu priests in India are strictly vegetarian.

In Britain the parents' generation in many families is vegetarian; equally, many Hindus in Britain enjoy non-vegetarian foods except beef. These family traditions are often challenged by the British-born youngsters.

Jay, a young Hindu, is now studying for his A' levels. His parents are vegetarian but since his secondary school days Jay has been eating fish and chicken. When he was 11 he developed a dislike of highly spiced, hot curry. He wanted to eat sausages and beans or hamburgers at weekends. His mother argued that she would not cook any such thing in her kitchen because of the household shrine there. Jay refused to eat spiced food and chose only rice, yoghurt, chapattis and fruit. Jay's father suggested a compromise. The household shrine was moved from the kitchen and installed in the parents' bedroom. Jay's mother agreed to prepare 'English' food for her son but refused to have beef in the house. The parents continue to be vegetarian.

Food that has come into contact with another person after serving, even accidentally, is unacceptable to Hindus. Each family member will have a large plate, or thali, on which separate helpings of food are placed.

Rohini is in her first year at college. Her parents came from Delhi, and for many years of their stay in Britain the whole family enjoyed thick nan bread, lentils and lamb or fish curries. Rohini, through her new friends' influence at college, decided to become vegetarian. Her parents still eat meat but now there are more vegetarian dishes in their diet.

Language

Language, not only the Indian language that the parents speak at home, but that which is used to conduct religious rituals, can bring about differences of opinion between the generations. Many first-generation Hindus are inclined to use their mother tongue at home, while their children have English as their first language. Children in many Hindu families learn to speak their parents' language, even though they cannot read or write it. This shortcoming is remedied by some temples where language classes for children are run. Some youngsters are embarrassed by their parents' Indian English sentences and Indian accents. When parents intersperse their English sentences with Indian words there is a breakdown in communication.

Many Hindu prayers and mantras – sacred phrases – used in worship and rituals are in Sanskrit, or regional Indian languages, which the youngsters do not understand. Often the parents or the priest conducting the ritual fail to explain the mantras in English, and as a result children become bored when attending religious rituals. After a while some young men and women begin to refer to the chanting of the mantras as 'a load of mumbo-jumbo' and try to stay away from elaborate rituals.

Young Hindus

Young Hindus make friends with their white British peers at school. Some of these friendships last a long time, but most seem to fade away when they reach the senior level in their secondary school. Parents want their children to do well at school and pass examinations, so the children are persuaded and even pressurized to give up socializing after school or at weekends. Usually the family will want to visit relatives or go to the temple. These weekend visits, or the school work and further studies, are plausible excuses used by the parents to protect their children from outside influences. Daughters are free to have other girls, white or Indian, as friends, but friendships with boys are not encouraged and sometimes forbidden. Sons have a little more freedom to continue friendships with other young men of their age, but girlfriends, if they are white, are not readily acceptable to parents. This does not mean that young Hindu men and women never have white, even Christian marriage partners. There are many marriages across the ethnic and religious divide, but they are a small minority. Having a daughter-in-law who has a different mother-tongue, or who has a different religion and cultural values, requires a great deal of adjustment on the part of the mother-in-law if the son is looked upon as an insurance for old age. Friendships between boys and girls are not encouraged, even when both are from the Hindu community. If such a friendship is likely to blossom into love and marriage, and if the young people are not from the same caste group, both sets of parents may consider it a disaster and put up stiff opposition. If the younger people continue their friendship in spite of the parental opposition and eventually marry, they may have to face the prospect of severing contact with both families.

Radha was born in East Africa and came to Britain 20 years ago when she was ten. After taking a degree in geography she now works in an office as a clerical officer. She says she likes to worship at the family shrine every day and she often visits a temple. 'Being a Hindu means showing respect for other religions. My father often reminds me of my duties but does not tell me what my rights are. Having lived in this country I have decided to earn my living and be independent. My parents have said that I should get married and have suggested many possible young men as marriage partners. They are all Hindus from hard-working families but I don't think any of them will be suitable for me. They look at me as a possible future possession and not as an equal partner. I have had a couple of dates with young white men. We enjoyed disco dancing and shared a meal afterwards, but they were looking for sex without commitment, while I was hoping for a genuine friendship. So, that was the end of that. I shall marry a man of my own choice. Because I hold these views of independence and free choice, that does not make me any the less a Hindu.'

What it means to be a Hindu is expressed in a variety of ways by adults and children, and these statements emphasize the fact that Hinduism is a way of life.

Gita is a Gujarati girl born in London. She says that because she was born in a Hindu family, she can visit the *mandir* (temple) every Saturday afternoon and meet other Hindu girls and their parents.

Rupal's parents came from India and speak Marathi at home. Rupal says that when some white children at school call her 'Paki' she feels hurt. She tells them that she is a Hindu because she can wear skirts or trousers and does not have to cover her head.

Madhu, a local government employee with a wife and a daughter, says: 'I recite the Gayatri mantra 108 times after bathing every morning. I work honestly at my job, provide for my wife and daughter and believe in God. I do not often go to a temple. My wife does the puja at our household shrine before she goes to work. We don't eat meat and I do not smoke. We visit our relations in India every four or five years and I send money to my younger brother when I can. As long as I don't cheat anyone and do my job well, I shall consider myself a Hindu.'

Children's games

A variety of games, sports and recreations are enjoyed by Indians of all ages, and the opportunities for these are provided by festivals, village fairs, full moon nights and the start of the monsoons. There are games needing individual skills, team games, games requiring expensive equipment, such as polo, cricket or tennis, and games that have no need of any equipment. Acrobatics and wrestling matches, along with cricket, are spectator sports in large cities and towns and villages. Indian children whose parents cannot afford any elaborate equipment choose and enjoy the traditional games.

Girls traditionally play a game with 12 dried berries which tests their skills in catching, picking up and neck balance. A group of girls sit in a circle with the right leg folded backwards. The berries are shaken in two cupped hands by one player and thrown like dice on the floor within the small circle. The girl tosses one berry high up, then picks one berry from the floor without touching any other, catching the first berry as it comes down using only one hand. This is repeated until she has picked up all the berries; each successful 'pick up and catch' earns one point. If she touches two berries while picking up, she loses her chance in that round and the next player takes over. Each girl gets her turn and collects points. The highest score wins the first round. In the second round, two berries must be picked up before catching the first berry, in the third round three berries are picked up, and so forth. The most skilful girls can pick up 11 berries in their final round – using both hands of course!

Other indoor games include blindfolding (like blind man's buff), chess and hide-and-seek. A game involving reciting verses from memory can be used for individual competitors or for two teams of 12–15 boys or girls. One person recites a verse in Sanskrit or the regional language. A player from the opposite team has now to recite a different verse beginning with the last letter of the first team's verse. The successful recitation earns no point, but if no member of the second team can recite a verse to match the first team's effort, the first team scores a point. A teacher acts as referee to make sure that a verse is not repeated by either team. In a classroom situation boys and girls can take part in this memory game, but normally the sexes are segregated.

Outdoor games that children enjoy include a game similar to hopscotch, in which each player hops on one leg over diagrams made on the ground, playing with marbles, games with stick and stub, and skipping and other rope games. Boys or girls separately enjoy swinging on rope swings at festivals or at village fairs. Tug-of-war and wrestling are popular with boys. *Kabaddi* is a team game which requires two teams of 12 and a pitch the size of a tennis court. One player stands on the centre line, starts saying, 'Kabaddi-kabaddi', and invades the opposition's territory. If he touches a player from the opposition with his fingers or foot and returns to the centre line still saying, 'Kabaddi-kabaddi', he scores one 'kill'. A player from the second team now invades the first and hopes to score a kill. Of course, if he is caught, he himself becomes the victim. The team with the larger number of survivors over a set period of time wins the game. There are leagues of kabaddi in different states and even interstate competitions. One such championship was recently shown on British television. A game of tag, either running or hopping, is also very popular.

Indian boys are keen on cricket and, in villages and towns, any open ground is used to play this game, perhaps with a piece of wood shaped like a cricket bat and an old tennis ball. In cities like Bombay, the game is played in narrow streets, and called '*gully* cricket' (gully means a narrow street); a batsman is out if he hits a tennis ball higher than first-floor level. This is good discipline for hitting the ball along the ground.

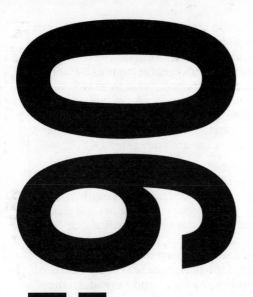

06 religion in the home

In this chapter you will learn:

- about the home shrine
- about puja and the 16-stage puja at festivals
- about food and fasting
- about women and religion in the home
- what sva-dharma is
- about the Divali festival
- about the social manifestation of caste
- about religious life in the villages.

Most Hindu rituals take place in the home. They include all life-cycle rituals, or rites of passage; festive occasions to commemorate the birth of certain deities, and regional festivals celebrating gods such as Ganesha or Durga, as well as those having national appeal such as Divali, Navaratri or Holi. There are many forms of worship in Hinduism; the most common form is called *puja* and many Hindus perform the daily puja at the household shrine.

In the following account, a Hindu woman living in Britain explains how she performs the daily puja, and describes her home shrine and the significance of this daily religious ritual to her spirituality.

I am Kamal. I came to London from Bombay 25 years ago with my husband Madhav and our daughter Shanta. Our son Shriram was born here five years after our arrival. Madhav and I run a newsagents' while Shanta looks after the sub-post office. Shriram is away training to be a teacher of physical education. We have a three-bedroom flat above the shop.

Because of the nature of our work, we all get up very early, then complete our ablutions and have a cup of tea. While Madhav and Shanta sort our newspapers and see to their delivery, I bathe and prepare the puja tray.

Our home shrine is arranged in a small wall unit in the kitchen. We replaced the door of the wall unit with a fretwork arch, so the shrine looks like a miniature temple. Behind the small altar in the shrine there is a framed picture of Ganesha. In a copper dish on the altar there is a stone Shiva linga, a murti of our family deity, the goddess Parvati, a rounded bluish stone, symbolizing peace, and representing God Vishnu, and a murti of Goddess Lakshmi. The two murtis of the goddesses are made of silver. On the altar there is a small conch shell on a brass pedestal to the left of the copper dish and a small silver hand-bell to the right. In the wall unit below the altar there is a shelf where I store the materials used for the puja.

On the puja tray I keep a copper beaker filled with cold water, a copper spoon, red kumkum, yellow turmeric, rice grains, an upright lamp with a wick soaked in ghee, some small flowers, and one joss stick. For food offerings I use milk or sugar crystals.

I sip water three times to purify myself, offer namaskar to the deities and ring the bell. The previous day's flowers and rice grains are removed from the copper dish. All the murtis, the conch and the bell are placed in another tray, and bathed and dried before they are returned to the copper dish on the altar. The conch shell, the bell and the murtis are anointed with the coloured powders and offered rice grains. The Ganesha picture frame is wiped clean and anointed with kumkum and turmeric. Flowers are offered. I light the lamp and the joss stick and offer light and fragrance to the deities. After the food offering I wave the lamp before the murtis while I chant arati verses, praising the deities. At the end of the puja I offer namaskar and prayers for the deities' blessing.

After seeing to the papers, Madhav and Shanta bathe, then offer namaskars to the deities, after which we have breakfast.

I spend no more than 20 minutes on the daily puja. Through it I remind myself that without God's blessing our work would not run smoothly, and we would not enjoy peace and harmony.

The type of home shrine described by Kamal is found in Brahmin households in small towns in India. Where more space is available, some families may set aside a small room for the shrine. In an Indian farmer's house in a village, a shrine set in a small alcove or an opening in the wall may contain only an embossed piece of copper showing a picture of the guardian deity of the village. In a small flat in a city where space is at a premium, a shrine may be set up on one side of a shelving unit fixed to the wall.

A daily puja is very simply performed, sometimes even without the chanting of the mantras. But an elaborate puja is performed for the consecration of a clay murti at the start of a festival such as the annual Durga or Ganesha festival.

Here a young Hindu, living in a small town in western India, describes how he performed the consecration puja to a murti of Ganesha on the first day of the deity's annual festival:

I am Vasant and my sisters are called Gauri and Padma. We live with our parents and grandparents in a fairly large house. Between the front door and our sitting room there is a small courtyard. In the wall of the sitting room facing the front door is an alcove, two feet wide, two feet deep and three feet high, with a semi-circular arch at the top. Four days before the Ganesha festival last year, my sisters and I removed books, newspapers and odds and ends from the alcove and swept it clean. My father painted the alcove and the surrounding area with a yellow emulsion paint.

Next day we three helped our mother to stick cut-out flower patterns of coloured paper into the small panels of a rectangular wooden frame. This decorated frame was to be fixed on two wooden pegs set in the wall on either side of the alcove, so that visitors would be able to see inside the alcove through the opening in the frame.

The day before the festival my father and I went to the sculptor, who makes clay murtis of different gods and goddesses for religious occasions. We paid 40 rupees for our murti, which had been ordered two months in advance. We brought the murti home and placed it in a copper tray on a small stool in the alcove. After the decorated frame was put in place and the electric light inside the alcove switched on, the smiling Ganesha could be seen clearly, even across the front courtyard.

Grandfather suggested that since I had undergone the thread ceremony six years earlier, I was well qualified to represent the family in any religious ritual, therefore I should do the consecration puja the next day. I could not possibly disappoint grandfather. I pointed out, however, that I did not know the mantras or the procedure, but I was assured that our Guruji would explain everything.

On the first day of the festival we all got up very early and bathed. Guruji, our family priest, had promised to conduct our puja at eight in the morning. Grandma, Gauri and Padma had arranged all the materials on two large brass trays. A basket held flowers and a variety of leaves especially needed for Ganesha worship. The puja utensils were made of copper. Three wooden boards were placed on the floor below the decorated alcove – one for Guruji, one for me and one for the murti.

I sat on the board facing the murti. Before me were a copper dish, a copper cup and long spoon. Another copper vessel had water inside and a coconut on top. There were a conch shell and a silver hand-bell as well. Guruji sat on my left; grandfather, father and my sisters sat near by and observed the puja. As Guruji chanted the appropriate mantras, I did the various rituals.

I sipped cold water three times to purify myself, speaking the names of God Vishnu. On the fourth name, water was allowed to trickle from my right hand into the copper dish.

I then joined my palms and offered namaskar to various deities, including those especially important to my family. Guruji then recited verses in Sanskrit praising Ganesha, Parvati, the Sun, Saraswati, and the trimurti.

The exact location and the time and day of the puja were announced. I had to repeat Guruji's words.

'I offer worship to God Ganesha, according to our family tradition, with my limited knowledge and with whatever is available, in order to gain for myself and for my family the blessings described in the *Puranas* and to fulfil the dreams and desires of all my relations assembled here, to ward off all evil from our lives and to secure well-being, stability, long life and prosperity for all!'

Worship was offered to the water vessel, representing the holy rivers, to the conch shell and to the bell. After the meditation prayer the 16 stages of the main puja followed.

The 16 stages of the puja are:

- **Invocation** rice grains were sprinkled on the murti. A blade of grass dipped in ghee was held near the murti, touching its eyes and heart. The spirit of god was believed to enter the murti at this stage.
- **Offering a seat** rice grains were spread in the copper dish below the murti.
- **Washing of the feet** the feet of the murti were touched with a wet flower.
- **Oblation of reverence** water and a mixture of milk, yoghurt, ghee, honey and sugar were offered. A drop of it was applied to the mouth of the murti.
- **Drink** fresh water was offered as a refreshing drink.
- **Bathing** the murti was bathed symbolically. A flower dipped in water and the honey-yoghurt mixture was used to sprinkle the image lightly. Saffron and sandalwood paste were also used for bathing.
- **Robes** a red cloth was draped round the neck and shoulders of the deity.
- **Sacred thread** a sacred thread was draped around the murti.
  (At this point, I lifted the copper tray with the murti and placed it firmly on the stool in the alcove. When the morning and evening pujas were done during the ten days of the festival, the murti was not to be moved. I continued the main puja standing up in front of the alcove.)
- **Sandalwood paste** and red and yellow powders were

applied to the murti's forehead.

- **Flowers and leaves** were arranged round the murti.
- **Joss-sticks** were lit and waved before the deity.
- **A ghee lamp** was lit and waved before the deity.
- **Food** copra and raw sugar were offered.
- **Fresh fruit** was placed before Ganesha. Some rupee coins were placed before the deity as a gift.
- **Circumambulation** was not possible, so I did a complete turn about myself in a clockwise direction. I begged Ganesha to accept the whole puja, which was offered with devotion, and to forgive any omissions.
- **Arati and flower offerings** using another ghee-lamp and camphor tablets, we performed the arati, singing verses which praised Ganesha, Devi, Shiva and Vishnu. Gauri and Padma played the brass cymbals to maintain the rhythm. After the arati everyone offered flowers to Ganesha and prostrated themselves before the deity in reverence. In conclusion, Guruji chanted the benediction verses. Before lunch, I placed 21 *modaks*, a special sweetmeat, before the deity. The sweetmeats were received back as prasad and given to everyone at lunch.

Food as Brahman

The vedic Aryans, during the early centuries of their stay in India, ate a rich diet including fish, meat, vegetables and milk products, and enjoyed intoxicating liquor. Their attitude to food was liberal, prompted by a philosophy of having healthy minds in healthy bodies. A later vedic text, called the *Taittiriya Upanishad*, equates food with Brahman. In modern practice, a verse used to say grace before a meal states that *Annam asti purna Brahman*, 'food is total Brahman', and that eating is not an act of merely filling the stomach but a religious sacrifice, in which oblations of food are offered to the fire in the stomach that consumes all. These two concepts explain why rinsing the mouth is considered an act of ritual purification.

Vegetarianism

As a result of the *ahimsa* (non-injury) religions, namely Buddhism and Jainism, meat-eating on religious occasions was declined. More and more Hindus favoured a vegetarian diet, which is more suitable for a hot climate. There are many Hindus who are strict vegetarians, orthodox Brahmin priests, for example; at the same time, meat, fish and poultry are enjoyed by many people in India and abroad. In some sects meat-eating and liquor are obligatory in certain rituals, but these are considered polluting by many Hindus. Onion and garlic are totally avoided by Brahmin priests, and food offered to deities in temples will not be polluted by these ingredients. They are, however, widely used on non-religious occasions for their medical benefits.

Food and pollution

Foods are classified as *pukka*, those deep-fried in ghee, and *katcha*, those cooked in water. Pukka foods last longer without refrigeration in a hot climate and do not pass on ritual pollution to those who eat them. Thus an orthodox family on pilgrimage can eat deep-fried food without it losing its ritual purity.

Katcha food not only goes off quickly but can also be polluted in many ways, and can pass on ritual pollution to those who eat it. Food cooked the previous night, cooked twice, or left over from a meal, is ritually impure. Food that has been touched or smelt by an animal or another human being is rejected. Most of these rules about purity and pollution applied to food seem to be based on rules of food hygiene, although they are expressed in religious terms.

Fasting

Fasting is a religious act undertaken voluntarily. Some people fast on a particular day of the week considered sacred to their chosen deity. For example, Monday is sacred to Shiva, Saturday to Hanuman, so people worshipping Shiva or Hanuman fast on those days. Some Devi worshippers fast on a Tuesday; other people fast on a particular day each month to propitiate god Ganesha. Motives for undertaking a fast are varied. Some do it to increase self-control, others to propitiate a deity. Women fast to bring religious merit and God's blessing to their family.

In Hinduism, fasting does not mean going without food altogether. Fasting foods include milk, yoghurt, fruit, certain root vegetables, dates and sago. But rice, wheat, millet, pulses, onion and garlic are excluded from the list. In spite of there being many permissible foods, many people allow themselves only water to drink between sunrise and sunset, and break their fast after the moonrise.

Women and religion in the home

Although major financial decisions affecting the welfare of the various members of a joint Hindu family are taken by the senior males in consultation with the senior womenfolk, women are largely free to decide how the various religious rituals are carried out in the home. The cooking of food and the ritual purity of the kitchen are domains of women. They arrange the food for the feast days to celebrate the rites of passage and festivals. They are ever-vigilant about the observance of fasts, not only for themselves but also for other persons in the family, and arrange for the appropriate fasting foods.

The wife performs the daily puja of the family deities when the husband is busy with his job. In some households husband and wife do the puja on alternate days. Women decide how the childhood sacraments for the new generation are to be celebrated. These include the naming of a baby, its first outing to visit the guardian deity of the village, and its first solid food.

Important religious rituals in which women participate prominently are the rites during pregnancy, which ensure the psychological and physical well-being of the mother. A woman experiences the spirituality of the faith at her own marriage ceremony as she goes through the rituals with her future husband. Her social and religious status changes when she marries.

The undertaking and performance of certain votive rites, and the fasting associated with them, are a woman's exclusive decisions. At her son's sacred thread ceremony her involvement is only partial; after sharing the ceremonial meal with her son, she takes no further part in the proceedings. At a thanksgiving puja, such as the *satya-narayan* puja, she sits to the right of her husband before the temporary altar, and jointly repeats the mantras to announce the reason for the puja and the blessings they hope to receive for the welfare of the family. She then retires to the kitchen to supervize the cooking for the ensuing feast, while her husband completes the puja under the direction of the priest. She has a great deal of freedom and authority over the practice of religion in the home, but a woman is not allowed to officiate in a priestly capacity at important occasions such as the sacred thread and marriage.

What is *sva-dharma*?

The *sva-dharma*, the personal code of religious practice of a family and its individual members, is determined by the *varna* (social category) and *caste* (jati) to which the family belongs. Each person's code of religious, social and moral duty is of prime importance, and takes priority over the general practice in the wider Hindu community. In the *Bhagavad-Gita* God Krishna says that it is better to perform one's own dharma badly than to do another's dharma well.

The sva-dharma of a family decides which deity is worshipped at home, which temples are attended for the *darshan* (viewing) of the deity, how the various Hindu festivals are celebrated at home, whether the sons experience the sacred thread, and who the marriage partners should be.

If the family belongs to one of the many sects of Hinduism, their personal practice may be different from that of other people belonging to the same varna. For example, certain orthodox Brahmins are strict vegetarians, while other families belonging to the same varna may occasionally eat fish. The celebration of festivals may differ from family to family in the same region. For example, the Genesha festival is celebrated as a public festival for ten days by the wider Hindu community in western India, but different families may celebrate the festival at home for two, five or seven days, depending on their sva-dharma traditions.

Sometimes an aspect of personal religious practice may be changed through a religious experience. A devout farmer, for example, may have taken a vow on a pilgrimage to give up eating meat, while other people belonging to the same farming community may continue to eat meat on certain occasions. Thus the sva-dharma practice of an individual or family may be different from that of the wider Hindu community.

Varna-ashrama-dharma

The word Hindu, derived from Sindhu, meaning the Indus river, was used by Persians to denote the people living beyond the Indus. The term Hinduism, used by Western scholars, refers to the religions of the Hindus. Hindus themselves describe their faith either as *sanatana-dharma*, the ancient or eternal way of life, or as *varna-ashrama-dharma*, meaning a way of life based on *varna* (social category) and *ashrama* (different stages of life). The explanation of the four ashramas, namely the celibate student stage, the married householder stage, the retirement stage and, optionally, the renunciation stage, can be found in Chapter 05.

The classification of people into social categories, called varna, originated among the vedic Aryans. A verse from the hymn called the *Purusha-sukta* found in the tenth book of the *Rig-Veda* says:

> When they split up Primal Man (Purusha), into how many parts was he divided? What did his mouth, arms, thighs and feet represent? The Brahmin was his mouth, the Kshatriya his arms, the Vaishya his thighs and the Shudra were born from his feet.
>
> (*Rig-Veda*: X.90, vv.11-12 Translation: Hemant Kanitkar)

A priest uses his mouth for reciting and teaching scriptures, a soldier needs the strength of his arms to defend his country from its enemies, a merchant or a farmer uses his thighs for transporting goods for commerce or for working in a field, while the artisan provides services to the three upper varnas just as the feet serve the body. The order in which the four varnas are listed in the verse was interpreted by Brahmin scholars to imply that the Brahmin was at the top and the Shudra was at the bottom of the social scale.

Some scholars have suggested that the verse in question was a forgery. Manu, the well-known lawgiver, codified the rules governing the conduct, duties and interrelations of the four varnas, which firmly established the concept and the order of precedence in Hindu society. The first three varnas are termed dvija (twice-born); they have a second spiritual birth when they receive the sacred thread, and can study the *Vedas*. The Shudras do not receive the sacred thread and cannot study the *Vedas*.

Some scholars put forward the theory that the Aryans differentiated themselves from the original dark-skinned Indian people on the basis of their lighter complexion. The Sanskrit word *varna* means colour, which, they suggest, is the foundation of the varna classification. The duties of the varnas are described in the *Bhagavad-Gita*, chapter 18, verses 41–44:

> O Arjuna, the duties of Brahmins, Kshatriyas, Vaishyas and Shudras have been fixed according to their qualities arising from their inherent natures.
>
> The natural duties of Brahmins are serenity, self-restraint, religious austerity, ritual purity, forgiveness, uprightness,

spiritual knowledge and belief in God.

The natural duties of a Kshatriya are bravery, splendour, fortitude, dexterity, courage in battle, generosity, and the exercise of authority.

The natural duties of a Vaishya are agriculture, cattle-rearing and trade. In the same way, rendering service through work is the natural duty of a Shudra.

(Translation: Hemant Kanitkar)

The Brahmins are priests and professionals; the Kshatriyas are soldiers and administrators, Vaishyas are the businesspeople and the Shudras are the artisans. The varna duties remain unchanged, but the duties of an individual change as he/she progresses through the ashramas.

Duties of a Brahmin householder

A Brahmin should earn a living and maintain a family by an occupation which does not affect other men's interest.

A Brahmin's speech and feelings must befit his birth, wealth, age and education.

No guest should be allowed to stay in a Brahmin's house without receiving hospitality, food, water and bed.

(Manu: 4.2,18,29)

Duties of Kshatriyas, Vaishyas and Shudras

A Kshatriya's first duty is to protect people and property. Agriculture, banking, commerce and dairy farming are suitable occupations for a Vaishya. Serving the three twice-born varnas is the duty of a Shudra. If a Shudra cannot get a good living by service, he may become a tradesman or learn a craft, but he should always serve the upper varnas.

(*Yajnavalkya*: 1.119-21 Both translations: Hemant Kanitkar)

Religion in the home of a dvija

The first three varnas are termed *dvija*. However, it is Brahmins in India who are most likely to progress through the ashramas, and experience the traditional 16 samskaras, or rites of passage. The popular rites of passage among British Hindus are: *seemanta*, a ritual performed during pregnancy to enhance the psychological and physical well-being of the expectant mother; the naming of a baby; a baby's first visit to the temple; the sacred thread, for boys in devout families; the wedding ceremony with mantras from the *Rig-Veda* and other scriptures; and cremation.

The daily puja of the family deities is performed either by the husband or the wife, where both are working full-time. In India the daily puja in a *dvija* household is usually performed by the senior male. Special puja is offered to various deities on the festival days dedicated to them. The birthdays of gods Hanuman, Rama, Narasimha and Krishna are festive occasions commemorated at sunrise, noon, sunset and midnight respectively, on the appropriate days in the Hindu calendar. The head of the household usually observes a fast on the day of the nativity, and a festival dinner is enjoyed by the family the next day. The regional festivals dedicated to Ganesha and the Goddess Durga are celebrated privately in *dvija* homes; they are also celebrated as public festivals by the whole community – Ganesha in western India and Durga puja in Bengal.

Brahmin and Vaishya families celebrate the major festivals at home; these are Navaratri, Dasara, Divali and Holi. The whole Hindu community is involved in Divali and Holi celebrations, with lights and fireworks for the former and bonfires for the latter. The religious aspects of these festivals are emphasized in *dvija* homes.

Observing various fasts on different days throughout the year, reciting evening prayers so that children learn verses praising different deities, telling stories from mythology to youngsters, and offering water to the sun at sunrise and sunset, are some of the religious practices found in the Brahmin households. Here the wife of a *dvija* describes how her family celebrated the Divali festival in their small flat in Bombay:

I am Tara; my husband is called Madhu and we have a 12-year-old son named Raju. My father is named Vishnu but Raju calls him Ajoba. Madhu's parents are Nana and Aji. Madhu's younger brother Sudhir is married to Rajani and they have two daughters. Madhu's three sisters are married, so they celebrated Divali in their own homes. Sudhir and his family live in their own flat in north Bombay. Nana and Aji came to Bombay for Divali from the small town where they live.

I had been busy the previous week preparing milk sweets and deep-fried savoury dishes for Divali. Raju had organized the small oil lamps and also made a lantern using bamboo slats and transparent coloured paper. Madhu and Raju did a lot of shopping, buying shirts, dhotis, saris, cloth for making blouses, hair oil, sandalwood soap, and fireworks (such as sparklers, crackers and bangers), not forgetting marigold and jasmine flowers for puja.

Our flat is one of 20 dwellings, built in two wings of ten flats facing each other, with an open quadrangle between the wings. All the flats open onto wide verandas, which were decorated for Divali with paper chains, and throughout the festival dozens of small oil lamps illuminated them. The quadrangle was swept clean and sprinkled with water, then small groups of girls drew *rangoli* designs of intertwining geometrical patterns, using different coloured powders. These colourful rangoli drawings and the rows of lights created a joyous atmosphere, which was enhanced by the fireworks.

On the first evening of Divali I prepared an oil lamp and placed it on the veranda just outside our front door, in such a way that the single flame pointed south to honour Yama, the spirit of death who rules over that quarter. For the rest of the year a single-flame lamp must never point in that direction.

On the second day we were up very early, and after our morning tea Aji and I applied perfumed oil to the head and upper body of Raju, Madhu, Ajoba and Nana before they bathed. Aji and I also applied oil to our bodies before bathing. First Madhu offered puja to the family deities and then Nana offered a special puja to the god Vishnu, to commemorate Vishnu's victory over the demon Naraka.

After this worship we all enjoyed the special Divali food for breakfast. That afternoon we invited some of our friends for refreshments, and we also visited their flats for snacks.

On the third evening I set up a temporary altar in our front room, to offer worship to Lakshmi, the goddess of wealth. On the altar table I placed some gold and silver ornaments, coins, ten rupee notes and our cheque books round a small silver bowl containing milk sweets. All of us offered red and yellow powders, rice grains and flowers to the goddess represented by the ornaments. Then I offered light and a joss stick. All our friends from other flats came to receive *prasad*. That evening we illuminated the verandas with lights and the children enjoyed the fireworks. We offered prayers to Lakshmi for her blessings throughout the next year.

We had invited all our relatives in Bombay for a festival lunch on the fourth day. To follow the tradition, Aji, Rajani and I received a present from our respective husbands. On this main day of Divali, King Balee is remembered for his generous nature. The story in mythology relates that god Vishnu restrained Balee and pushed him into the nether world, but granted him a boon by which the King would be remembered on earth during Divali.

The fifth and last day of Divali is celebrated as sisters' day. Madhu, Sudhir and Raju visited their sisters and cousins for lunch and gave them cash presents. The illuminations and fireworks continued for another week or so, after which our lives returned to normal routine.

Jati

Jati is the most important category for most Hindus; this word is translated as caste, derived from the Portuguese word *casta* meaning breed, race or kind. Most scholars hold that by the seventh century BCE northern Indian society, formed through the intermarriages between Aryans and the original inhabitants, was changing, and had gradually begun to add a fourth varna, called shudra, to the earlier threefold division. New settlements needed new skills, which the artisans developed, as well as providing goods and services to the three earlier groups. There were many families doing 'unclean' jobs, such as tanning leather and removing dead animals from the villages. These people belonged to the fifth group, and were excluded from the varna categories.

As centuries passed, different occupational groups (castes) evolved, fitting into varna groups. The skills of each craft were guarded within the families and passed on to the sons, who began to follow the occupations of their fathers. In the early period, however, it was possible for some people to change their occupations, and to move either up or down the first three varnas. In some cases the Shudras moved up the varna scale; some became petty chieftains, thus following the Kshatriya occupations. But those doing the 'unclean' jobs forever remained at the bottom of the social scale.

As time went on, various occupations became exclusive, and each group created a vested interest in its own particular occupation, thus making it very difficult for people to change their jobs. Occupations became hereditary and exclusive to certain groups, giving rise to rules prohibiting intermarriage and dining between castes. A hierarchy of castes within the varna system emerged; this ranking was not uniform all over India, although the varna ranking was. For instance, the *dhobi* (washerman) caste might rank above the barbers in some regions, but below them in others; nevertheless, both remained

Shudras and always ranked below the three upper varnas. Varna and jati are therefore not interchangeable terms. Varna is a larger group comprising smaller caste groups doing different jobs and maintaining different family traditions. A family priest, a temple priest and a funerary priest all do their jobs differently within the Brahmin varna.

The social manifestation of caste (jati)

Ritual pollution

Members of the upper castes consider the lowest castes to be ritually unclean. They feel they can be polluted by the proximity of the low castes, by eating the food cooked or touched by them, or by using the same well. The former untouchables now call themselves *Dalit*, and untouchability has been abolished by law.

Eating together

Members of the same caste eat together, and only fellow caste-members are invited to a meal in the home. Forbidden foods such as meat, fish, onion and garlic, eaten by low castes, are believed to pass on ritual pollution. Different castes in a village, at a wedding feast, for example, sit in different rows, thus eating at the same time but not eating together. Food cooked by Brahmins is acceptable to all castes.

Marriage within the same caste

A marriage partner for a son or a daughter is generally chosen from the same caste, but intercaste marriages are legal. The choice of a marriage partner from the same caste ensures common ritual and cultural traditions.

Hereditary occupation

In modern India, greater educational opportunities offer training in different fields, and young people can apply for jobs regardless of caste, although those from professional homes are still more likely to follow their fathers' professions. Nevertheless, people do not necessarily follow the traditional varna/caste occupations: for example, a Brahmin may work as a bank clerk, own a grocery shop, or become an officer in the armed forces. A Kshatriya may prefer to farm the family land, or run a haulage firm transporting goods by road. A Vaishya may be a senior Customs officer, or become an airline pilot. A Shudra can take advantage of the special educational opportunities, and become a doctor or a lawyer, or may become an MP and eventually a Minister in the State or Central Government.

Economic interdependence

In the past, certain castes such as the barber or the washerman performed services for the higher castes, and were paid in kind at harvest time. Priests were also paid in kind as they provided services to Kshatriyas or Vaishyas. This system prevails in some villages, but the cash wages earned in factories or government offices diminishes this aspect of caste in modern times.

Varna and caste today

For the past 75 years at least, caste barriers regarding social mixing and eating together have been broken down in large cities. In 1950, untouchability was abolished by law, and temples were 'open' to all Hindus. The underprivileged are given preferential treatment in education and jobs. But caste and varna are still important in relation to marriage. Caste loyalties are activated during elections or when applying for jobs.

The varna-ashrama-dharma is, in reality, alive only in orthodox Brahmin families. Brahmins always know they are Brahmins. Shudras and Dalits always know that they are considered to be on a lower level in society. The two in-between varnas, the Kshatriyas and the Vaishyas, are not very clear about their varna status but they know which caste they belong to. A Hindu is born into a particular caste and stays in it, even though he/she may change religious loyalty. Former Hindus now converted to other faiths find that the change of religion has not improved their social status. Caste gives its members a sense of belonging, but the caste label sticks in spite of economic success or political power. The caste system is peculiar to India, and affects all religions and regions.

Religious life in the villages

In many villages there are a few Brahmin households, although the majority of Hindus earn their living as farmers, farm labourers or artisans such as bricklayers, carpenters, blacksmiths, basket makers or barbers. The majority may not be conversant with the religious observances that take place in a Brahmin home, yet they have a religious life of their own which is important to them. In some homes there might be a picture of the guardian goddess of the village embossed on a piece of copper placed in a small alcove. This symbol of the divine is offered flowers in worship on certain days and joss-sticks may be lit at the same time. There might be a picture of Ganesha or

Hanuman printed on the calendar which will receive reverence. A picture of Sai-Baba, or some regional holy man, will receive similar homage.

While bathing in the local stream the people utter the name of Ganga (Ganges) or say '*Jai Bhagawan*', 'victory to God'. Going to the Mata shrine or visiting the Hanuman shrine is a popular act of devotion for many people in the village. Village deities have their annual festivals called *Jatra* (fairs), at which time many people will make offerings to the deity, and dab their foreheads with the holy ash kept near the murti, as a mark of receiving God's blessing. These fairs are occasions for enjoyment; there are wrestling contests and folk plays. On the day of the serpent festival, young boys and girls enjoy themselves on rope swings which are suspended from the branches of banyan trees. Snake charmers bring live cobras to the village square, where many women offer flowers and milk to them. There are hardly any instances of snake-bite on that particular day!

The Holi festival is celebrated in hundreds of villages with great enthusiasm. When the Holi bonfire is lit at dusk, pieces of coconut are offered to the fire. Going round the bonfire is considered sacred. The next day the men of the village play games near the dying bonfires and children sprinkle everyone with coloured powders or coloured water, in fun. In all these activities there is a religious element, which reminds people of the existence of the superhuman power which they call *Bhagawan*.

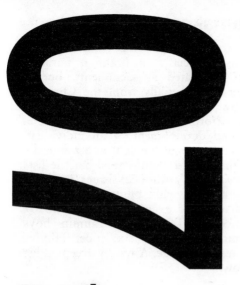

07

family rituals
and ceremonies

In this chapter you will learn:
- the traditional 16 samskaras
  – life cycle rituals
- about naming a baby and
  the childhood sacraments
- about marriage and the
  Hindu wedding
- about death and cremation.

Traditional 16 samskaras

Among family rituals and ceremonies, the samskaras are considered very important, especially in Brahmin families. Samskaras are sometimes translated as sacraments, but in Hindu use the term differs substantially from the Christian concept, as indicated below. Samskaras are rites of passage, comprising various rituals performed during a person's lifetime. These mark the growth and development of an individual, purify and sanctify the body, ennoble the soul and refine the personality. Traditionally there are 16 samskaras, but the lists given in various sacred texts are not always consistent. Regional practice stresses some rites as vital, while omitting minor ones such as learning the alphabet, for example. Only orthodox Brahmin males experience all 16; many Brahmin boys experience about ten, and girls about six; most Hindus experience at least three rites of passage. A widely accepted list of sacraments is given below.

Hindu samskaras

Before the birth of a baby

1 Conception
2 Prayers for begetting a son
3 Hair-parting

Childhood sacraments

4 Birth ceremonies
5 Naming a child
6 A baby's first outing
7 First solid food
8 A boy's first haircut
9 Piercing the upper part of the right ear
10 The sacred thread ceremony
11 Starting to learn the scriptures
12 End of vedic education

Rites for an adult

13 Marriage ceremony
14 Householder stage of life
15 Retirement stage of life, ritual performed on 60th birthday
16 Cremation

Naming a baby

The naming ceremony is called *Namakarana* and is performed on the 12th day after birth. Many Hindu families in Britain celebrate this rite of passage. The mother and child are in a state of ritual pollution for ten days after childbirth, and no one except the midwife has physical contact with them. This period of ritual pollution prevents any infection from reaching them.

Many Hindu women in small villages have their babies at home, and the ten-day period of segregation of the mother and child from the rest of the family is a wise precaution against infection. Well-to-do women in large cities can afford to have their babies in hospitals or private nursing homes, where infection is easily prevented, and so the segregation is not strictly observed. The birth of a baby is joyfully welcomed in all families, but Hindus celebrate the occasion with greater enthusiasm if the new arrival is a son. The naming ceremony is both a religious and a social occasion. The modern tendency among rich city-dwellers in India is to perform this ceremony in a hired hall witnessed by many relatives and friends, who stay to enjoy a lavish dinner afterwards.

Orthodox families usually follow the procedure given in texts that deal with religious rituals in the home. The parents and the baby are dressed in new clothes, and the baby is held by the mother on her lap as she sits on the right of her husband. The family priest conducts the ritual. Rice grains are spread on a metal plate which is kept in front of the couple. The father, using a gold ring or a piece of gold wire, writes the name of the family deity, followed by the date of birth of his child and the proposed name. The father whispers the name into his baby's right ear. All those present bless the child and the priest receives a cash gift.

In many families the ritual is quite informal, and mainly attended by women in the late afternoon on the 12th day after the child's birth. The baby is dressed in new clothes, with a soot mark on its forehead to avert the envious eye. It is placed in a cradle which is suspended from the ceiling. Some families light 12 oil lamps and place them under the cradle. The name of the baby is announced by the senior woman in the family. The assembled women then sing cradle songs in which the new name is inserted at the appropriate place. Everyone is given cooked chick-peas and refreshments. In many families the village goldsmith is invited for the occasion; he pierces the baby's earlobes with fine gold wire, which is made into a thin ring.

Personal names

The scriptures recommend that boys' names should be of two or four syllables, while girls' names should be of one, three or five syllables. In ancient days the male names were suffixed by specific words; Sharma for Brahmins, Varma for Kshatriyas, Gupta for Vaishyas and Dasa for Shudras. Thus the names might read Vishnusharma, Mahendravarma, Devagupta and Devadasa. Such names in modern Hindu society do not necessarily indicate varna or jati.

Girls could be named after certain constellations, rivers or birds, and in the past names such as Rayvati, Rohini, Ganga, Yamuna and Maina were quite popular. Names chosen by modern Hindu parents for their children are not so traditional, and may come from the worlds of film, music or literature.

The births of all Hindu children in Britain are registered, as the law demands for all; but in India this is not always the case, which can give rise to problems in later life regarding passport applications, school or college enrollment, or pension claims. Many parents in India get round this difficulty by having horoscopes cast for their children, which show not only the date but also the time of birth. These are acceptable to Indian officials, but such documents may not prove adequate in Britain without further documentation; and it is often difficult to get this from India.

Important childhood sacraments

If a Hindu woman has her baby in a hospital or a private nursing home, the first journey from the hospital back home has no religious significance. The rite of the first outing is performed in the third or fourth month after birth, so that the child becomes aware of its surroundings. The scriptures suggest that this rite should be done in the light half of the month, when the moon is clearly seen. On the day of the ritual, the parents and the baby bathe early. The father offers puja and special prayers to the family deities at the home shrine; the child is dressed in new clothes which are of dark colours, and a small dab of lamp-black or soot is applied to its forehead and cheek. This is designed to avert the eye of envy from women who have no children of their own. The baby is taken out of the house and shown the sun for a few seconds; care is taken not to harm its eyes through overexposure.

In a city, a baby is taken to the nearest temple, but in a village it is taken to the shrine of the guardian goddess to receive blessings. The mother and baby are accompanied by other female relatives who carry flowers, a piece of new cloth and a coconut which the mother offers to the goddess with prayers for a long and healthy life for the baby. In the evening, the child is shown the moon. A four-month-old baby is made aware of light, darkness, shapes and colours through this ritual.

The rite of the first solid food is performed seven or eight months after birth. In well-to-do families, the father offers special prayers to the family deities as he performs the morning puja. The child is first fed a small quantity of boiled rice mixed with yoghurt, ghee and honey by the father, using a spoon. The mother then completes the feeding. A child from a poor family may be given only some rice and milk as its first taste of solid food. The rich, Westernized families in India probably use special baby-food from an expensive tin for this ritual.

The time for the first haircut of a boy is chosen after his first birthday, and the ritual may not be performed until the third year if the child is weak. Nowadays, only the orthodox Brahmin families perform this rite elaborately. The barber is paid cash and a quantity of rice and millet. The head is not completely shorn; a small tuft of hair is left at the front. Most boys, however, follow the Western fashion. In some parts of India, young girls also experience this ritual. A medical text from about 180 CE recommends periodic shaving of the head to promote a strong growth of hair.

Until the beginning of this century, many Brahmin boys had the upper part of their right ear pierced when they were about six years old. This ritual enabled them to wear an ornament consisting of a golden ring with pearls, but the custom has steadily gone out of fashion. A child's earlobes are pierced either on the day of its naming ceremony or when it is a few months old.

These rites mark the important stages in a child's growth. The most significant rite of passage is the sacred thread, which marks the end of childhood. A young Hindu's experience of his thread ceremony is given in Chapter 01 of this book.

Marriage

Marriage is perhaps the most important event in a Hindu family. It is a significant rite of passage for a young man or woman since it changes their *ashrama*, or stage in life. For a woman, it is also a major religious ritual marking adulthood since women normally do not experience the sacred thread ceremony.

Arranged marriage: a cultural phenomenon

In Western culture the majority of marriages take place because the couple have fallen in love with each other and have mutually decided to marry. In India the majority of marriages are arranged or assisted by people interested in the welfare of the couple. Because 82 per cent of India's population is Hindu it is assumed that only Hindus have arranged marriages. In fact, it is a cultural phenomenon that applies not only to Hindus, but also Sikhs, Jains, Muslims and Christians.

The need for such a practice

Where a young couple have themselves chosen each other as marriage partners without any assistance from either family, and intend to set up a nuclear home, either in Britain or in India, they are not likely to have day-to-day contact with other members of the extended family. Of course, they will meet the others for short periods on special family occasions. But in their home in a large city, the young wife will have the freedom to run the small household to suit her husband and herself, and develop her own lifestyle.

But when a young bride comes into her husband's family and has to live in a large household where two or three generations live under the same roof, she has to adjust to the cultural pattern in her new family. The senior woman, probably the mother-in-law, runs the household, supervizing all domestic matters such as cooking, the daily puja, washing of clothes and the celebrations of various religious rituals. If the young bride comes from a family which does not have cultural traditions and patterns of behaviour similar to those in her new home, she will find it hard to adjust to the new lifestyle, and there will be minor clashes with almost all members in her new home. A daughter-in-law, for example, may favour wearing *shalwar-khamiz* (trousers with a long overshirt), though her new family may insist on a sari; she may use garlic in cooking, which could be a polluting food for her husband and his relations; her ritual observations may not be in harmony with those of her husband's family. For these reasons a young man's parents and other senior relatives will undertake a long search to select a bride for him from a family with similar religious, cultural and financial traditions and capabilities as their own. For example, problems would certainly arise should a young man from a village background, studying agriculture at university in order to increase output from the village landowners' farms, fall in love with and marry a sophisticated urban graduate, and expect her to adapt to a rural lifestyle. In a society full of wide status and custom divergences, as modern India is, arranged marriages safeguard family unity and prosperity to the benefit of husband and wife, their children and relatives, and their community.

The match-makers

Both parents of a marriageable young woman begin their search for a suitable bridegroom by speaking about it to their close friends, who in turn spread the word among families of similar religious and cultural traditions with marriageable sons. In these preliminary soundings, details of the prospective bride's caste and varna, age, physical appearance, skin complexion, accomplishments, education, paid employment if she has one, and the financial status of the family, are given to the possible bridegroom's family. The search may continue for months, even a couple of years. Many candidates are rejected: perhaps because they are very rich, or not suitably educated, because they are rich and highly educated but belong to a lower varna, because they have some physical defect or because some member of their family has leucoderma, diabetes, or some other hereditary disease.

Sometimes the search is very short and the parents quickly find a prospective bridegroom from a family of equal standing to their own. A meeting of the two families is arranged. If the young people like each other, their parents enter into serious negotiations. At this stage, the family priests of both sides study the birth horoscopes of the bride and bridegroom, and if they match, the betrothal takes place, a suitable auspicious day for the wedding is chosen, and the preparations begin in earnest.

Advertisements in the matrimonial sections of prominent Sunday newspapers in India are quicker match-makers because they cut out the middleman and directly reach those seeking marriage partners. Families from all five religious groups mentioned above who are seeking suitable partners for their sons or daughters, and some Europeans living in India, take advantage of the 'matrimonial columns' service provided by newspapers such as *The Hindu* in Madras or *The Times of India*, in Bombay.

Matrimonial advertisements

BRIDEGROOMS WANTED *The Hindu*
Enquiries invited from middle-class Andhra Brahmin parents of sons between 28 and 32, professions India/UK/USA for Andhra Brahmin, smart graduate girl 25, height 158 cm. Doing postgraduate study in the UK. Reply with photo and horoscope. Box 123, c/o The Hindu, Madras.

Alliance invited for a Tamil Iyer girl 33, MA. A divorced graduate with sound income and no children will also be considered. Reply with photo and horoscope to Box 629, c/o The Hindu, Madras.

Kerala Muslim girl, 32, graduate, college lecturer. Well placed, pious family, invites alliance. Box 792, c/o The Hindu, Madras.

BRIDES WANTED *The Times of India*
A handsome Parsee doctor, 28, height 180 cms, earning 15,000 RS. per month in Bombay invites enquiries from parents of well educated, fair and attractive daughters. Photo. Apply box – M121, The Times of India, Bombay.

Indian Christian computer engineer, 35. American citizen. Own house in New Jersey. Wants sophisticated girl, any caste. Apply with photo. Box T35 US. c/o The Times of India, Bombay.

Austrian businessman, carpet exporter, central India, 38. Height 175 cm, fair hair, blue eyes, seeks very attractive, well-educated Westernized Hindu girl. Complexion and caste immaterial. Send photo c/o Box AB95, c/o The Times of India, Bombay.

A Kshatriya government officer with car and flat in Bombay, 27, height 168 cm seeks bride from a high caste Hindu family. Must be a graduate, with a light complexion. Photo. Box KG854 c/o The Times of India, Bombay.

In the specimen matrimonial advertisements given above, four factors are considered as important in almost all of them. Can you say which they are? Most of these advertisements found in Indian newspapers are placed by the families of the prospective brides or bridegrooms. Orthodox Brahmin families usually ask for the horoscope of the prospective bride or bridegroom. As the

Tamil girl in the advertisement is in her thirties, her family cannot be choosy, and are prepared to consider a divorced graduate. Invariably these advertisements refer to skin complexion and caste, either directly or indirectly. In contrast, such advertisements from men and women seeking partners also appear in British newspapers, but here they are placed by the individuals themselves. They mention personal interests such as music, theatre, wining and dining, country walks and the like, which the advertisers hope to share with their partners. Indian newspaper advertisements do not mention any personal interests of the young men and women concerned.

The third type of matchmakers are the matrimonial agencies found in Indian cities. These charge a fee for providing full information about prospective brides and bridegrooms and their families to their clients. The agencies are approached by parents, who supply details about their son or daughter and state their own expectations. From the hundreds of completed forms in the files of the agency, the parents then receive details of possible partners for their children. These agencies in India invariably introduce *families* to each other, which underlines the fact that Hindu marriages are unions between two families rather than two individuals.

There are introduction agencies in London and Leicester which specifically cater for professional young Hindu men and women. The people who run these introduction parties, which include dinner and disco dancing, are well known to the parents of the young people attending the parties. The organizers and the participants belong to the same caste associations. It is the young people wishing to find suitable marriage partners who enrol their names with the agencies; although their parents do not attend the parties they are reassured by the knowledge that the organizers will act as watchful, but almost invisible, chaperones to ensure responsible behaviour by the young participants.

Here, Nisha, a young Gujarati woman, who works as a computer programmer, describes an introduction party she recently attended:

Introduction party

I registered my name with 'Introductions Select' nearly three months ago. My parents had been suggesting for quite a while that I should think of getting married but I had told them that I did not want an arranged marriage. When two of my friends, Gita and

Pushpa, told me that they had enrolled their names with the agency called 'Introductions Select', I registered with the same agency. When there was no early response, I thought that I had wasted my £10. I had almost given up. Then the invitation came through the post. The same day Pushpa phoned to tell me about her invitation, and told me that Gita had also received a similar one.

The party was arranged from 7 to 11pm at a small hotel, and included soft drinks and chat for an hour, followed by a formal dinner and a disco afterwards. We were greeted by the Gujarati couple who organized the party. There were about 15 women and maybe 20 men. Each of us had to wear a lapel card with our name. Over the soft drink cocktails I chatted to three young men. One spoke Hindi, which created a kind of barrier between us since I speak English and Gujarati, but not Hindi. One or two girls seemed shy and the adult staff took the trouble to introduce them to some young men. I got on quite well with the other two men, and I must say I rather liked one of them called Raman. He spoke Gujarati and was also into computers. We sat next to each other at dinner and talked non-stop. He was a good dancer too. I enjoyed myself at the party, and the evening cost £20.

Before leaving, Raman asked me for my phone number. Whether he phones me or not, I intend to attend more parties to widen my choice. I have decided to wait until the right man comes along. After all, I am only 24.

As has already been indicated, not all Hindu marriages are arranged. Many young men and women, particularly from Westernized families living in the cities, find their own marriage partners. In India, such self-choice pairings are termed 'love marriages', and these may be between men and women from different religions, or, if both are Hindu, they may not belong to the same caste. Many young people in cities meet their future partners at college, at their place of work or at amateur drama groups. In these situations they tend to be drawn to those with family backgrounds similar to their own, and their love marriage is approved by their respective parents, because the parents' expectations of having a son- or daughter-in-law from the same caste are automatically fulfilled.

In Britain, many young Hindus exercise their freedom of choice with active encouragement from their parents, and there are many cases in which a Hindu man or woman has married a partner who is Christian and white. In most cases the European daughter-in-law is warmly welcomed into the Hindu family whether she becomes a Hindu or retains her Christian faith. Now European sons-in-law, too, are becoming more readily acceptable to Hindu families.

Wedding preparations

After the young son or daughter has found a suitable partner and agreed to marry, both families begin their preparations. Although the practice of dowry has been made illegal by Acts of the Indian Parliament, some sort of financial agreement is often made between the families. An auspicious day for the wedding is chosen and a priest is selected. Not all families worry about selecting an auspicious day, but orthodox families will consult the Hindu almanac, which lists propitious days for weddings. In India marriages are usually celebrated during the eight months from December to July. The months from August to November are unsuitable because of the monsoons and the celebration of major festivals, such as Navaratri and Divali. Traditionally, the wedding takes place in the bride's home, and all expenses are borne by her family. In most cases nowadays a hall is hired to accommodate a large number of guests, and caterers are appointed to provide the wedding feast. The bride's family buys her various gold ornaments, such as necklaces, bangles and rings, but the wedding necklace of black beads is given by the bridegroom on the day of the ceremony. Wedding invitations are printed in regional Indian languages, but for a Hindu wedding in Britain the invitations are usually printed in English.

Pre-wedding rituals

In India, since the 1955 Hindu Law reform legislation, all Hindu marriages are to be registered, though this is not always the case in practice, especially in rural areas. In Britain, all marriages between Hindus are subject to formal registration because the hired halls used for the religious ceremonies are usually not registered for the solemnization of matrimony. A few days before the main ceremony, worship is offered to Ganesha and the family deities by the parents of the bride and the bridegroom in their separate homes. Prayers are said in the hope that the couple may be blessed with wealth, prosperity, children, long life and happiness, and that the wedding day will be free from any obstacles.

A specimen invitation for a Hindu wedding in Britain

(Reproduced with the permission of the bridegroom's family)

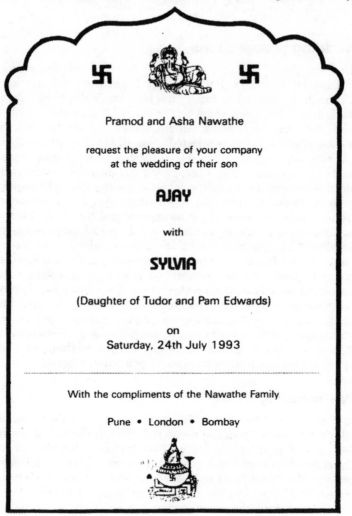

Pramod and Asha Nawathe

request the pleasure of your company
at the wedding of their son

AJAY

with

SYLVIA

(Daughter of Tudor and Pam Edwards)

on
Saturday, 24th July 1993

With the compliments of the Nawathe Family

Pune • London • Bombay

the above invitation shows that the bride is not a Hindu
the picture of Ganesha, the swastikas, and the water vessel with a coconut
on it and a lamp beside it are auspicious Hindu symbols usually printed on
wedding invitations
the bridegroom's family is settled in London, but maintains close contact
with other relatives living in India

The wedding day

The length of the religious service has always depended on the scholarship of the priests, and has varied enormously in the past. Time was when Hindu weddings lasted for four or five days, with a couple of religious rituals performed each day, the rest of the time being devoted to feasting! But now the religious service is shortened and streamlined. The service explained below contains mantras from the *Rig-Veda* and other scriptures, which are recited in Sanskrit to accompany and emphasize rituals with religious significance. The whole service lasts for about three hours, which leaves sufficient time for an elaborate wedding feast before the hired hall has to be vacated.

Meaningful participation in the service by the guests is determined by the design of the hall. Usually the assembly area is used for dining and the service is conducted on the stage at one end. This is not a very satisfactory arrangement because the guests sitting towards the back of the hall cannot see the rituals or hear the mantras clearly. If a school hall is hired for the day, the dinner can be served in the school dining hall and the main assembly hall can be used for the religious service. Ideally, a temporary altar is set up in the middle of the hall, on which are arranged the murtis of Ganesha and the family deities and the two water vessels with coconuts. The metal container for the sacred fire and other materials can be laid out near the altar. The guests can be seated on chairs on all four sides of the altar, so that everyone can see the rituals and hear the mantras clearly. The bride and her parents sit before the altar facing east, and purify themselves by sipping water as the priest utters 24 names of Vishnu. The following 15 rituals are performed on the wedding day as the priest recites the appropriate mantras:

Invocation of Ganesha The hired hall is considered the temporary home of the bride. The bride's parents invoke the family deities, the river goddess represented by the water vessels, and god Ganesha, to be present at the place of the wedding, to remove all obstacles and to bless the couple. The priest recites a mantra from the *Rig-Veda* to invoke Ganesha. A simple puja is then offered to the deities.

Worship of Parvati The bride then withdraws to a small room to offer private worship to Parvati and Shiva and to seek blessings for prosperity, long married life, health and children, especially sons.

The bridegroom arrives   The bridegroom arrives at the place of the wedding with his parents. He is welcomed at the door of the hall by the bride's mother who has a sacred light to ward off evil spirits. The priest recites a verse praising Vishnu, for on the day the bridegroom and the bride are likened to Vishnu and Lakshmi and given due honour. The bride's parents and the priest bring the bridegroom into the hall and give him a seat of honour near the altar.

Honey and welcome   He is then given honey by the bride's father to sweeten the welcome, while the priest recites a mantra from the *Yajur-Veda*.

A daughter is given in marriage   The bride's parents formally give their daughter in marriage and she is accepted by the bridegroom and his parents. By this action parental consent is made open and public, being witnessed by the guests. In this ritual three generations of ancestors of the young couple are mentioned three times by name.

The bride says: 'Dear friend, you must not offend against me in your observance of *dharma* (religious and social duty), *artha* (the earning of money) and *kama* (enjoyment of the good things in life); you must be moderate.'

The bridegroom replies: 'Fortunate one, I promise to be moderate in dharma, artha and kama.'

After having her bridegroom's promise of moderation, the bride will be happy to promise in return, at the 'seven steps' ritual, that she will support her husband in his lawful endeavours.

The young couple and their parents stand facing each other holding hands, while making a vow of friendship.

Expressing three wishes   The couple stand facing each other, holding rice grains in their left hands, each alternately expressing the hope that their three wishes be fulfilled. As the bridegroom expresses his wish the bride puts rice grains on his head and says, 'So be it', voicing her support. The bridegroom similarly voices his support when the bride expresses her wish: 'I hope for increasing good fortune, plenty of money and healthy children.' The bridegroom then says, 'I hope to be able to perform *yajna* (*havan*) and other rituals, fulfil my dharma and achieve success and fame through my occupation.' This ritual indicates that the marriage will thrive only through mutual co-operation.

Symbolic marriage bond The couple sit opposite each other. The bridegroom ties a piece of soft cotton thread tinged with yellow turmeric (or with a piece of turmeric root entwined in it) round the left wrist of the bride. The bride ties a similar thread round the bridegroom's right wrist. This ritual symbolizes their marriage bond. This thread with the turmeric root is used as an amulet to exorcise evil spirits, to enable the couple's relatives to prosper, and to bind the couple in mutually dutiful affection.

a bride and bridegroom offer roasted rice and ghee to Agni, the God of Fire at their wedding ceremony

The marriage necklace The bridegroom then fastens a necklace of black beads round his bride's neck to bring them good fortune, love and affection, and lifelong friendship. Black beads are used to avert the evil eye.

Taking the bride's hand The bridegroom takes his bride's right hand in his right hand and repeats the mantra which the priest first recites. The mantra means: 'I take your hand to bring us good fortune. I hope you grow old with me as your husband. The gods have entrusted you to me so that I may fulfil my duties as a married householder.'

Offerings to the sacred fire The couple sit before the sacred fire, which is kindled in a metal container. The materials for oblation, namely darbha grass, sacred woods and ghee, are placed in front of them. The bridegroom sprinkles water over the materials to purify them. As the priest recites the appropriate mantras, the bridegroom offers darbha grass to the fire which is meant for god Skanda (son of Shiva). The bride touches his right hand as he makes the offerings. The sacred wood is then offered to Agni, god of fire.

Then follow the seven oblations of ghee, the first to Prajapati, the second to Soma and the remaining five to Agni.

Roasted millet offering, circumambulation and stepping on a stone slab This three-part ritual is performed three times. The first oblation of roasted millet is given to Agni. The sacred fire and the water vessels are circumambulated, the bride following the bridegroom. The bride is asked to step on a stone slab and be firm as a rock. This order is repeated twice more.

The second oblation of roasted millet is given to god Varuna and the third to the Sun god. The next two rituals are performed after each offering. Before each circumambulation the bridegroom says: 'My bride, I am sky, you are earth. I am the melody of the *Sama-Veda*, you are the hymn of the *Rig-Veda*. Let us marry and have children. Dear to each other, radiant, well disposed, let us live for a hundred autumns.'

'Seven steps' ritual In the past, when the religious ceremony was the only requirement for a valid Hindu marriage in India, the 'seven steps' ritual was crucial to the completion of the marriage wherever this ritual was included in the service. A marriage could be declared null and void at any stage before this ritual. It is an important stage in the service, but in some cases it is not performed in Britain.

The scriptures demand that the 'seven steps' ritual be performed to the north of the fire in a straight line, where the priest makes seven small heaps of rice, about 30 cm apart. The bridegroom should put his right hand on the bride's right shoulder. When the bridegroom speaks the mantra the bride takes a step forward with her right foot, onto one of the heaps of rice, and brings her left foot forward to stand still. Each step is taken with the right foot in a slow march as the mantra is repeated.

The couple stand side by side, and before each step the bridegroom says, 'My bride, take the first step for a plentiful supply of food. Support me in my endeavours.' The bride takes the step and says: 'I will support you in your righteous undertakings.'

The mantra is modified as necessary and the seven steps are walked together by the couple:

Take the second step for strength,
Take the third step for wealth,
Take the fourth step for happiness,
Take the fifth step for children. May we be blessed with many sons. May they live to a ripe old age.
Take the sixth step so that we may enjoy seasonal pleasures together.
Take the seventh for a lifelong friendship.

Prayers to Agni   One more oblation of ghee is given to Agni. The couple stand before the fire and offer prayers.

'Grant me, O Agni, the conveyor of oblations, faith, intellect, success, understanding, learning, wisdom, riches, strength, long life, power and good health.'

The priest sprinkles the couple with water, reciting a mantra:

'With the inspiration from god Savita, with the arms of the Ashvins, with the hands of god Pushana, with the brightness of Agni, with the lustre of the Sun, with the power of Indra, I sprinkle you with this water mixed with gold, so that you may be blessed with strength, riches, success and food. May this action turn out to be a sprinkling with nectar. May there be peace, prosperity and contentment.'

The marriage ceremony is brought to its conclusion by the bride's parents.

Verses of blessing   Now that the bride and the bridegroom have reached the status of wife and husband, the assembled guests give their blessings.

The bridegroom stands facing west. A silk cloth decorated with the sacred symbols, Om and swastika, is held by two close friends of the families as a screen in front of the bridegroom. The bride, escorted by her maternal uncle, arrives and stands opposite the bridegroom, facing east. They cannot see each other. Rice grains tinged with red kum-kum are distributed among the guests. Eight verses of blessing are chanted by the priests and others. At the end of each verse after the refrain the guests symbolically shower their blessings upon the newlyweds by throwing a few grains of rice.

At the end of the verses of blessing, the silk screen is removed. The couple give each other garlands and put a few grains of rice on each other's head.

Blessings, good wishes The bride's parents advise their daughter about her duty to her new family by saying:

'My daughter, be a queen with your husband's father, be a queen with your husband's mother, be a queen with your husband's sister, be a queen with your husband's brothers' (implying that she should win over their hearts by her charm and modest behaviour).

The priest blesses the newlyweds with the following three mantras:

'Remain and act as a couple without any difference of opinion. May you be blessed with long life. May you happily live in your home playing with your sons and grandsons.'

'May your hearts hold similar intentions and thoughts. May you act with one mind. May your actions reflect unity of purpose.'

'May you progressively prosper and live to enjoy 100 autumn, winter and spring seasons. Worship and propitiate the gods Indra, Agni, Savita and Brahaspati. They will grant you a further 100 years.'

With these blessings ends the wedding service.

In the evening the couple offer prayers to Ursa Major and the Pole Star. When the bride enters her new home, she is asked to kick a pot of grain at the threshold so that the grain will spill into the house, symbolically bringing prosperity into her new home. Then the bride is given a new first name symbolic of a new beginning.

(All mantras given in quotation marks in this wedding service translated by Hemant Kanitkar.)

a bride and bridegroom walk the 'seven steps' together at their wedding; each step is taken with the right foot after speaking the relevant mantra

Cremation

The final rite of passage is cremation, which is the normal practice of disposing of the dead. However, very young babies, who are not yet named and therefore not full members of the family, are not given ritual cremation, but are buried. So are the *sannyasins* (world-renouncers), since they have no relatives to perform the cremation rites.

When a Hindu villager dies a natural death, the local doctor or the subsidised medical practitioner (equivalent to a paramedic), signs the death certificate, and the nearest male relative of the deceased has to arrange the funeral. In large cities, the corpse can be conveyed to the cremation in a motorized vehicle, and is burnt using gas or electricity. But in small towns and villages a different method is employed:

Who performs the funeral rites?

Deceased person	The performer
A married woman	The husband
A widow	(eldest) Son
An unmarried woman	Father, or elder brother
A married man/widower	(eldest) Son, grandson
An unmarried man	Father, brother, uncle

Ramji's story

I am Ramji and I am a farmer in a village in the Maratha country. The nearest market town is five miles away. I own two fields of six acres each, where I grow millet and sugar cane. I have two bullocks, a bullock-cart, one buffalo and my own wooden plough. Most of the millet provides our bread for about eight months in a year, but I sell the sugar cane crop to the sugar factory for cash, which is sufficient for us to buy clothes and extra food.

I was married to Manju for 20 years, but two months ago she died of a stomach illness. I have two sons aged 16 and 12 and both help on the farm.

Manju had been ill for about three months. Our local medicine man began treating her but she didn't improve, so I took her to hospital in the market town. The doctor there told me that Manju had some illness in her stomach for which he had no cure. He gave her some medicine to reduce the pain.

Poor Manju! She suffered a lot. One day she said that I should give her some Ganga water and some basil leaves. I went to Pandit Govind, our village priest, who had a small copper bottle with Ganga water. I came home, opened the bottle and gave Manju the holy water. She said it was Bhagwan's (God's) wish. My two sons and I sat near her that night. She seemed to be asleep. Suddenly she opened her eyes, touched our hands and said, 'Rama, Rama'. Then she closed her eyes and grew cold and lifeless. Our medicine man came and said that she was dead. We had to control our grief and prepare for her final journey.

I sent my eldest son and a neighbour in our bullock-cart to the hospital in the town, to tell the doctor of Manju's death and get the death paper. I had also asked them to bring wood fuel for burning the body. It was the middle of the night when the bullock-cart left for the town and it would not be back until noon the next day. In the morning I went to Pandit Govind, who agreed to say the mantra words on the cremation ground near our local stream.

The wives of neighbours came to bathe Manju's body and dress her in her new sari. Two neighbours went to cut the bamboo poles from the thicket on the edge of the village. I had already bought a piece of white cloth since I knew that Manju would not live long.

The bullock-cart returned at 11 o'clock with the death paper, dry wood fuel and cowdung slabs. Now Pandit Govind came with some flowers, joss stocks and camphor tablets. When the bamboo poles arrived, we prepared a stretcher, placed Manju's body on it and covered it with the white cloth, leaving the face open to the sun. I put some red and yellow powders on Manju's forehead, and placed flowers on her body. I walked in front carrying an earthen pot with live coals. Three neighbours and my elder son lifted the stretcher. Manju's feet pointed in the direction of the cremation ground. We all chanted the name of god Rama throughout Manju's last journey. The wood fuel and the cowdung slabs had arrived before us. With the help of my friends I built a pyre. The body was placed on it, feet pointing south. Pandit Govind placed the sandalwood joss sticks and camphor tablets on the pyre. He said the mantra as I lit the pyre on all sides, pouring vegetable oil on it. Pandit Govind drilled a hole in the earthen pot and filled the pot with water. I walked round the blazing pyre holding the pot. Water dripped onto the ground making a line. Then I stood with my back to the pyre and flung the pot backwards. It fell near the pyre and broke into pieces. The pyre blazed for an hour, and when we heard the skull crack, we bathed in the stream and went home. We were in mourning for ten days. On the third day Pandit Govind and I went to collect the ashes. On the tenth day he helped me to offer cooked rice balls to Manju's soul. Pandit Govind does only funerals and charged me 25 rupees. Even after two months we three walk with heavy hearts.

In Britain Hindu funerals are carried out in the same way as other funerals, the corpse being placed in a coffin and left in the funeral parlour at the undertakers' until it is time to take it to the crematorium, where the cremation is by gas. Pandit Sharma relates his experiences:

I officiate as a priest mainly at Hindu rituals and ceremonies such as thanksgiving puja, festivals, the sacred thread and marriage. I normally do not conduct any funeral rites because they are spiritually polluting. But there is a shortage of Hindu funeral priests in Britain, so occasionally I have to perform funerals. On such rare occasions, I do not charge a fee and certainly do not accept any gifts, because the sins of the deceased are believed to cling to such gifts.

Close relatives come to the funeral parlour, where the chief mourner is asked to wind soft cotton thread round the coffin. This acts as a boundary round the soul, so, it is believed, that it will not come back to earth as a ghost and haunt the living. In some cases, six *pindas*, balls of dough made with wholemeal flour, are placed on the body in the coffin. Water mixed with sesame seeds is poured into the mouth of the corpse. Many unlit joss sticks are placed round the corpse, or alternatively, sandalwood. A flower garland is placed round the neck of the corpse. The relatives and friends who come to the funeral parlour offer a flower to the deceased to say good-bye. After this ritual, the coffin is closed and brought to the chapel at the crematorium.

When the mourners have taken their seats, I read ten verses from the second chapter of the *Bhagavad-Gita*, which describe the nature of the soul and advise the mourners not to grieve because death is natural to all who are born. The close relatives are asked to place flowers on the coffin. Then I recite the funeral verse from the *Veda*. As the coffin slowly begins to slide through the window, all the mourners stand and chant the name of god Rama.

When I return home, I put all the clothes I am wearing into the laundry bag, and bathe to purify myself. The clothes are immediately washed. I advise the relatives of the deceased to send a cash gift to a medical charity such as Cancer Research, or the British Heart Foundation, in remembrance of the dead.

The ashes are collected from the crematorium by the relatives, and are either sent to India to be deposited in the Ganges or committed to the sea here.

The shraddha ceremony

On the 11th day after death an offering of ten *pindas* (balls of cooked rice, moistened with milk and water) is made, which is believed to help the deceased to acquire a new body for the next existence. These immediate post-cremation rites are inauspicious and spiritually polluting.

The shraddha ceremony is the annual homage paid to the departed ancestor, and the procedure is described in special texts called *Shraddha-Kalpa*. The annual homage rites are auspicious. Many Hindus try to perform the first annual shraddha at a holy place such as Hardwar on the Ganges; thereafter the ceremony is performed at home by devout Dvija families. Each invited Brahmin represents a departed ancestor on the day of the ceremony, and many families commemorate all departed ancestors on the same day. All close relatives are also invited to share the offerings, which consist of sesamum, water and pinda. The Brahmins are fed before the relatives. Other food is also served according to local custom, along with the pinda. Very close relatives receive a portion of pinda, with sesamum and water; remote relatives receive only sesamum and water. Each Brahmin is given a cash gift at the end of the meal. Many Hindu families in Britain take care to observe the shraddha ceremony after the death of a relative.

Rebirth

Some scholars hold that the idea of transmigration of the soul was adopted by the vedic Aryans from the original inhabitants of India. It was first mentioned in the *Shatapatha Brahmana* text and later developed in the *Upanishads*, the laws of Manu and the *Puranas*.

Hindus believe that the individual *atman*, the soul, passes through a long cycle of existence occupying different bodies and experiencing repeated births, deaths and rebirths. This cycle is called *samsara*; it is what every Hindu tries to break to reach *moksha* (liberation).

This concept may become clearer if we think of samsara as a post to which is tethered a calf, representing the individual soul. The rope that ties the calf to the post is the restricting and controlling force of *karma*.

The word karma is used in different senses to mean action, deeds, destiny, fate; but in the context of rebirth karma means the consequence or the result of actions. The universal order, rita, which is the foundation of dharma, is governed by the natural law of cause and effect. Action is unavoidable for all beings, for it is through actions that life is sustained.

Even unconscious actions such as breathing, or thought processes, produce results. There are actions undertaken with a particular motive and actions that are essential to fulfil one's social position or to satisfy one's nature. Every kind of action produces some kind of effect, good or bad.

The sum total of an individual's desires, feelings, thoughts and actions constitutes his/her karma. It is karma in a previous existence that determines the kind of body occupied by the atman in the next existence. It is possible to cut the ropes of karma and escape from the post of samsara.

The different paths that reduce the burden of karma are: the knowledge of Brahman, atman and the universe; selfless actions; deep and single-minded meditation and exercise; and total and complete surrender to God to receive divine grace, which will neutralize karma.

Thus the law of karma, which adjusts debit and credit for good and evil actions, determines rebirth. It can be said that man is punished by his wicked actions, not *for* them.

08

scriptures

In this chapter you will learn:
- about *Rig-Veda*, the oldest holy text
- about the Shruti texts
- about the Smriti texts
- about the role of the written word in Hinduism.

Scripture doesn't play the central part in Hinduism that it does in some other faiths. The student might search in vain in a temple for a sacred text, but it will not be found in the form of a book. It will be there in the words spoken by the priest performing the ritual.

The earliest scriptures of the faith now known as Hinduism are believed to have been composed between 1200 BCE and 1000 BCE, by the Aryans who began to settle in north-west India in about 1500 BCE. This was the start of the vast amount of literature produced during a period of 1000 years between 1200 BCE and 200 BCE. This period is known as the vedic Age since the scriptures are called the *Veda*, which comprises four different compositions. It is strongly believed that these texts were received by inspired scholars from God; they learnt them by heart and passed them on to the next generation by word of mouth.

The vedic texts are traditionally called *shruti*, 'hearing', for two reasons: they are believed to be eternal, and were 'heard' by scholars directly from God. For centuries they have been received by pupils orally from their teachers who recited them. The pupils repeated the words and intonation of the teacher exactly as they heard them, so that they have been preserved orally for thousands of years. The earliest manuscript of the *Rig-Veda* dates from the 15th century CE. Modern scholar priests prefer to recite a vedic text from memory, even though it may be available in printed form. The shruti texts are composed in the older form of Sanskrit, called the vedic.

Shruti texts

The *Vedas*: (1200–1000 BCE) These are four separate compositions called the *Rig-Veda*, the *Yajur-Veda*, the *Sama-Veda* and the *Atharva-Veda*. Each *Veda* has four parts: chronologically these are the *Samhita*, the *Brahmanas*, the *Aranyakas* and the *Upanishads*.

The *Samhitas* contain hymns praising God under different names. They constitute the main body of each *Veda* and are the most ancient part.

Rig-Veda Samhita: This is the oldest of the four *Vedas*. The text is divided into ten books (called *mandalas*) and has 1028 hymns praising ancient deities. Some of these deities have been mentioned in Chapter 04. Many hymns from the *Rig-Veda* also occur in the next two *Vedas*, but they are differently arranged for ritual purposes.

Yajur-Veda Samhita: This was used as a handbook by the priests performing the vedic sacrifices. The present text is in two collections.

Sama-Veda Samhita: This consists of chants and melodies, and indicates tunes for the singing of the hymns at special sacrifices.

Atharva-Veda Samhita: This has preserved many pre-Aryan traditions dealing with spells, charms and magical formulae.

Many mantras from these texts are used in modern Hindu worship and ritual. The *Gayatri* verse from the *Rig-Veda* is widely recited in daily worship. Hymns describing god Vishnu and Purusha, Cosmic Man, are recited during the performance of an elaborate puja. Verses from the first two *Vedas* are used as mantras in the sacred thread and marriage ceremonies.

The *Brahmanas*: (800–500 BCE) These are prose manuals of ritual and prayer for the guidance of priests. They form the second section of the vedic literature and were composed after the *Samhita*. There are seven important *Brahmana* texts.

The *Aranyakas*: (400–200 BCE) These resulted from discussion in the forests about worship, meditation and ritual. They form the third section of the shruti. There are only four texts surviving, which are attached to the first two *Vedas*.

The *Upanishads*: (400–200 BCE) These compositions contain mystical concepts of Hindu philosophy. The word *upa-nishad* means 'near-sitting', which indicates that these texts were tutorials given by Gurus to their chosen pupils, who sat near them to receive the mystical teaching.

These texts were composed towards the end (*anta*) of the vedic period and form the basis of what is therefore called Vedanta philosophy. Although composed later than the other three sections, some of them are incorporated in the *Brahmanas* and the *Aranyakas* and have similar names. The *Brahmanas* deal with ritual performance but the *Upanishads* are concerned with philosophical knowledge. Traditionally, there are 108 texts, but only 15 are considered important.

Some of the most important Hindu philosophical ideas are contained in these texts. They are:

• the individual soul (*atman*) and universal soul (Brahman) are identical

- Brahman is without form and is eternal
- the visible world is an illusion (*maya*)
- the soul passes through a cycle of successive lives (samsara) and its next existence is determined by the consequences of its actions (karma) in the previous existence
- the soul is capable of achieving liberation (moksha)
- there is a unity of all things in the created universe.

Smriti texts

The popular Hindu epics, the *Mahabharata* and the *Ramayana*, are classed as *smriti* texts, which include religious, moral and educational writings based on 'remembered' tradition. These texts were composed from 500 BCE onwards. Most devout Hindus accept the teachings of smriti texts as long as they do not conflict with those of the shruti. The shruti texts, believed to be the direct word of God, remain the supreme authority.

The *Bhagavad-Gita* is very popular with many Hindus, and although a smriti text, it is believed to be the word of God, since Krishna is an important incarnation of the God Vishnu.

The *Bhagavad Gita*, which might be translated as 'The Song of the Adorable One', is part of the sixth book of the *Mahabharata*, the world's longest poem. However, many scholars think that it has been inserted into the *Mahabharata* and date it between 200 BCE and 200 CE.

The *Bhagavad Gita* takes the form of a dialogue between prince Arjuna and his charioteer, Krishna, who turns out to be an incarnation of the supreme God, Vishnu. The setting is the battlefield of Kurukshetra, where the great and terrible war was fought. The sons of King Pandu are preparing to fight their cousins, the sons of Dhritarashtra. Arjuna, a Pandu prince, decides to turn away from the battle. He envisages the carnage that will ensue and has no wish to kill his kinsmen. Krishna tells him bluntly that it is his dharma to fight.

Dharma, it will be remembered, is a word of many meanings. It is the nearest term to the word 'religion'. Hindus call their religion the *sanatana* dharma, the eternal dharma. It also means custom, or way of life, and duty. Arjuna is a kshatriya, a member of the warrior varna, and as such he has a reponsibility to fight in a just war, *dharma yuddha*, a struggle in the cause of righteousness. The war against those who tricked his family out of their kingdom (which the enemy, the Kaurava princes, had done), is just.

The thread of dharma runs through the *Gita*, so that even in the last chapter Krishna says:

> Better to do one's own caste duty (sva dharma), though devoid of merit, than to do another's, however well performed. By doing the works prescribed by his own nature a man meets no defilement (18:47, cf. 3:35).

Caste duty is laid upon a person at birth and by birth. Throughout the *Gita* Krishna warns against the confusion which must necessarily develop in the divinely ordained order of things if individuals take it upon themselves to reject their own place for that of another.

However, dharma is not the *Gita's* only theme. A dominant theme is that of bhakti, loving devotion to God and the love of God. Krishna teaches that:

> Whoever bears me in mind at the moment of death accedes to my own mode of being. Then muse on me always, for if you fix your mind and soul on me you will come to me set free from doubt (8:5).

This idea is perhaps taken further than in any previous writing, for Krishna also says:

> Whoever makes me his refuge, though he may be base-born (of low caste), even a woman or a shudra, theirs it is to tread the highest way (9:32).

They need give only a flower, the merest token of love, in the spirit of bhakti for Krishna to accept them. He suggests that it is even easier for Brahmins to come to him, thus further suggesting that it is not the purpose of the *Gita* to undermine the *varna-ashrama-dharma* in the process of offering liberation, moksha, to everyone.

The *Bhagavad Gita* mentions the words *samkhya* and *yoga*, two of the orthodox schools of Hindu philosophy, which may be translated literally as 'theory' and 'practice'. The systems are closely, if not inseparably, related. Samkhya provides the analysis of reality, yoga the method of attainment. In the *Gita*, as in the earlier *Svetasvatara Upanishad*, Samkhya-Yoga is theistic. The teaching and method are endorsed in the *Gita*, however, the goal is not isolation but becoming Brahman, and the 'highest Brahman' is Krishna.

Action, *karma*, is also a subject of discussion. Actions cannot be avoided but they should be performed without desire and offered sacrificially to Krishna: then they will benefit the one who performs them. Done with selfish motives, even if they *seem* praiseworthy, they will not have good karmic consequences.

As natural as the theme of action in a dialogue set in the context of war, is the subject of the fate of the soul after death. Arjuna is assured that it does not die with the body, but will be reborn. The prospect is horrifying:

> Birth after birth in this revolving round, these vilest of men, strangers to good, obsessed with hatred and cruelty, I ever hurl into devilish wombs. They never attain to me and so they tread the lowest way (16:19).

Grace is offered to those who behave morally and rationally, but there is a need for human effort. This tempers the doctrine of predestination enunciated by Krishna when he is persuading Arjuna to fight. The fate of the combatants has been decided; Arjuna is merely the agent. In commending devotion to Krishna the *Gita's* author touches on the worship of other gods. They possess reality but are inferior in a sense to Krishna. He says:

> Whosoever worships the gods will surely go to the gods, but whosoever loves and worships me will come to me (7:23).

The perceptive worshipper of any god will realize that the one who is really being worshipped is Krishna.

> Those who devote themselves to other gods and sacrifice to them filled with faith, really worship me (9:23).

The focus of the *Bhagavad Gita* is Krishna, the main character in the dialogue. Defence of dharma seems to be a subordinate theme to commending a devotion to Krishna – which involves the observance of dharma. Arjuna must fight. A hidden purpose of the book may be the repudiation of non-theistic Buddhism, which permitted king Ashoka to embrace pacifism and reject dharma.

Much of popular literature is in the form of stories and poetry, and it is the source material for plays and pageants performed during the celebration of many festivals. The rules of behaviour for different categories of people given in a smriti text can be altered to suit changing circumstances. This enables Hindus to adapt their *dharma*, or personal code of behaviour, according to the needs of the times.

the drawing shows God Krishna, the Divine Teacher, in the *Bhagavad Gita*, driving Arjun's chariot as the warrior prince sets out for the battlefield

---

Smriti texts

1 The educational texts composed after the *Veda*, but considered essential to its study. They deal with the performance of rituals, law, astronomy, grammar, phonetics and literature.
2 The texts explaining the six orthodox systems of philosophy.
3 The epics, the *Bhagavad Gita*.
4 The texts on Hindu mythology. These are called the *Puranas*.
5 The texts of various Hindu sects worshipping Vishnu, Shiva and the Mother Goddess.

Various authors composed the sacred texts at different historical times, and the ideas about God, what is right and wrong, and the forms of worship from the earlier texts, were re-explained in later compositions. This helped to continue the religious and cultural traditions. As has already been mentioned, the early scriptures were in the vedic and Sanskrit languages, but from about the seventh century CE, they were brought to the ordinary people through writings in regional Indian languages.

Sacred literature in regional languages

The religious and philosophical thought contained in the *Vedas*, the shruti texts, was a closed book to many men and women because they were outside the pale of the twice-born, who had a right to study the *Vedas*. Tulsi Das, Tukaram, Mirabai, Dadu, Jnanadeva, Eknath and many other Indians, often of low caste, made available the teachings of Hinduism in poetry, composed in regional languages, to people who were not twice-born or literate. These poets were inspired by their deep personal experience of God. Like the sculptors who worked on some of the magnificent medieval temples, they did not hesitate to employ the imagery of erotic love to describe their relationship with God. *Bhajans*, or devotional songs, composed by some of these poets can be found in the chapter on bhakti (Chapter 12). Others included the Maharashtrian bhakti poets of western India, who composed their works in the regional language, Marathi, to bring the teachings of the *Bhagavata-Purana*, the *Bhagavad-Gita* and the *Upanishads* within the reach of ordinary men and women, and include Jnanadeva, Namadeva, Tukaram, Eknath and Ramadasa.

Namadeva (14th century CE), a tailor by trade, stressed through his many songs that caste status was no barrier to complete devotion to God. Jnanadeva (1275–1296 CE) wrote a book on the *Upanishads* and over 1000 devotional songs, and his commentary of 9000 verses on the *Bhagavad-Gita*, written in old Marathi, is highly popular. It combines devotional philosophy and musical poetry, the two qualities that have kept the book ever-fresh for 700 years.

Eknath (1533–1599 CE) edited Jnanadeva's great work, which had become corrupted since its compositon in 1290 CE, and wrote a commentary on the eleventh chapter of the *Bhagavata-Purana*, which is held to be a classic in Marathi. His devotional songs express his mystical experiences. He made no distinction between brahmin and outcaste and preached Bhakti to all. He re-wrote the *Ramayana* in Marathi.

Ramadasa (17th century CE) is best known for his book, the *Dasabodha*, which is much influenced by the teachings of the *Bhagavad-Gita*. He was a devotee of god Rama and wrote his Marathi version of the Rama story.

The epic *Ramayana*, by Valmiki, is in Sanskrit, and for many centuries was beyond the reach of men and women who spoke only their regional languages. Various poets between the 9th and the 17th centuries CE produced the Rama story in Tamil, Marathi, Hindi, Gujarati and Bengali. All these writers insisted on using regional languages to bring the earlier religious tradition from Sanskrit works within easy reach of ordinary people. Their commentaries, devotional songs and other writings in regional languages have the same sanctity and authority as the earlier scriptures written in Sanskrit.

There were many *bhagats* (devotees), often of low caste, who rejected the caste system, wrote about what they had experienced, and declared that God's liberating love was available to everyone.

Other sacred literature

The story of Hindu sacred literature has no end, only the occasional update. Many Hindus might consider Gandhi's commentary on the *Bhagavad-Gita* inspiring. They would certainly treasure the words of Sri Ramakrishna (1836–1886 CE), the influential Hindu mystic of the 19th century. The writings of A.C. Bhaktivedanta (Prabhupada), the founder of the International Society for Krishna Consciousness (ISKCON) – the Hare Krishna movement, are popular beyond the Hare Krishna devotees, and are used in the religious education of young Hindus of Indian origin growing up in Britain.

The role of the written word in Hinduism

Although the correct performance of various religious rituals is firmly based on scriptures, the physical presence of the scripture in the form of written words is very often non-existent. The worshipper or the officiating priest learns the procedure and the mantras from the written texts, commits them to memory and recites them at the appropriate time in the ritual to accompany the actions.

Orthodox Brahmins recite from memory the Gayatri verse and other mantras from the *Rig-Veda* when they perform daily Sandhya, the worship of the sun, offering water oblations to it. Professional priests officiating at the sacred thread or marriage ceremonies hardly ever look at the written words of the mantras from the *Vedas* or the *Grihya Sutras* (texts giving the procedure and mantras of home based religious rituals). They prefer to recite the mantras from memory to accompany the actions of the participants.

The mantras for the daily puja, either at the home shrine or at a temple, are taken from the *Puranas*. A householder who is not conversant with the Sanskrit mantras will of course look at the written word, but both family and temple priests will recite the puja mantras from memory. Puja is offered to a deity such as Ganesha, Durga, Lakshmi, Vishnu or Shiva at the celebrations of certain festivals, for which recitation from memory is the normal practice.

There are some occasions, however, when the written word becomes important. When a householder performs a *satyanarayana* (thanksgiving) puja with the assistance of a priest, the puja mantras are recited from memory, but the story of the origin of a ritual is read by the priest from the written word while everyone present listens to the spoken word. The people attending the puja consider it more important to hear the words of the sacred text spoken by the priest than to read the story themselves.

When god Krishna's birthday is celebrated in many temples in India, the priest reads the story of Krishna's birth from the written text of the *Bhagavata Purana* and the people present experience the spirituality of the occasion through hearing the words.

During the Ganesha festival, in many homes and temples in India and in Britain, there is daily reading of different portions of the *Bhagavata Purana* for seven days, which is attended by many Hindus. For most people attending these readings, hearing the words of the scripture spoken by the priest is an act of devotion.

Of course, learned Pandits will read and re-read the texts to increase their understanding of the subject, but for most Hindus the spirituality lies in the hearing of the sacred words, whether the priest recites them from memory or reads the written word.

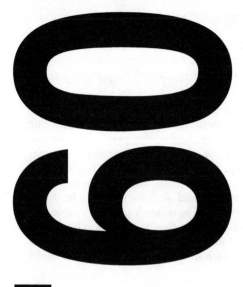

09

pilgrimage

In this chapter you will learn:

- about different sites of pilgrimage
- about the purpose of going on a pilgrimage
- the sacred locations – rivers, mountains, lakes, famous shrines dedicated to Vishnu, Shiva and the Mother Goddess.

Pilgrimage (Yatra)

Hindu religious rituals are classified into three categories: Nitya, Naimittika, and Kamya.

Nitya rituals are those occurring every day, such as offering water to the Sun in the morning, or performing puja to the family deities at the home shrine. These Nitya rituals are essential to Hindu practice. *Naimittika* rituals are important but they only occur at certain times during the year, such as the celebrations of different festivals, the performance of a special thanksgiving puja when good fortune smiles on the family, and, of course, the celebrations of the various life-cycle rituals such as naming a baby, the sacred thread and marriage. The third kind of rituals are called *Kamya*. These are highly desirable but optional, and pilgrimage falls into this category. The 19th-century Hindu reformers condemned pilgrimages and ritual bathing in holy rivers, along with untouchability, caste and child marriage.

For many people in India, going on a pilgrimage and experiencing the physical hardships that are necessary to reach their destination is almost a normal way of life. During certain festivals such as Navaratri, dedicated to the Mother Goddess, many people go on a short pilgrimage to visit a shrine of the goddess, which is perhaps situated on a hill near their town or village. The journey is made on foot, and the effort of climbing the hill might take a couple of hours. The physical exertion enhances the spirituality of the experience. Obtaining *darshan* (viewing the Murti) and offering flowers, a coconut and cash at the shrine are the main objectives of these local pilgrimages. A particular day during the festival is set aside for the visit, and the whole village may be involved in such a local pilgrimage.

Many people in western India walk up to 200 miles to visit a historical temple at Pandharpur, about 150 miles south-east of Poona, which is dedicated to the god Vishnu, locally known as Vithoba. This particular pilgrimage takes place twice a year, in July and November, and thousands of Hindus from towns and villages in Maharashtra walk to the shrine in groups, singing devotional songs, some of them carrying on their heads small pots of the holy basil plants. Hindus from different varna and jati groups, such as priests, office workers, shopkeepers, carpenters, leatherworkers, washermen, married women, widows and college students, intermix and eat together as they walk towards their goal. Caste awareness recedes into the background during the pilgrimage, but grows in significance as they return home.

People also go on very long pilgrimages to distant holy cities and famous shrines, spending many hours, even days, in crowded trains, and walking the last stage of their journey to reach the pilgrimage site. The distances really are vast. For example, Bombay to Varanasi is nearly 1000 miles; Delhi to Tirupathi, near Madras, is even longer. Although pilgrimage is optional, it is very popular in India, and many tour operators specialize in arranging group travel to distant sacred sites.

Why do people go on a Yatra?

There are many motives for a Hindu Yatra. Bathing in a pool or a river at a sacred place is believed to cleanse the spirit of sinful thoughts or actions, and thus increase spirituality and accumulate *punya*, religious merit. In Hinduism the seven sacred rivers are the Ganges, Yamuna, Sindhu (Indus), Sarasvati (which is underground), Narmada, Godavari and Kaveri. The most sacred of these is the Ganges, and thousands of Hindus travel to north India to places like Hardwar, Varanasi or Allahabad (Prayag) to bathe in the Ganges. To bathe at the confluence of two or three sacred rivers is even more meritorious. Ganga, Yamuna and Sarasvati form a triple confluence at Prayag (Allahabad), so Prayag is very popular as a place for ritual bathing. But these north Indian places are too distant for those living in the south, so people there do their ritual bathing in their local river on full-moon days in October and February.

Special bathing fairs (*Kumbha-Melas*) occur every 12 years at Hardwar on the upper Ganges and at Nasik on the Godavari. As many as 100,000 Hindus from all walks of life gather at these places for ritual bathing, sincerely believing that their sins will be washed away.

After the ritual bathing and spiritual purification comes the important religious moment and, in a way, the culmination of the exhausting pilgrimage. The devotees may have to stand in long queues for hours before they find themselves at the entrance to the inner sanctum so as to obtain darshan of the deity. After viewing the murti, they make cash offerings, receive the sacred light from the lamps held by the priest and gain god's blessing in the form of prasad.

All pilgrims perform *pradakshina*, or circumambulation, walking round the main shrine in a clockwise direction so that the shrine is always on their right-hand side. Hindus maintain that the right-hand side of the body is spiritually purer; this is why the right hand is always used for making religious offerings, for eating and for giving and receiving money.

Many Hindus go to a place of pilgrimage either to deposit the ashes of a deceased relative in a sacred river such as the Ganges at Varanasi, or to perform the first *shraddha*, the annual remembrance ritual.

Atonement for sin is a powerful reason for pilgrimage to certain shrines. If a person breaks the law he/she is punished by the courts, but breaking a sacred religious rule, such as killing a cow or damaging a murti in a temple, necessitates making amends. The atonement may involve suffering some physical hardship, giving money to charity, or performing a special puja at a place of pilgrimage.

Some Hindus may visit a distant shrine in the hope of finding some relief from pain caused by an incurable disease.

Important places of pilgrimage in India

Hindu sacred sites of pilgrimage are often situated near a river or the sea, or on a hilltop. Some shrines are high up in the Himalayan foothills, 10,000 ft (3,000 m) above sea level. There are literally hundreds of temples all over India, but the following shrines are important as well as popular places of pilgrimage.

Shrines dedicated to the Mother Goddess

The Mother Goddess at the temple in Calcutta is known as Kali. At Varanasi she is called Vishalakshi. The Mahalakshmi temple at Kolhapur in Maharashtra is popular with the devotees of the Mother Goddess. In her temple at Kanchipuram in south India she is named Kamakshi, while she is popularly worshipped as Meenakshi in her magnificent temple at Madurai, also in southern India.

Shrines dedicated to the God Vishnu

The Badrinath shrine is situated 10,350 ft (3150 m) up in the Himalayan foothills in Uttar Pradesh. At Dwaraka in Gujarat, the god is called Krishna. At Puri in Orissa, in eastern India, Vishnu is worshipped as Jagannath and at Tirupathi he is named Balaji, while at Trivandrum in Kerala he is Padmanabh.

Shrines dedicated to the God Shiva

The god Shiva is called Amarnath at his shrine in Kashmir. His shrine at Kedarnath is 11,750 ft (3580 m) up in the Himalayan foothills in Uttar Pradesh. At Varanasi he is worshipped as Vishveshwar (Lord of the Universe), in Gujarat he is Somanath and at Nasik in Maharashtra he is called Trimbaka. His southernmost shrine is at Rameshwaram. At all these shrines Shiva is worshipped in a phallic form called the lingam, but at Chidambaram in Tamil Nadu he is worshipped at Nataraj, the Lord of the Cosmic Dance.

Pilgrimage – a personal experience

Here a British Hindu describes his experience of the pilgrimage to Yamunotri, Gangotri, Kedarnath and Badrinath in the Himalayan foothills in Uttar Pradesh, northern India. This mountainous region is known as Uttara-Khanda.

Day 1   I was able to join a group of 22 people; 19 of them were Brahmins and of these, eight were men and 11 were women. We planned to go on a pilgrimage to four holy places in the Himalayan foothills. Various members of the group travelled from the USA, Canada, Britain and distant cities in India such as Coimbatore, Madras and Hyderabad, to Delhi, where the organizers had chartered a bus for our journey. We were complete strangers to one another, but we were linked by a common goal.

When everyone had reached Delhi, one member performed a simple puja to the god Ganapati in the evening, with prayers for a trouble-free journey, offered sweetmeats to Ganapati and received them back as prasad. That blessed offering was shared by everyone, and the act of worship strengthened our sense of belonging to a group.

Day 2   We left Delhi in the early morning and after a hot and dusty journey of 200 km, including a break for lunch at Cheetal Grand Hotel in Muzafar Nagar, reached Haridwar (or Hardwar) about 2.30 in the afternoon. We had a short break for refreshments and then went on another 24 km to Rishikesh. Our rooms were booked at the Hotel Ganga Kinaré ('On the Bank of the Ganges').

There was only half an hour for a quick bath, change of clothes and tea or coffee before we went back to Haridwar to witness the arati of the goddess Ganga. Our coach had to be parked nearly a mile away from the *ghat* (steps leading down to the river). I was rather put off by the dirt and excrement on the footpath. After a little hop, skip and jump we managed to reach the paved path near the river. Even here we had to avoid the many cooking fires which the pilgrims had lit to prepare their evening meal. Some holy cows had also left their calling cards in places!

However, nothing daunted, we threaded our way through the throng of pilgrims towards the Ganga temple. We had to leave our sandals at a booth, for a small charge, since leather footwear causes spiritual pollution at a temple or a holy ghat. Now the crowd was really pressing; everyone was trying to protect their wallets, keep their balance and crane their necks to get a glimpse of the arati flames. Fortunately we could hear the verses sung in praise of the river goddess on the public address system. When the arati ceremony was over, our group moved to one side to enable the crowds to thin a little. Then most of us managed to climb down the slippery steps to reach the water's edge. Our tour guide had managed to locate about four priests, who assisted a number of us in offering puja to the goddess Ganga. I made an offering of 51 rupees in charity to the priest, after I had placed rice grains and flowers in the sacred river, and prayed for the material and spiritual welfare of my wife, myself and all our relatives, friends, dependants and domestic pets. I stood in the water of the Ganges while doing this puja and praying.

There must have been at least 10,000 people on the ghat at Haridwar on that evening, but remarkably no one was hurt or drowned. There were many devout souls bathing in the holy river, hoping for the goddess's blessing to lead them to moksha, spiritual liberation. People from different varna and caste groups from various regions of India had gathered to pay homage to God, before whom all stood equal.

Day 3 The day dawned bright and warm in Rishikesh. Some pilgrims said their morning prayers sitting on the steps near the river behind our hotel. After breakfast, which was prepared and served by the two cooks and four helpers who travelled with us, we set off to visit the famous meditation centres situated within a few kilometres of Rishikesh. An exciting bus ride along a winding mountain road took us to a temple, where a murti of Lakshmana alone is seen. Normally, Lakshmana is shown with Rama and Sita in many temples dedicated to god Rama. Our tour guide related a story which said that since Lakshmana had killed Ravana's son in battle, he had incurred the sin of killing a Brahmin. Lakshmana therefore had to expiate his sin through penance, and the temple is built near the place where he is believed to have performed this penance. Nearby is a suspension bridge called Lakshmana Zula. The earlier footbridge, made of rope and wooden slats, collapsed in 1925. A substantial donation by a rich merchant, and active support by the British Raj resulted in the steel suspension bridge being constructed between 1927 and 1929. It is a remarkable feat of British engineering. There is a second steel suspension bridge of post-independence construction, called the Rama Zula.

The Ganges was in full flood, but the rushing water was quietly making its progress downstream towards the sea when I walked across the Lakshmana Zula. There are many 'business' temples of recent origin, where unwary but devout pilgrims place money in the *dana-peti* (donation box), which supports the people running each temple.

Here, too, the Divine Life Society is to be found; this is an *ashrama* founded in 1936 by Swami Shivananda, which has temples, lecture halls, a meditation centre and a hospital. The *swarga ashrama* is a complex of buildings consisting of inexpensive accommodation for pilgrims; it has a temple dedicated to the *Bhagavad-Gita*.

Our return journey to the hotel for lunch was quite a hair-raising experience. Our tourist coach had to join a long queue of heavy goods vehicles across a bailey bridge, which had temporarily replaced a recently damaged road bridge. The driver displayed great skill in taking the coach along the narrow bridge and over the rough and pot-holed road to safety. The morning outing had been rather tiring, so I opted out of the organized activities for the rest of the day and evening. It had been a scorching day, but a spiritually fulfilling one nevertheless.

Day 4   We had to leave Rishikesh early when it was still dark, and without breakfast because of the (peaceful) political protest and the area-wide strike in the northern part of Uttar Pradesh. Our coach was able to get away from the trouble spot and stop for breakfast and lunch along the way. We reached Dev Prayag and saw the confluence of the rivers Alakananda (rising near Badrinath) and Bhagirathi (rising at Gangotri). After this confluence at Dev Prayag the combined waters of the two rivers are known as the Ganges. Next we stopped at Rudra Prayag to look at the breathtaking turbulence caused by the confluence of the rivers Alakananda and Mandakini (rising at Kedarnath); thus between Rudra Prayag and Dev Prayag the river is known as Alakananda. Just before we reached the village of Rampur, we had another occasion to admire the daring and skill of our driver. There was a landslide across the mountain road which had broken the surface, creating an incline of 45°. We asked the driver whether we should get out of the coach. 'No need', he replied, 'we are on a pilgrimage and God will protect us. Trust in Him. Besides, I have driven this coach through worse obstacles before.' With remarkable skill and judgement he drove the coach, slowly but surely, over the damaged road and brought us to safety.

Late in the evening we reached Rampur. In our guest-house the facilities were poor: no electricity, damp walls and damp beds. The evening meal was taken in dim candlelight. Physical discomfort and hardship is supposed to enhance the spirituality of the experience on a pilgrimage.

Day 5 After a damp and restless night we got ready for the day in candlelight, ate breakfast in buffet style and set off for Gauri Kund, about 30 km away. On the way we saw the spuming waters of Son Ganga and Mandakini at the confluence of Son Prayag. Many of us walked down the steps and dipped our feet in the refreshing water. Bathing at a confluence is believed to increase religious merit, so our partial effort probably increased our religious merit by a fraction! When our coach reached Gauri Kund we were surrounded – by about 100 eager young men seeking business. They were looking for customers who wanted to hire a horse or a *doli* (litter) to climb the mountain. After a lot of shouting and stick-waving our guide managed to push the crowd away from the door of the coach, then arranged for us all either a litter, which is carried by four strong men, or a horse, which one may ride or use to carry the back-pack.

I hired a horse, put my back-pack on the saddle and started to walk up the path. A few yards further on I bought a strong, metal-tipped bamboo stick to help me keep my balance on the slippery path and continued to walk. Gauri Kund is about 6500 ft (2000 m) above sea level, while our goal, Kedarnath, is 11,750 ft (3580 m) high. The winding path up the mountain is 14 km long. About six or seven people from the group decided to walk; others opted for a litter or a horse. As the altitude increases, the air becomes thin and has less oxygen, so it is necessary to inhale through both nose and mouth in order to get adequate oxygen into the lungs.

As I walked up the path I had a truly spiritual experience. Some unknown power prompted me to recite the *Gayatri* mantra aloud, which meant I was taking in sufficient oxygen to maintain my energy level. I recited the mantra and walked on without feeling any altitude sickness. The young man whose horse I had hired kept on urging me to ride, but I became more determined to walk the whole distance. Honestly, I did not think about the rarefied air. I simply kept on reciting the mantra and stopped only when I touched the steps leading to the Kedarnath temple. When I walked into the hostel other members of the group greeted me with loud cheers. I was the only one to have walked the whole distance from Gauri Kund to Kedarnath.

I discovered that at least six people needed oxygen to combat altitude sickness. The hostel had a resident doctor and oxygen cylinders, so medical help was promptly obtained. After a much-needed cup of coffee and some snacks, I went outside to stand and look at the majesty of the mountain. The peaks behind the temple were covered in snow, which glistened in its silvery brightness in the rays of the setting sun. The thin string of the river Mandakini was frozen white on the upper reaches of the slope as if the god Shiva had been experimenting with a giant tube of icing sugar, while the crystal-clear water further down tumbled joyfully over the rocks and gathered momentum on its downward journey.

The temple of Kedarnath is very old; it houses a black phallic-shaped rock, about 1 m tall – the symbol of Shiva. We were able to obtain darshan (view the lingam) from the doorway, but could not enter the holy of holies. Afterwards we were given sugar crystals as prasad. It had been a memorable and spiritually satisfying day.

Day 6   We got up in the early hours to get ready to attend the puja at the Kedarnath temple, which was to start at 5 am. Each of us was supplied with a bucket of hot water to bathe, because we could not possibly attend the puja without bathing. In our enthusiasm we forgot to take precautions against exposure to the cold mountain air. It was a recipe for disaster, and some of us caught chills and colds that persisted for a few days. Since it was very cold at Kedarnath and some members had suffered from altitude sickness, it was decided that we should leave after breakfast and seek shelter at a low altitude in Rampur.

The temple of Kedarnath is built in black stone, and set against the magnificence of the snow-covered Himalayan peaks. It is very clean inside and the surrounding paved courtyards are free from litter.

After breakfast we offered namaskar to the god Shiva, and began to climb down towards Gauri Kund. In three or four places water was rushing across the path, so I decided to ride the horse for

7 km to a village called Rambada where we stopped for lunch. I walked down the rest of the mountain path to Gauri Kund. From there onwards our journey was fraught with unforeseen difficulties, both natural and man-made.

We arrived at Gauri Kund to face a general strike, and the bus station was full of stranded vehicles. Our coach was parked further away out of sight of the protesters, so we were able to get in and drive off, but at Son Prayag we came to a halt because of a barricade. Fortunately, all the horses we had hired were from Rampur, so we were able to ride back there. Then the heavens opened and we progressed in driving rain towards Rampur. Everything, including our back-packs, was thoroughly drenched. Before leaving Rampur we had deposited our suitcases in a different guest-house where there was electric light and the rooms were clean and dry, so changing into dry clothes and drying the wet ones was fairly easy. The cooks prepared excellent food for our evening meal and we had a restful night. Every bone in my body ached as a result of my first-ever horse ride.

Day 7 Because of the general strike we had no option but to stay at Rampur, so we made the most of this enforced rest-day. The sun shone brightly and all of us were busy washing clothes and hanging them out to dry. It was the first day of the Ganesha festival, which we celebrated by offering prayers to the formless Ganesha before breakfast and then by singing devotional hymns in Sanskrit and Tamil. Three people were unable to participate in the hymn-singing because they spoke only Telugu. Mango sweets were also given to all as prasad. After a hot bath and a good lunch our tiredness diminished and our spirits were revived.

Day 8 We were up very early and left Rampur at 5 am to travel to Badrinath. We retraced our steps to Rudra Prayag; then we turned north and travelled almost parallel to the river Alakananda, where we enjoyed the beauty of its confluences with other smaller streams.

The Pindar merges with the Alakananda at Karna Prayag; the river Nandakini meets its waters at Nanda Prayag; and Vishnu Ganga embraces it at Vishnu Prayag. Our coach travelled along the steep but well-maintained mountain road through spectacular scenery, and after a 13-hour exhilarating journey we reached the town of Badrinath, which is 10,350 ft (3150 m) above sea level. The accommodation at the Paramarth Loka Hostel was adequate, but there was no electric light. After freshening up we walked to the temple of Badrinath to obtain darshan of the deity before the

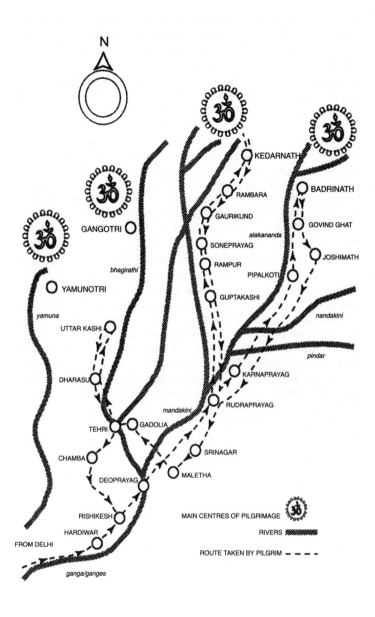

map showing the route followed by the pilgraims and main sites of
pilgrimage

temple closed at 7.30 pm. The evening meal by candlelight was enjoyable, and a warm bed was even more welcome after a tiring journey.

Day 9 At Badrinath the main town and the temple are separated by the river Alakananda, over which there is a suspension bridge. Not far from the temple, which is dedicated to god Vishnu, there is a hot water spring that fills four stone-built pools, two of which are used by men and two by women for their ritual bathing. Many young men from the town carry large cans of this hot water to the hostel for the pilgrims' morning bath and charge five rupees per bucket (about 10p). My day started with a refreshing bath before I went with others who wanted to bathe at the spring. About 10 feet (3 m) away flows the river with its ice-cold water. While at the spring I witnessed the second naming ceremony of a young girl, who wanted to have the ritual repeated in holy surroundings.

Some members of the group, after bathing at the spring, went on to a special area on the ghat to offer pindas (balls of cooked rice) to departed ancestors. When we went to the temple, we placed rupee coins in front of the deity; these were blessed by the priest and returned to us to be kept in our home shrines. It is believed that such blessed coins bring continued prosperity to the family. There were many stalls in town near the suspension bridge selling books, maps, brass and copper utensils for puja, different types of rosaries and many other religious artefacts. I bought a copper plate which showed embossed images of Badrinath (Vishnu) and Kedarnath (Shiva) for our home shrine. I also bought two sealed copper bottles of Ganga water.

In the afternoon all the pilgrims went for a short walk to the source of the river Alakananda; we saw it emerge from an opening in the mountain, gushing out forcefully in its milky magnificence. Although the day had been spiritually fulfilling and warmed by the Himalayan sun, at dusk it was chilly, and after our candlelit meal it became decidedly cold.

Day 10 The Badrinath temple shows the influence of Nepali and Tibetan Buddhist architecture. The popular belief is that the present murti was originally that of the Buddha seated in a lotus posture, but that during the Hindu renaissance it was thrown into a pond, where it remained for many years. The first Shankara restored it to its present position as the murti of Vishnu and named it Badrivishal. The murti is made of black stone and is not well defined, but the deity is seen seated in a lotus posture. In

Hindu mythology, the Buddha is considered the ninth avatar of Vishnu.

Many of us attended the early morning puja, and after a quick breakfast we left Badrinath at 9 am to enjoy a truly spectacular drive through the Himalayan foothills.

We reached Jyotir Math in two hours, where, in the present monastery, there is a cave; here the Adi-Shankara, the Vedanta scholar, first established the monastery. There is also a Lakshmi-Narayan temple. We passed through many small towns during our journey before reaching Srinagar in the Gadhawal district, where we stayed the night at Prachi Hotel. It was sheer luxury to have modern amenities and electric light again (provided by the hotel's own generator) for the first time since leaving Rishikesh.

Day 11   Our morning was free; there was no organized activity. Our suitcases were packed and loaded on the roof of the coach by 11 am. After 'brunch' we left the hotel and began our journey to Uttar Kashi, a distance of 125 km through the mountains, along well-maintained roads. However, we did hit a stretch where the road was rough and dusty.

When we reached Uttar Kashi at 6.30 pm, we learnt that the roads to Gangotri and Yamunotri were blocked by landslides, slippery and very dangerous. We had to consider the welfare of some senior citizens in the group. It was decided that we should stay at Uttar Kashi for two nights.

Day 12   Today there was no long coach journey. Our feet were to be on firm ground, so after breakfast we began to explore the town of Uttar Kashi (3500 ft) (1000 m), which is situated on the banks of the river Bhagirathi, which rises at Gangotri. Thus far, from the start of our yatra, our coach had climbed and descended 16 high mountains.

In the morning we visited the Kashi Vishwanath (Shiva) temple and offered puja and prayers individually. Within the same precincts there is a Shakti-Devi (Mother Goddess) temple, inside which is a 30-ft (nine-metre) tall carved stone pillar that cannot be moved with force, but can be slightly pushed away from the vertical with just one finger. At the top of the pillar is a stone axehead and above it a trident. It is very ancient; no precise date can be ascribed to it. Near the Devi temple there is a very large *yajna-shala* (place of fire-sacrifice) where a few years ago a large and prolonged *havan* (fire-sacrifice) was performed with prayers for world peace.

That night there was a blackout in town to avert political protests, but the river Bhagirathi quietly flowed downstream in the dark towards Dev-Prayag, to meet the Alakananda.

Day 13 The trips to Gangotri and Yamunotri were considered impossible, so it was decided to go to Mussoorie and to stay there for three nights. But after leaving Uttar Kashi we learnt that there was a curfew round Mussoorie, so we made our way to Chamba and checked in at Hotel Trishul Breeze, which is on top of a high mountain, affording a panoramic view of many peaks.

the Vithoba (Vishnu) temple at Pandharpur in western India; it is a popular pilgrimage site in July and November each year

The night stop at Chamba was restful, but it was very cold during the hours of darkness. There was a general strike at Chamba as well, so our coach was halted for a few hours the next day.

Day 14 The manager of the hotel went into the town of Chamba and negotiated with the protestors a safe passage for our coach to Rishikesh. Soon after lunch we left Chamba and made our way down the mountain to Rishikesh. The journey was without much incident; however, 100 buffaloes had claimed the right of way ahead of our coach. Their own *bandh* (strike) had also checked our progress for a while.

When we reached Hotel Ganga Kinaré all of us clapped with enthusiasm to express our appreciation for the efforts and skill of the driver, Mr Kuldeep Singh, and Mr Joshi, our tour manager and guide. All of us breathed a sigh of relief to have concluded our pilgrimage safely. The memory of the great mountains and the temples in their isolated holiness will remain with all who shared this yatra; some regretted ever having to descend to the mundane matters of daily life, though we all carried with us God's blessing.

10

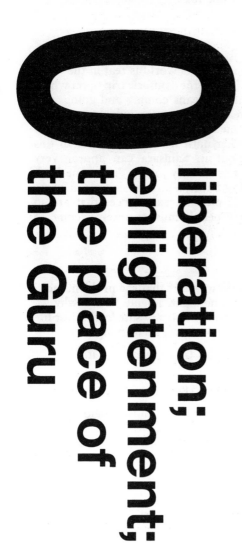

liberation; enlightenment; the place of the Guru

In this chapter you will learn:
- the place of the Guru
- about reality and unreality
- ways of liberation
- about the Guru as teacher and spiritual guide
- about the death of a Guru.

Liberation from what?

Hindu family life, the gods and their stories, fascinating and enjoyable festivals and dietary matters must not distract us from realizing that what matters ultimately is belief. If we forget this then we have fallen into the snare against which Hindu teachers and scriptures continually warn us: we are in danger of confusing the ephemeral with the real.

What is unreality?

The short answer is that it is the world of the five senses; it is materialism; it is the illusion that this world is real in the sense that we can enjoy it forever. This is the samsaric trip upon which we embarked at birth. Samsara means coming and going, and embodies the idea that our real self, the atman, which is spiritual and non-material, is imprisoned in our body and is destined to pass from one body to another until we become aware of this fact and do something about it, Samsara can appear very enjoyable. Many of us say, not entirely joking, 'If I come back I'd like to be a world class footballer, a jazz musician, the prime minister'. We forget that the pleasant experiences that are so attractive in the lives of these people must themselves come to an end.

Reality has no end

Indian religious traditions tend to assert that the problem faced by all human beings is one of unenlightenment. That is why we mistake the unreal, temporal and temporary satisfactions of life for those that are permanent and eternally satisfying.

As one of the Hindu scriptures (an *Upanishad*) puts it:

> Lead me from the unreal to the real, from darkness to light, from death to immortality (Brihadaranyaka 1:3:28).

The illusory goals are those against which most religions warn: wealth, power, sexual satisfaction, greed, pride – in short, all those things that dupe us into believing life is so pleasant that we need look no further for happiness.

The goal of liberation

The goal, liberation (*moksha*) of the spirit, soul or *atman*, from an apparently endless series of rebirths, is envisaged in a number of ways. Some Hindus will offer the analogy of a drop of rain entering a stream and progressing back to the ocean from which it came. Others speak of many inter-related atoms moving around one another. There may be a focus, like the sun as centre of the solar system, or there may be none. There is no uniform view as to whether the individual atman becomes one with Brahman or remains in some respects distinct. Others still may refer to the process of rebirth as the shedding of the various sheaths that imprison the soul. These must be removed if liberation is to take place. Even the wish for personal survival into eternity is one that Hindus might consider selfish and therefore to be relinquished. Can there be any better goal than to be united with Eternal Reality, however that Being, the Absolute, or God, may be understood?

The ways of liberation

Hindus believe that there is more than one path to liberation. The sannyasin, who forsakes even his name when he enters the final stage of life, and cremates an effigy of his body to show that the past is totally dead, is practising the rejection of earthly attachments so that he may realize Brahman. This is one of the traditionally acceptable ways of pursuing moksha, though it was one which Gandhi and Nehru tended to reject. Nehru, attempting to build the new independent Indian State, said, 'Aram haram hai' (To rest is forbidden). He felt that withdrawal from the world was not something that would benefit the country – but then, he was not a religious person. Others value the lifestyle of sannyasins highly, providing them daily with food as they make an alms round. Most Hindus, however, follow a less rigorous path, by performing religious actions, *karma marga*, which includes selfless deeds and puja, or *bhakti marga*, or loving devotion, in which faith and God's grace are important as the means of deliverance. (Some of these are discussed in greater detail in Chapter 12). A third *marga* is the philosophical one, that of knowledge (*jnana*). It may seem strange to some people that knowledge can have any saving worth whatsoever, especially when the word 'philosophy' is attached to it. However, this is the term that Hindus prefer over 'theology'; it revolves around *darshanas*, ways of seeing reality or the truth. The purpose of Hindu philosophy is to enable the believer to attain spiritual liberation, not to play intellectual wordgames as Western philosophy sometimes seems to do!

Some years ago the BBC broadcast a programme about atheism in which some participants suggested that it is a Western rather than an Eastern religious problem. This is certainly not true for Sikhism, but Buddhism, Jainism, and Hinduism are religions in which it is perfectly possible and respectable to be an atheist. Let us consider how an atheist can achieve liberation. If one takes a completely materialist outlook, believing that only the material world exists, then there can be no liberation. There is no non-material essence to be liberated from its material bonds. However, with the existence of the atman, which somehow or other has become imprisoned within the material body, and which is destined to suffer reincarceration until the bonds are finally broken, liberation is a possibility. Through ascetic techniques, which subdue the material world, or yogic meditation which enables the practitioner to transcend it, the atman can be freed. The atman, which escapes the gravitational pull of the material world, goes into orbit around the Absolute, or plunges into it/him/her, and thus liberation is achieved. There are six philosophical schools which are described as orthodox (*astika*), that is, which claim to be based upon the *Vedas*. They will be discussed more fully later, but some reference is appropriate here. Of these the two that are most important are *Advaita Vedanta*, non-dualism, and *Vishishtadvaita Vedanta*, qualified non-dualism.

Advaita teaches that the material world is an illusion, ultimately unreal. When this intuitively becomes clear, we realize the identity of Brahman and atman. As it says in one *Upanishad*, '*tat tvam asi*', 'that (Brahman) is what you are'. Once grasped intellectually, the task is to realize and base one's life upon this truth. (The chief exponents of the two major philosophical schools will be discussed in Chapter 11.)

For many Hindus the path to spiritual liberation lies in following the teachings of a *Guru*, the kind of master (they are usually male), or adept, which Muslim mystics, Sufis, and Christians also regard as essential. In fact it is widely held that the path should not be undertaken without a personal teacher.

The Guru

Two very important features of Hinduism are the place of oral teaching and the emphasis upon spiritual experience. The *Rig-Veda*, the earliest scripture of Hinduism, may be dated earlier than 1000 BCE, but it was not written down fully for over 2000 years (until about 1400 CE). A belief that the sanctity of the spoken word would be affected by putting it into writing may be one reason for this delay; another may be a belief that the word should be transmitted or communicated by men who knew its meaning intuitively and empirically. These men were mostly Brahmins. A collection of laws known as the *Laws of Manu*, dating from about 200 BCE, would suggest that this was because only Brahmins had a right to study and teach the *Vedas*. However, there is evidence in the *Upanishads* of non-Brahmin teachers. Those who were Brahmins might also have acted as priests, but it is their role as spiritual teachers that is of concern here. The name used for such men, and today some women, is *Guru*. A Guru is a spiritual preceptor, not a teacher in the normal sense of the word. However, he not only provides spiritual guidance; he may also advise on careers or marriage. After all, the whole of a person's life is directed at the attainment of moksha, and choosing an inappropriate form of employment might hinder or even prevent it being achieved. The importance of husband and wife walking this path together is mentioned in the marriage service. The word Guru is often explained by splitting it into two parts. *Gu* means darkness and *ru* means light. A Guru is one who dispels spiritual darkness and gives light to the disciple (called a *chela* or *sishya*). Guru can also be linked with a word meaning heavy. He is a person who removes the burden of doubt and ignorance, the karma which the disciple brings. To be effective, a Guru must traditionally possess four essential qualities: he must be *shratiya*, well versed in the scriptures; he must be *brahmanishtam*, established in brahman (this means he must have realized the spiritual goal himself); he must be *akamakita*, unsmitten by desire; and he must be *nishkalamika*, stainless, free from guile. Only such a person can enable the seeker to achieve liberation. As the Guru Chaitanya (1486–1533) said:

> The Guru is the skilful helmsman, divine grace the favourable wind; if with such means man does not strive to cross the ocean of life and death, he is indeed lost.

A helmsman who does not know the way across the ocean of birth and rebirth *samsara*, is actually worse than useless, and can cause untold spiritual damage.

Hinduism teaches that God, Brahman, is within everyone, but that the natural state of humanity is one in which this awareness is made impossible through ignorance. The *sadhu*, the wandering ascetic or holy man, may have overcome ignorance and become liberated and yet have no calling to share enlightenment with others. The Guru, however, is convinced of a divine vocation. The chelas, for their part, are equally sure of the Guru's ability to help them achieve the same status of *Brahma vidya*, knowledge which is intuitive as well as intellectual, and the realization of Brahman.

Gurus often trace their lineage to God. Chaitanya is often considered at a popular level not only to be a devotee of Krishna, but also his incarnation. In the *Mundaka Upanishad*, Brahma, the first of the gods, taught the science of Brahman to his eldest son. Eventually this knowledge was handed down to Angiras, the Guru whose teaching the *Upanishad* contains. In other words, Brahma is the Adi Guru of the *Mundaka Upanishad*. The very word *Upanishad* means 'sit-down-near', and describes the posture of the student who approached the Guru in the hope of being allowed to sit at his feet in study.

As the words of Chaitanya state, the Guru is essential to the achievement of moksha. This is a belief that most Hindus would share. There are those who put their trust in the practice of austerity, but even sannyasins often have a spiritual director. Hindus who emphasize the path of ritual action karma may often combine it with following the teaching of a Guru who will guide them in which actions they should undertake and what foods they should eat. The priest who officiates at religious ceremonies and the Hindu who performs them (and attempts to fulfil his dharma perfectly) are aware that there is esoteric knowledge, truths that cannot be committed to books, mantras, and techniques of meditation that are too intimate to be make public. It is the Guru who possesses these.

Some Guru movements have emerged as distinctive Indian religions: Jainism, Buddhism, and Sikhism – largely because the teachings of their originators were not based on the *Vedas* and have always been critical of their authority and that of their interpreters, the Brahmins. Most, however, have remained within the Hindu tradition, even though they may not have had Brahmin Gurus. For many Hindus it is not orthodoxy of teaching that matters but how the Guru matches up to the devotee's prayer; a great medieval Guru called Kabir illustrates this idea:

> The pearl is found in the oyster, and the oyster is in the sea. The diver brings it up. No one else has the power to do this.

In other words, the Guru only helps us to achieve self-realization, to become what we really are. He does this by giving darshan. This is more than the audience which a king grants a subject. It is a gracious glance. It bestows grace. It penetrates our very being and goes to the heart of our needs. When a disciple says, 'My Guru knows everything', she or he may be making a statement about his omniscience, but is probably affirming that he knows what they need before they ask him. He is like a perceptive parent. In fact, some scholars have suggested that the Guru is of major importance in Indian religion because the nature of the extended family encourages dependence rather than independent initiative. He is a father-figure upon whom all burdens may be cast, But he is probably much more than this.

Darshan, the gracious glance, may not be received by everyone who visits a Guru. They may not yet be ready for it, and the Guru will recognize this. He may ignore them, as (in one Hindu myth) Shiva ignored someone who performed the great ascetic act of standing on one leg outside the cave where he (Shiva) lived, for 1000 years. Only after this period of penance was he ready to receive what Shiva could impart. On the other hand, he may give them a menial task to do because he knows they need to be prepared for the obedience which discipleship entails.

Initiation

When the seeker is finally ready to become a chela, the Guru will confer initiation, or *diksha*. This usually entails the giving of a special word or Sanskrit verse to the initiate, with an instruction to meditate upon it regularly. The verse or word, which is whispered in the chela's ear, should be kept secret; it is personally chosen and not to be shared. If it is told to someone else its power will be lost. Like all religious experiences it is a private matter. Hindus will not give personal testimonies of the way God has become active in their lives in the way that members of some other religions do. This would be to betray a trust.

Upon initiation, the disciple takes certain vows relating to various aspects of his or her lifestyle. This vow may be of celibacy, of abstinence from using drugs including alcohol and tobacco, or it may be to adopt a vegan diet. Gurus often have two kinds of initiated chelas. There are disciples who give up all aspects of their previous lives to live permanently in the ashram. Others continue their occupations and live with their families, but are available immediately, should the Guru summon them to undertake some act of seva, and will keep certain lesser vows to those of chelas living in the ashram. Their employer would know that their first duty was to the Guru, and should not express annoyance at their absence from work, however much he might be inconvenienced. (Often he would have the same Guru as his employee.) They will probably keep the same dietary rules, and perhaps abstain from sexual intercourse except for purposes of procreation.

The death of a Guru

When a Guru finally departs for his heavenly abode ('dies' would not be a word normally used), his body will not be cremated. It is likely to be buried in a seated lotus posture, and a monument known as a *samadhi* may be placed over him. It will become a venerated site. If the Guru is aware of his approaching death he may appoint a successor and even induct him as Guru. Otherwise the disciples will have to agree who should take his place. A Guru might state that there will be no successor, but more often than not a cult is established. The successor must, of course, know the teachings perfectly intuitively as well as intellectually. He must be at one with his Guru – so much so that he may even take the Guru's name. Spiritual enlightenment is the principal requirement, of course. No one can carry the burdens of others who is weighed down himself by karma. It might be prudent if the community already respects him, but this is not essential; the conferred authority of the outgoing teacher should be sufficient.

The other kind of Guru is one who appears for the first time and has no acknowledged master. He may undergo a personal experience in which he becomes certain that God has called him to be a Guru. It may be that his family or friends detect special qualities in him and seek his advice on matters of concern, including spiritual development. When someone has chosen to become his disciple and has been accepted then the man becomes a Guru. If he is a Brahmin he will probably gain devotees from all classes, depending on whether he makes himself available to low caste men and women or not. A low caste Guru would have to be a remarkable person to win the devotion of Brahmins and other high caste people. It would be even more difficult for a woman to win chelas. Her support might come from non-Hindus, or Hindus who were indifferent to traditional ways of thinking, or perhaps Westerners. She might well be the subject of unwarranted gossip. The Guru will set up an ashram or compound of buildings which will be his base, and where some disciples will settle and others come at the weekend or other convenient times.

The teachings of a Guru

Spiritual liberation is the main provision that a Guru makes for disciples. The *sadhana* or means of achieving this end may vary. Concentration may be on a particular method of meditation. Nowadays service in Indian society is frequently stressed.

A day in an ashram

This is just one account. Other ashrams may have different ways of life, but there will always be some form of discipline, or ashram dharma.

3.30 Rise and bathe.

4.30 Arati and chanting *bhajans*, devotional songs.

7.00 Breakfast. A simple meal of sliced bread and tea.

8.00 *Seva*, selfless service, that is, offering work to God as a form of worship. It might take the form of washing the dishes, cleaning latrines, gardening, or generally keeping the ashram clean. Devotees must do what is required of them. Through this they learn obedience.

11.45 Chanting

12.00 Lunch, followed by rest. This is essential in the hot Indian climate.

2.00 Return to seva. Seva might include going from the ashram in a jeep or lorry to give service in the wider community: manning mobile clinics, providing milk and food for children.

During this afternoon period the Guru gives darshan. Members who wish to receive darshan gather seated in an open area in the Guru's presence. When attendants tap them on the shoulder with a fan (*chauri*), they may approach the Guru for an audience. The Guru will know who is in need of darshan and what the nature of the need is.

6.30 Tea, followed by arati and evening chanting.

9.15 Bedtime.

Several festivals will be celebrated in ashrams, depending upon the teachings of the Guru. In those devoted to Shiva, it is likely that there will be a *yajna*, or sacred fire ceremony, lasting as long as ten days, or to Ganesha; a Shanti yajna to remove evil and secure peace and tranquillity.

When the Guru gives public teaching the address is unlikely to be sophisticated. It is the quality of the message that counts. The Guru's ideals will be emphasized. Perhaps devotees will be encouraged to recognize God in each other, to seek to be free from suffering by rejecting all attachments, and to attain bliss (*anand*) by obeying the Guru, meditating, and practising seva.

Nowadays there are many Gurus whose disciples are to be found worldwide, including Westerners as well as people of Indian origin. Occasionally they appear on television and give a message which is so simple that audiences find it unconvincing. This is because they are looking for deeply philosophical homilies and, disciples would say, are not on the wavelength of the Guru. Only those who enter into the intimate relationship and perceive that the Guru in his teaching will pass beyond the limits of their ignorance, receive darshan and enter upon a new life. The great philosophers Shankara and Ramanuja were Gurus as well as highly intellectual teachers.

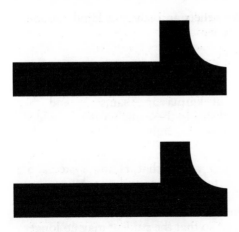

11
Hindu philosophy

In this chapter you will learn:
- about the six systems of Hindu Philosophy
- about the Yoga Sutra and the eight steps of yoga
- arguments for whether God exists.

When questioned about the beliefs an orthodox Hindu should hold, the reply tends to include:

- belief in one ultimate reality
- belief in the authority of the *Vedas* (which includes the *Upanishads*)
- belief in the principles of karma and samsara, and the eventual attainment of moksha; to these might often be added the performance of *dharma*, right conduct and the observance of caste duties.

With these in mind, we may assert that Hindu systems of philosophy, and religious movements and teachings, are motivated not merely by the purpose of discovering Truth but also by realizing Truth in life. In other words, the teacher analyzes the nature of Reality, so that the student may no longer be caught up in the cycle of rebirth but may achieve moksha. Hindu philosophy is therefore perhaps nearer to Western theology than to Western philosophy. However, the philosophy that concerns us in this chapter is distinctive and should be studied in its own right. The main purpose of philosophy might be regarded as the elimination of suffering, rather than the explanation of evil or of creation and existence, though these themes are often discussed.

The six systems of Hindu philosophy

There are six orthodox schools of Hindu philosophy, or darshanas, which are based on the *Vedas* (including, of course, the *Upanishads* and *Gita*). These are known as *astika* or orthodox. The most famous *nastika*, or unorthodox schools, are the Carvakas, Buddhism and Jainism, which reject the authority of the *Vedas* as divinely inspired and provide their own alternative world views and paths to liberation.

The six astika schools are now usually grouped in pairs, but this was not necessarily the original arrangement, and the pairs do not always complement one another. They are:

- Nyaya and Vaishesika
- Samkhya (sometimes spelled Sankyha) and Yoga
- Mimamsa and Vedanta.

All these systems can be traced back beyond the Common or Christian Era. *Nyaya* means logical analysis. By the use of perception, including the senses and insight, inference, analogy, and verbal testimony – which came to include the authority of scripture (shruti) as the system was developed – valid knowledge resulting in moksha could be acquired. *Vaishesika* is said to derive from a term meaning 'a category of knowledge denoting essential difference, individuality, particularity'. Great importance is attached to the concept of substance, which is comprised of the five elements of earth, water, light, air and ether, in addition to time, space, the essence of being (the atman) and mind. Everything has its unique essence, its particularity, and release is obtained by recognizing the atomic nature of the universe, the difference between matter and soul and the separation of the two. Ethical conduct was important in achieving this goal. The system in its original form had really no place for Brahman but Ishvara was added later in response to criticism.

Samkhya

The oldest astika system is that of *Samkhya*. Its origins are obscure and it may originally have been materialistic (though it regards matter as eternal and atheistic, but in the available written forms it tends to be theistic and linked with yoga as the method of release. The classic treatise on samkhya is the *Samkhya Karika*, dated to about the second century CE; that on yoga is the earlier *Yoga Sutra* of Patanjali of the second century BCE. Earlier references are to be found in the *Gita*. It must, therefore, be about 2300 years old. The principle behind Samkhya is the complete cessation of suffering. This is attained through yoga. Samkhya teaches that individual souls (*Purushas*) and matter (*Prakriti*) have existed since time immemorial: both are uncreated, Purusha is neither produced (created) or productive. Prakriti is also unproduced but is productive. Thus it changes and evolves, although it can never be destroyed.

'The complete cessation of pain is the complete goal of humanity.' These words are attributed to Kapila, the sage who is regarded as the originator of Samkhya.

Pain is to be understood in the Indian philosophical and spiritual sense as an awareness of dissatisfaction, alienation from the cause of bliss or peace, craving after illusory goals, or wrong attachment. It does not necessarily relate to physical suffering. Hindus will tell many stories of people whose lives were materially enjoyable and who were never exposed to physical pain, but who were acutely aware that they were suffering. Gurus and philosophical teaching often begin by diagnosing the causes of suffering, and then prescribing a remedy which leads to its cessation, the attainment of spiritual liberation described as nirvana, or *moksha*. The Hindu philosopher has been traditionally a doctor of the spirit. Samkhya is sometimes described as the oldest known philosophical system in the world and can be traced back the the Indus Valley civilization, which came to an end about 1700 BCE, even though the writings of its legendary founder, the *Samkhya-karika*, only belong to the third century CE. It is mentioned in the *Svetasvatara Upanishad*:

> Eternal among eternals, conscious among the conscious, the One among the many, he disposes over desires: he is the cause, he can be comprehended in theory (samkhya) as in spiritual exercise (yoga); knowing this God a man is from every fetter freed.

and in the *Bhagavad Gita* where Krishna tells Arjuna:

> This wisdom has been revealed to thee in theory (samkhya); listen now to how it should be practised (yoga): if by this wisdom thou art exercised, thou wilt put off the bondage inherent in all works.

Samkyha means 'enumeration', probably because of the detailed way it analyzes human personality, though it is not unique in this respect. It is a dualistic system that postulates two ultimate or eternal realities, *purusha* and *prakriti*. Its diagnosis of the cause of pain is based upon the view that the soul or cosmic spirit (purusha) is not identical with the body or matter (prakriti). The purusha is essentially free, but is so caught up with matter that it appears to be in bondage to it, hence the sense of pain. Evidence for the existence of purusha takes the form of the awareness that human beings have of a state that transcends the realities of phenomenal experience, and the desire to attain it. The existence of prakriti is self-evident. Samkhya divides prakriti into 24 parts (26 if prakriti itself is included), of which the most important are the three *gunas* or strands, like those of a rope; these are responsible for the tendency to evolution or change, which characterises prakriti. As already stated, purusha is neither produced nor productive, but prakriti, though unproduced, being eternal, is productive. The three gunas are *sattva*, *rajas* and *tamas*. Sattva is potential consciousness, goodness, pleasure, pain, bewilderment. Though it might be described as good, it nevertheless binds the purusha to things like wisdom and joy, thus apparently depriving it of freedom. Rajas is activity or passion. It leads to craving and desire. Tamas is darkness, the coarse quality which results in ignorance.

Liberation is obtained by freeing the purusha from the influence of sattva, rajas and tamas, which coil around it like a rope, or hold it in bondage like a chain. Once it is set free, the purusha can enjoy *kaivalyam*, isolation, as one monad among many.

The dualism of samkhya is not between good and evil, or between the real and the unreal, but between the unchangeable and the constantly changing. It is a non-theistic system with no outer agency (God or God's grace) to help the process of liberation. In fact, such help as there is comes from prakriti, which not only causes bondage but also provides the experiences that lead ultimately to detachment and freedom.

In the *Svetasvatara Upanishad* and the *Bhagavad Gita*, samkhya may be translated as theory or knowledge. In its earliest traceable forms there is no God, nor is there any advice on how *kaivalyam* might be realized. Traditionally, however, the way of liberation has been through the combining of samkhya analysis with yoga practice, for which it provides the metaphysics, though among the six astika schools yoga is given a place of its own. In its theistic form samkhya adds a twenty-sixth category to prakriti: Ishvara, the Lord. However, theistic samkhya still teaches the goal of kaivalyam, not union with Ishvara, which is itself detached: as the *Yoga Sutra* puts it:

Concentration is attained by devotion to Ishvara. Ishvara is a special kind of Purusha, which is untouched by affliction, karma, fruits, or hopes. In him the seeds of omniscience is perfect. He is the Guru of the ancients unlimited by time.

He is merely an object of devotion or a focus for meditation. Such a Lord is very different from the medieval development of tantric yoga, in which purusha (male) becomes Shiva and prakriti (female) becomes either Shakti, or the Lord of the *Gita*, Krishna, who offers integration rather than isolation. Yoga is the means of achieving liberation. In its unliberated state the purusha appears to be subject to subtle changes in the body, to moods and effects brought on by tensions between the three gunas. In reality it is free, but this freedom has to be realized in practice. The categories outlined in samkhya have to be controlled and their influence eliminated. This is done through a disciplined process. The philosopher Patanjali described eight steps or limbs (*angas*).

1 Abstention This includes such things as non-injury (*ahimsa*), speaking the truth (*satya*), celibacy (*brahmacharya*) and the rejection of greed and theft.

2 Observance This includes positive attributes and attitudes such as self-discipline, purity, equanimity. The *Gita* says:

> The one whose mind (buddhi) views friends, comrades and enemies in the same way, is outstanding.

Simplicity, awareness of one's own personality and motives, seeing God in everything, and accepting all the experiences that God provides, also play central roles.

3 Posture (*asana*) This is important so that it is possible to concentrate on meditation without distraction. The posture should be steady and pleasurable. The amazing contortions often associated with yoga in the Western mind are not advocated.

4 Breath control Anyone who is at all self-observant will notice how they breathe rapidly when they are upset and how the advice 'take a deep breath' helps composure. In yogic practice breathing is highly disciplined, but has the same purpose and effect.

5 Sense withdrawal Switching the mind off from its normal functions, as we do when sleeping so successfully that we do not hear a clock strike – i.e. making the senses serve the mind.

6 Concentration Mastering the mind so that it is bound to one object of attention, instead of flitting aimlessly out of control.

7 Meditation Filling the mind with the single object upon which one is concentrating.

8 Contemplation This is known by a number of names such as self-realization, a state of higher consciousness or illumination. It is reached when the thought supply is exhausted and the individual continues to look attentively without desire or thought or will. It is something like a 'penny-dropping' realization after long thought. In this state of independence (*kaivalya*), the self exists in isolation, like the lotus in a dirty pond, unbesmirched by the surrounding grime and pollution. The stage beyond this is moksha.

Yoga is one of the six astika schools of philosophy. The description of its purpose above may come as a surprise to some Westerners, for whom yoga is only a physical disciplines. Although one may see Hindus in amazing postures, it is important to realize that none of these is necessary; control of the body is merely the third stage in the list and can be achieved by sitting in a comfortable chair!

Ishvara

One category has not yet been mentioned: Ishvara, which means Lord. He is mentioned in the *Yoga Sutra*. There may not need to be a place for a creator, but this concept recognises the value which the worship of God might have for some seekers after perfection. It describes Ishvara thus:

Ishvara is a special type of spirit, untouched by suffering, works (karma), or the result of works or impressions. In him is the highest knowledge of everything. He was Guru of the ancients and is not limited by time.

This twenty-sixth category of yoga leaves a place for *bhakti* (see Chapter 12) within the philosophy, though the texts do not speak so much of reciprocated love as of an object of devotion, a help to meditation and concentration, and a model of perfection.

As we have seen, Samkhya-Yoga has developed over the centuries. Its advocates were sometimes critical of vedic teachings and rituals, though they are included in the orthodox schools of philosophy. This may say something about the eclectic nature of Hinduism. It may also suggest that the origins of samkhya and yoga lay outside the Aryan tradition, which produced the Vedas and were survivals, which eventually found acceptance in the great tradition, from the earlier civilization which flourished in the Indus Valley region.

Mimamsa

'Enquiry' is coupled with Vedanta, but was merely an exposition of the *Vedas* rather than a way of liberation. Eventually, it affirmed that moksha was to be obtained by respect for the *Vedas* and observation of the rituals included in them. It later tended to merge with Vedanta, and was therefore sometimes called *Uttara Mimamsa*, or later *Mimamsa*.

Vedanta

Vedanta is probably the area of Hindu philosophy best known in the West, through writers such as Christopher Isherwood. Vedanta means the *Veda's* end, and has also been described as complete knowledge of the Vedas and is used to refer to the philosophies which began with the *Upanishads* (which are themselves philosophical treatises in the form of the teachings of Gurus to their disciples).

What we shall now consider are two particular and differing interpretations of the *Upanishads*. The first is that of Shankara.

Shankara

Shankara, a south Indian, Tamil, and devotee of Shiva, was born in 788 CE; he became a sannyasin as little more than a child and died at the age of 32 in 820. His opponents accused him of being a crypto-Buddhist because they could see no difference between his teaching on Brahman and the *sunya* doctrine of Buddhism. Other Hindus noted that his name meant 'auspicious' and was one of the epithets of Shiva, so they claimed that he was an incarnation of that deity. He has often been described as Hinduism's greatest philosopher. Besides being a philosopher he composed some hymns to Shiva and devotional books. He regarded belief in Ishvara as a useful, but lower, path to that of knowledge, *jnana*, and founded four colleges which have survived to the present day, at Dwarka in the west, Puri in the east, Badri in the north, and Shringeri in the south, as well as an order of monks known as Dashanamis.

Shankara's philosophical system is known as *advaita vedanta*, non-dualism; it is based upon an unequivocal belief in the authority of scripture, *shruti*. A verse in the *Chandogya Upanishad* (6:10:3) reads, '*tat tvam asi*', 'that you are'. Shankara took it to mean that the individual soul or atman, and Brahman, are one. This monistic doctrine took some justifying. After all there seems to be a considerable distinction between one person and another.

This is actually an illusion based on ignorance (*avidya*). The Absolute, Brahman, is *sat-chit-ananda*, pure being or truth, pure consciousness, and pure bliss – unconditioned by time, space or causality. Anything less must, by definition, be less than Absolute. The personal self, atman, must possess the same properties, otherwise it cannot be eternal.

Ignorance causes us to look at a shining object on the beach and say it is a piece of silver when it is merely a shell, or to conclude that a partly submerged stick is bent when it is actually completely straight, or stand terrified as we see a snake in our path only to discover that it is only a rope, or to believe that the sun turns red as it disappears over the horizon. We are victims of *maya*, illusion. Sense experience and even the intellect mislead us. Proper perception is only possible when we intuitively accept that Brahman alone is real, the world is false and that the individual is Brahman and nothing else. Until we reach this position we will continue to superimpose our false perceptions upon the Real, and we will persist in error.

Of course, Shankara was not concerned about such trivial things as ropes and shells; he was interested in liberating people from the bondage of suffering. Bondage and liberation, he said, exist in the mind only, but the ignorant attribute them falsely to the atman itself – just as they say the sun is darkened when it is merely covered by a cloud. The Brahman, the one without end, the unchangeable reality, remains unattached. It is pure consciousness.

Dualism, reliance on actions and individualism had no place in the teachings of Shankara. Brahman, the one reality, could only be realized when the penny dropped, when the enlightened mind perceived its unity with the One. When this happened suffering would cease because it would be seen to be unreal.

The teachings of Shankara seemed to leave no place for bhakti, devotion to a personal God, or to any kind of emotional element in religion. True, as has been mentioned, he composed hymns and was in some respects a devotee of Shiva, but worship of Ishvara was a lower order than intuitive direct experience.

However, one man, more than anyone else, challenged Shankara's interpretation of Reality.

Ramanuja

Ramanuja is said to have lived from 1017 CE to 1137, but his birthdate may have been altered to enable him to be placed directly after Yamuna as the head of the Shrirangam temple, which he entered after an unsuccesful marriage. He certainly was in charge of it for much of his life, although this did not prevent him from travelling widely elsewhere in India, converting people to Vaishnavite Hinduism, repairing temples and engaging in disputation. He wrote commentaries in Sanskrit on the *Vedanta Sutra*, the *Gita* and the *Upanishads*. The choice of Sanskrit was probably intended to convince an intellectual readership, who might have shunned his writings had he used the regional Tamil language favoured by the Alvar bhakti poets. Of course, most Hindus elsewhere in India would not have access to any regional language other than their own. Sanskrit was the national language of the brahminical tradition. Unlike the Alvars Ramanuja did not disregard caste, as is seen in the ritual handbook for his temple, which he organized along caste lines, though accepting the bhakti teaching that all castes could reach God. There was a place for Shudra servants and Shudra ascetics in the ritual life of the temple.

Ramanuja was faced with three tasks. These were:

- to reject Shankara's concept of higher and lower levels of truth
- to answer Shankara's argument that the world is illusory
- to accept some kind of unity of Brahman and atman.

He could not accept the non-theistic, dualist, samkhya analysis, which in any case emphasized liberation through knowledge and the detached and detaching practice of yoga. He believed strongly in dependence upon God and the real existence of the world. To show this he used the following analogy. We possess a body which is subservient to the self, to 'me'. We say, for example, 'my body'. The human being and the world are the body of Brahman. A person has also two aspects, consciousness and bodily states. The cosmos is the body of Brahman. Here Ramanuja's analogy faced a problem: Buddhists criticized theists by pointing out that the cosmos is in a state of constant change – how could there be a changeless God? Again he used the personal analogy. We say, 'I remember . . .'. This suggests the existence of something permanent and beyond change, the 'I' which is capable of observing. God is, by analogy, changeless.

Ramanuja argued that there are many individual selves, but that they are not completely free and independent. God is the inner controller, and any freedom which finite selves possess is God-permitted. In Ramanuja's teaching God has some need of human beings and cannot maintain himself without them. The words of the *Gita*, 'The man of wisdom is my very self', (7:8), mean just this. 'Tat tvam asi' means that the atman has divine attributes. At liberation the life *monad*, the *jiva*, realizes its essential Godlike properties, and so enters upon an eternal life of bliss derived from dependence of God. Taking Shankara's analogy of the lotus growing in water but being unaffected by it, Ramanuja pointed out that the lotus does have a dependent relationship with the pond. It needs water to sustain it. This more accurately describes the Brahman-atman connection than that of the *advaita* school. Ramanuja's system was known as *vishishtadvaita vedanta*, or qualified non-dualism. Like Shankara, he was concerned about dualist philosophy, but he also saw danger in complete monism. Monism seemed to provide no essential link between the individual soul and God; dualism denied the existence of such a link. Ramanuja argued from experience that deity, Brahman, is real and independent and that souls, atman, are also real but totally dependent on deity. With Samkhya in mind (which claimed that both the Spirit and Matter, Purusha and Prakriti, were eternal), he wrote in his commentary on the *Gita*:

> The body, being a perishable entity, cannot be imperishable, and the atman, being an imperishably entity, cannot be perishable . . . nobody can kill the atman; the verb 'to kill' means nothing but 'to separate the atman from the body'.

The world, and therefore all spiritual and material entities, constitute the body of Brahman; they are the products of Brahman's creative power. Thus they are parts of Brahman. The individual atman is dependent on Brahman, but moksha does not mean the end of an apparent but unreal distinction, as Shankara taught. *Tat* is 'that', the absolute, the first cause, *tvam* is 'you', the inner controller modified by the embodied soul. This is qualified non-dualism, *vishishtadvaita vedanta*.

Ramanuja's teaching upon a degree of distinction between the atman and Brahman, and the idea of the soul being dependent upon God, enabled him to justify *bhakti* (devotion), the lower way which Shankara had grudgingly acknowledged. Whereas Shankara had written a commentary upon the *Gita* unenthusiastically, only because it was such a popular scripture, but had found its emphasis on bhakti distasteful, Ramanuja welcomed the opportunity to express his views as being the true interpretation of the book, noting its acceptance of the need for ritual action as a step on the path of devotion, and its acceptance of bhakti with its stress on surrender and grace but also effort. The question of the relationship between grace and human effort, which he did not resolve, eventually caused a split among Ramanuja's followers. One group the *marjara* (cat) school, interpreted Ramanuja as teaching that the devotee is the passive recipient of God's grace, delivering the atman as a mother cat does her kittens, by grabbing them by the scruff of the neck. The *markata* (monkey-hold) school believed that it was necessary for the devotee to make an effort, to cling onto the mother as a young monkey does. But both agreed that grace was essential.

Ramanuja also gave considerable attention to arguments or proofs for the existence of God, but considered that knowledge of God is not achieved as the result of human reasoning. However, his main contribution to Hinduism is his justification of bhakti and his provision for it of intellectual acceptability and rationality. Bhakti has always been the most popular religious path because everyone can follow it, women as well as men. However, it was often regarded as irrational emotionalism, to be despised by those of superior intellect who might also be anxious that it might provide a justification for flouting the varna-ashrama-dharma. In Ramanuja bhakti found a champion, a Brahmin impeccable in his observance of the shastras.

Does God exist?

As we have seen, there are forms of Hindu philosophy that did not originally postulate the existence of God. These offered explanations of the cosmos, and paths of liberation that did not necessitate belief in God as the source of creation or of salvation. There were also Jain, Buddhist and Charvaka philosophers to contend with. The teaching of this last group may be summed up in the words: 'while you live, live well, even if you have to borrow; for once cremated there is no return'. These hedonists ridiculed the *Vedas* and the Brahmins as well as rejecting caste. Thus, long before the Common/Christian Era, emergent Hinduism was confronted by a denial of the basic vedic and Upanishadic teachings that there is one ultimate Reality.

The theists based their defence on the following arguments:

• awareness of order in the universe; for example, phases of the moon do not occur in a random, unpredictable manner (our example); this means there must be an intelligence that is the source of this order
• human intuition also points to existence of this intelligence.

They might, of course, have argued from the authority of the *Vedas*, when discussing existence, with other philosophers who would accept their authority. For example, the *Vedas* speak of Rita (pronounced like 'bitter'), the cosmic order that the Gods must protect, especially Varuna. This order is moral as well as scientific. Book One of the *Vedas* includes the words:

That which is One the sages call by many names (1.64.46).

In Book Ten is the interesting assertion that:

> With their words the wise poets shape the One into many
> forms; agni, Yama or Matarishvan (10.114.5).

The famous *Hymn of Origins* states:

> In the beginning there was neither existence nor non-
> existence;
> Neither the world nor the sky beyond.
> What was covered over? Where? What gave it protection?
> Was there water deep and unfathomable?
>
> Then was neither death nor immortality,
> Nor any sign of day or night,
> That One breathed, without breath, by its own impulse;
> Other that That there was nothing at all . . .
> In the beginning was love,
>
> Which was the primal germ of the mind.
> The seers searching in their hearts with wisdom
> Discovered the connection between existence and non-
> existence . . .
>
> The Gods are later than this world's creation –
> Therefore who knows from whence it came?
> That out of which creation came,
> Whether it held it together or did not,
> He who see it in the highest heaven,
> He only knows – or perhaps even He does not know
>
> (10:129)

This is a very late hymn, but, nevertheless over 3000 years old.
It demonstrates the existence of philosophical speculation. Its
agnosticism, however, seems less akin to later Western thought
and more an example of questioning the original existence of
the dualities (which it mentions), and asserting a primordial
unitary reality that cannot be comprehended further.

12 the path of loving devotion

In this chapter you will learn:
- what Bhakti is
- about the *Upanishads* and the *Bhagavad Gita*
- about Islam in India
- some famous Bhaktas.

Bhakti, the belief in the possibility of a relationship with God based on love, can be traced back in literature as far as the *Svetasvatara Upanishad* (C5/4 BCE), in which this verse occurs:

His form cannot be glimpsed, none may see him within the eye: Whoso should know him with heart and mind as dwelling in the heart, becomes immortal (6:20).

It ends with the statement that the teaching of the *Upanishad* can be understood only by 'the great-souled man who loyally and greatly loves (bhakti) God' (6:23).

The *Bhagavad Gita* declares that God's gracious love is available to anyone who comes to him, including outcasts and women (9:32-34):

Whosoever makes me his haven, base-born though he be, yes, women too, and artisans, even Shudras, theirs it is to tread the all-highest way.

How much more should it be the way for the Brahmins, pure and good, and royal seers who know devoted love (bhakta). Since thy lot has fallen in this world impermanent and joyless, commune with me in love (bhaj).

On me thy mind, for me thy loving service, and to me be thy prostrations: let thine own self be integrated, and then shalt thou come to me, thy striving bent on me.

Some verses earlier, God Krishna, says:

Be it a leaf, or flower, or fruit, or water that a zealous soul may offer with loves devotion (bhakti), that do I willingly accept, for it was love that made the offering (9:26);

and

Those who commune (bhaj) with me in love's devotion (bhakti) abide in me and I in them (9:29).
(translations from R. C. Zaehner, *Hindu Scriptures*, Dent)

The Alvars, Vaishnavite bhakti poets (devotees of Vishnu) who flourished in southern India during the Gupta period (c.5 CE), must not be forgotten either, but it is of Chaitanya, Tukaram, Mirabai, Kabir, Tulsidas, and others such as Guru Nanak and Ravidas that many Hindus think today, when the bhakti movement is mentioned.

Two questions face the student of bhakti: the first is where its origins lie. It is not vedic and it appears, somewhat suddenly and unheralded, in the *Svetasvatara Upanishad* and the *Bhagavad Gita*. It may be that it was part of the indigenous tradition associated with the Indus Valley (see pages 140, 158–9) which was submerged by Aryan influence, only to re-emerge centuries later. Secondly, its period of greatest prominence coincided with Muslim penetration of northern India. Whether this flowering of devotional poetry would have occurred without the existence of Islam is again a debatable question. What can be said is that these and other bhaktas made God available to low caste and 'outcaste' men and women, those outside caste on grounds of pollution, to the extent that conversion to Islam as the only way of gaining spiritual satisfaction was not necessary. Many low-caste people did convert, some for religious reasons; often, however, the motive was social mobility; the hope of escaping from the rigidity of the caste system. Islam, however, failed to provide this relief, as did conversion to Christianity during the period of the Raj, which succeeded the Mughal Empire.

Islam in India

Islamic contact with India first came through Arab traders. It was not until 1001 that Islam made a strong impact upon the subcontinent through Mahmud of Ghazni, whose raids led to the destruction of Somnath and the occupation of Punjab. However, only with Babur, the first Mughal emperor, in 1526, was the permanent conquest of the north achieved.

Mughal rule was generally tolerant. The *jizya* (poll-tax on non-Muslims) was imposed from time to time, but often Brahmins were exempt, or paid a reduced amount. Rulers intermarried with Rajput princesses, and Hindu customs were countenanced at court. Temples received government grants. Much of this has been forgotten by those twentieth-century Indians who wish to demonstrate the alien nature of Islam, and by religious leaders who link Hinduism with Indian nationalism. For all of them the Emperor Aurangzeb (1658–1707) typifies Mughal rule. He demolished temples and replaced them with mosques, imposed the jizya relentlessly, and closed Hindu schools. His piety also alienated Muslims, for he imposed a strict code of Sunni morality upon his Muslim subjects who, along with Hindus and Sikhs, had been used to the relaxed and tolerant régime which flourished most completely during the reign of Akbar the Great (1556–1605). The long decline of Mughal power began with the

Emperor Aurangzeb, whose expansionist policies paradoxically almost took the empire to Cape Camorin, the southern tip of India, but resulted in widespread rebellions against his rule.

Some famous Bhaktas

Chaitanya

Chaitanya 1485–1533, was a Bengali Vaishnavite Brahmin, whose devotees regarded him as an incarnation of Krishna. Part of his catechism reads:

Question	Which knowledge is highest of all?
Answer	There is no knowledge but devotion to Krishna.
Question	What is counted wealth among human possessions?
Answer	He is immensely wealthy who has love for Radha-Krishna.
Question	What is the heaviest of sorrows?
Answer	There is no sorrow except separation from Krishna.
Question	Among songs what song is natural to creatures?
Answer	It is the song whose heart is the love-sport of Radha-Krishna.
Question	What is chief among the objects of worship?
Answer	The name of the most adorable couple, Radha-Krishna.

Little has survived of his poetry. He is best known today as the inspiration of the Haré Krishna movement (see page 110).

Mirabai

Mirabai ('bai' is an honorific term often attached to a woman's name) was born about 1498, and was a Rajput princess. (Some scholars place her a century earlier.) The Kshatriya culture of Rajasthan was one in which, if menfolk were defeated in battle, their wives committed *jauhar*, mass suicide, to prevent them from falling into the hands of the enemy. Chastity and obedience were highly valued virtues. Mira's family were devotees of Vishnu. Her great-grandfather founded the city of Jodhpur and her grandfather won victories over the advancing Mughals. It is said that as a child Mira was given a murti of Krishna by an ascetic; soon afterwards, when a marriage was being celebrated nearby, she asked who her own bridegroom was to be. She was told by her mother, pointing towards Krishna, 'There is your bridegroom'. In 1516, however, she married the son of the ruler of Mewar, leader of the Rajputs.

Legend surrounds Mira's life and her marriage. It is said that on her wedding day she performed the marriage rituals with the murti of Krishna before performing those with her husband, and on entering the family home she refused to give up worship of Krishna for Durga, their ishtadevata. When she attended the temple it is said that she danced and sang in public, often with men and women of low caste, an act unheard of among Rajput aristocrats. Mira's husband died but she refused to become a sati; then her own father and father-in-law died fighting the Mughals. The new king tried to kill her and she left the palace to live a life of wandering as a worshipper of Krishna. She died in 1546.

Mirabai deserves attention because she is a rare example of a woman bhakta, as well as for the intrinsic quality of her devotional poems which, of course, were composed during her wanderings, and not written down during her lifetime. The attraction of her poetry lies in her ability to identify with Krishna at a personal level, with all her awareness of his beauty and the experience of his presence, and an ability to express the deep pain of separation from him. She regarded herself as a bride of Krishna.

Sometimes she described herself as a lover waiting, suffering pain when Krishna does not come.

> I am longing for you, O my Lord, for the season of the swing has come but you are not beside me.
> Clouds gather on my brows and my eyes shed heavy shadows.
> My parents gave me to you, I have become yours for ever; who but you can be my Lord?
> This separation troubles my breast; make me your own; make me perfect like you, O Lord of Perfection.
> (from A. J. Appasamy, *Temple Bells*, YMCA Calcutta, n.d.).

> Look how he wounds me again.
> He vowed to come and the yard is empty, food flung away, like my senses.
> Why must you shame what you say?
> You've wisped yourself away, lifter of the mountain, left me here to splinter.

Yet she can also affirm:

> My love,
> he is here
> inside
> He does not leave,
> He doesn't need to arrive.

Daringly, she even compares the Supreme God, Krishna, to one of the lowest of human beings, a washerman. His love made clean the souls of all devotees:

> Hari is a dhobi, takes in all stained clothes.
> In the river of his love, with the soap of his peace glowing iridescent in the sun he washes everyone.
> No envious smear returns.
> The souls he's done are like muslin when worn, says Mira.
> (These translations are taken from *In the Darkness of the Heart*, ed. Kerry Brown and Sima Sharma, Harper Collins, 1995. Those which follow are again from *Temple Bells*.)

Kabir

Kabir 1398–1518, was a low-caste weaver of Varanasi. His *julaha* weaver caste had probably converted *en masse* to Islam some time before his birth in the hope of improving their status. He is an example of a bhakta who refused to accept the titles of Hindu or Muslim. Another was Guru Nanak, a younger contemporary, whose teachings are, however, quite independent of Kabir's. Kabir said:

> If God be within the mosque, then to whom does this world belong?
> If Ram be within the image which you find upon your pilgrimage, then who is there to know what happens without?
> Hari [a name of Vishnu] is in the east: Allah is in the west.
> Look within your heart, for there you will find both Karim [a name of Allah, meaning Generous] and Ram;
> All men and women of the world are his living forms.

Tulsi Das

Tulsi Das (d. 1623) was a Brahmin who spent most of his life in Varanasi where he composed the *Ramacharitmanas* (Sacred Lake of the Acts of Rama), in Hindi rather than Sanskrit, which would have been inaccessible to most people – and all those of lower caste.

Many are the means of crossing over the ocean of transmigration which the pure words of the *Vedas* speak of. But Tulsi says: 'Real happiness of heart cannot be attained without giving up the ideas of "I" and "mine".'

Tukaram

Tukaram, 1607–1649, a Maharashtrian Shudra, regarded pilgrimages and other external practices of religion as ineffectual. The only source of liberation was God's grace.

> No deeds I've done nor thoughts I've thought;
> Save as your servant I am nought.
> Guard me, O God, and O, control
> The tumult of my restless soul.
> Ah, do not, do not cast on me
> The guilt of mine iniquity.
> My countless impurities, I, Tuka, say,
> Upon thy loving heart I lay.

The poems of Nobel prize winner Sir Rabindranath Tagore (1861–1941), and *My Sweet Lord* by George Harrison, might also be included in the bhakti tradition, which has no end any more that it had a clear beginning.

13 the beginnings of Hinduism

In this chapter you will learn:
- about the vedic religion of the Aryans
- about the cosmic principle of Rta and the importance of sacrifice in relation to Rta
- about pre-Aryan people
- about the Indus people
- Hindu concepts taken from the pre-Aryan people
- about fertility cults and the Mother Goddess
- about some conflicting interpretations by scholars.

We have noted the diversity of Hinduism, and the apparent tension which sometimes exists between one expression of the religion and another: for example, the strength of the emphasis upon caste, purity and pollution, as opposed to the statements, particularly from the bhakti traditions, of the effectiveness of God's grace, which can provide liberation for even Shudras and women, to paraphrase the *Bhagavad Gita*. It is now time to ask what the origins of Hinduism are, and how its diversity and seeming contradictions are to be explained.

To provide answers, it is necessary to begin with the known and proceed tentatively to the unknown. The known is the religion which is to be found in, or clearly developed from, the *Vedas*. We must then look at what is left unexplained and ask whence it might have come.

vedic religion of the Aryans

vedic religion is the religion of the Aryans, and the main source of our knowledge about it comes from the *Vedas*. The Aryans were a people of European origin, who spread westwards as far as Ireland (Eire) and eastwards into such areas as Iran and India. They entered India in about 1700 BCE and replaced the dominance of the Indus Valley culture with their own.

The nature of vedic religion is known from the *Vedas*; these are four in number. One of them, the *Atharva Veda*, differs from the rest and can be dismissed from discussion at this point, since it may throw more light on non-Aryan ideas than it does on vedic religion, although it does contain some hymns to the gods of the vedic pantheon. The principal vedic text is the *Rig-Veda*. It was recited by the *hotars*, the priests who were responsible for the fire sacrifices. We know, therefore, that the focus of worship was sacrifice, sometimes using animals, and that there were officiating priests who attended the fire, and chanting priests, the *Udgatars*.

The content of the *Vedas* varies considerably. There are hymns to the gods who were worshipped by the Aryans. These were mostly male, and the concerns expressed were related to such natural phenomena as storms and rains. As many as a quarter of the hymns were dedicated to Indra, who helped the Aryans overcome the Dasa people of the Indus valley as well as Vritra, the force who holds back the light and the rain. Another important god was Varuna, the universal monarch responsible for the moral order.

The Aryans brought the caste system with them to India, though not in its fully developed form. One scholar named Basham believed that it was a two-tier structure of nobles and others; another, Dumezil, claimed that it has three parts; the Brahmins, the Kshatriya warriors, and the Vaishyas, who were the ordinary people. One of the hymns of the *Rig-Veda*, the *Purusha Sukta*, or hymn to Purusha (primeval man), composed after the Dasa people had been assimilated into the varna system, gives it divine origin. It states that the Brahmins were created from the mouth of Purusha; the Kshatriyas from his arms; the workers, Vaishyas, from his thighs; and the Shudras, or serfs, from his feet. The same hymn says that the sun came from the eye of Purusha, the gods Agni and Indra from his mouth, and the earth from his feet. Thus, something of the monism, which emerges strongly in some of the *Upanishads*, is also to be found in this hymn.

Another strand, usually reckoned to be late (the *Vedas* may be the product of 500 years or more of religious development), is one of sceptical philosophical enquiry. Part of it reads:

Neither not being nor being was there at that time. There was no air-filled space, neither was there sky beyond it. What enveloped all? And where? Under whose protection? Neither was there death nor immortality at that time. There was no distinguishing mark of day or night. That One breathed without wind in its own special manner. Other than it, indeed, and beyond, there did not exist anything whatsoever . . .

Wherefrom this creation has issued, whether he made it or whether he has not he who is the superintendent of the world in the highest heaven he alone knows, or, perhaps, even he does not know.

(Book 10:129)

Despite the multiplicity of gods there is more than a hint of unity. The *Rig-Veda* in fact explicitly affirms this:

To what is One, sages give many a title; they call it Agni, Yama, Matarisvan.

This is echoed in the *Yajur Veda*:

For an awakened soul Indra, Varuna, Agni, Yama, Aditya, Chandra all these names represent only one basic power and spiritual entity.

The Aryans believed in a cosmic principal, Rta. This was precarious, and had to be sustained by sacrifice as well as by the proper performance of dharma, its corresponding equivalent in earthly terms. Hence the proper ordering of things which was the responsibility of the priests, and the reason why the *Vedas* (and the ritual system which has given rise to them) were eventually to be supplemented by the *shastras* – manuals or treatises which ranged from the conduct of rituals to the ordering of society and which included philosophical tracts, especially the Laws of Manu.

Much of the emphasis in Aryan religion was upon a successful happy life here and now; however, the *Vedas* may mention an after-life (scholars are not agreed on this), with the righteous going to the World of the Fathers, and the wicked to the House of Clay. The transmigration of souls was not part of vedic teaching, but it does appear in one or two later passages, doubtless as the result of non-vedic influences. From such examples, and the incorporation of the *Atharva Veda* into the corpus of *shruti* (that which has been heard), the direct revelation of Brahman, there is some indication of the power of the Indus Valley tradition, or perhaps of the eclecticism which becomes one of the characteristics of later Hinduism.

We must now try to establish the source of important aspects of religion not found in the *Vedas*; for example, the Mother Goddess and the female element in Indian religion; and yoga, and bhakti, the strong devotional strand based on belief in a personal and loving God.

Indus people

When the Aryans arrived in India they came across people whom they described as '*Dasa*' or '*Dyas*' – dark-skinned, snub-nosed worshippers of the phallus whom they clearly regarded with derision. They were defeated by the Aryans who were inspired by the Gods Indra and Agni, upon whose appearance 'the dark-hued races scattered leaving behind all their possessions'.

Archaeology may have revealed more information about them. In the Indus Valley there have been found the remains of an urban civilization which flourished in the valley region of the river Indus in what is now mainly Pakistan, between about 2500 and 1700 BCE. Its nature and extent are known largely through excavations carried out since 1920. The vedic references are thought to indicate these people whom they conquered, and with whose survivors they probably intermarried. The principal Indus Valley cities were Mohenjo-daro and Harappa. Other sites at Kalibangan, Lothal and Surkotada have been examined since the 1960s, and work is still proceeding.

The only direct literary evidence for Indus religion is the vedic reference to phallic worship cited above. It provides an interesting link with the discovery of phallic symbols and other artifacts which might have associations with fertility cults, such as figurines of women which might represent the mother goddess. Most importantly, there is a seal bearing the image of a horned, three-faced male with erect phallus, seated in a yogic posture, surrounded by a goat, a tiger, an elephant, a bull, a cobra, and a rhinoceros. This figure has been identified as the god Shiva Pasupati, Lord of Beasts. However, the link must be conjectural in the absence of further literary evidence, but reasons for making it are as follows:

- The vedic mention of Dasa phallus worship is significant; the lingam is associated with Shiva in later Hinduism.
- Shiva is not one of the vedic gods. It is attractive to postulate his existence as an Indus deity, and his later incorporation into post-vedic Brahminism. He is the subject of one of the principal *Upanishads*, the *Svetasvatara*.
- Fertility cults, part of developed Hinduism, are not Aryan. Their existence might be explicable as an Indus survival associated with Shiva.
- The vedic statements of the destruction of the Dasas does not stand up to archaeological scrutiny. Not all excavations, by any means, have yielded evidence of destruction. If, as seems likely, there was intermarriage between Aryan warriors and Indus women, it is conceivable that it resulted in a cultural synthesis.

The kind of extrapolation provided by this example is the method that scholars have to use to try to discover the nature of the Indus religion. Taking this case further, the bhakti tradition of devotion to a loving and gracious God is not found in the *Vedas*, being first encountered in the *Svetasvatara Upanishad* mentioned above. It is attractive to see this too as part of the Indus legacy.

Several other archaeological features have given rise to similar speculation. An open space with what may be a sacrificial square and statues, found in the same context, suggest the possibility of temple worship, which was not practised by the Aryan nomads. The other most important find was the discovery

of a great bath at Mohenjodaro. The complex, which had side
rooms and statues associated with it, may indicate the practice of
religious bathing to remove the taint of pollution. Again, it may
have links with fertility rites; the suggestion has been made that the
rooms were used for the purposes of cult prostitution. More
definite is the link with the ceremonial importance of water, which
would be natural in a riparian civilization (that is, one living on the
banks of the river), and which is an extremely significant aspect of
later and modern Hinduism.

Conflicting interpretations by scholars

Many scholars have been inclined to look at the Hinduism that
becomes identifiable as such between about 200 BCE and 200 CE,
to take from it what is clearly Aryan, using the literary source of
the *Vedas*, and say that what remains must have come from the
Indus Valley culture. Such speculation is tempting, especially
bearing in mind the eclectic nature of Indian religion, and it may
be the only way in which the content of Dasa religion can be
deduced, for even if a bilingual text enables the Indus seals to be
deciphered, this does not constitute a considerable amount of
literary material.

It is necessary, however, to add a word of warning. Other
influences may account for some – even much – of the non-
Aryan practices of Hinduism, especially in the early southern
cultures of Karnataka and Andra Pradesh. Moreover the lack of
literary evidence makes statements about beliefs particularly
risky. It may be that the belief in rebirth, samsara and karma
(scarcely found in the *Vedas*), and yoga philosophy, as well as
bhakti beliefs, are Dasa in origin, but certainty is not yet
possible and perhaps never well be. If they are not indigenous
and the product of the Indus Valley culture, we are left so far
with no other source to which they may be ascribed. Some
nationalistic Hindus may be encountered who play down the
Aryan effect completely, ascribing the origins of Hinduism
completely to beliefs and practices found within India; and
others have claimed that to find them we should not look to
northern India at all but to the Tamil-speaking south. This
language is the true tongue of Hinduism, they say, thus rejecting
attempts to make Hindi the spoken language of the subcontinent. The attempt to mould scholarship to ideology is not
exclusively a Western phenomenon ...

ethics

In this chapter you will learn:

- about caste and family influence and about the positive discrimination included in the Indian Constitution to deal with the practice of 'untouchability'
- about the changed status of Hindu women
- about the preference for a male child
- about medical ethics – drugs, alcohol, food and fasting
- about wealth and work
- about care for the needy
- the five great sins.

Even in days when individualism seems to dominate, children from meat-eating families anywhere in the world are likely to be unquestioning carnivores. This is their way of life. Similarly, the offspring of parents whose ancestors have served for generations in the armed services will probably regard the army as a natural vocation. Not all decisions are matters of personal ethics. The family and caste influence is especially strong in Hinduism. Mahatma Gandhi's vegetarianism was originally the result of his Vaishya upbringing. In England, where he encountered meat on the menu for the first time in his life, and flirted with eating it, his vegetarianism did eventually become a matter of conscience. His rejection of cow's milk, once he saw how India's sacred animal was treated, was an ethical matter; but it is doubtful whether many other Indians ever considered this issue as ethical, certainly until Bapu (as Mahatma Gandhi is sometimes known) made his decision. *Ahimsa*, non-violence, was a Jain teaching, related to keeping pure; Gandhi linked the emphasis on it to the ethical principle of reverence for life, and related it to the political principle of non-violent resistance. Incidentally, the *Mahabharata* (written possibly between 300 BCE and 300 CE) asserts:

> That mode of living which is founded upon total harmlessness towards all creatures or (in the case of necessity) upon a minimum of such harm, is the highest morality.

It might often seem more appropriate to think of the Latin word '*mores*' in preference to the word ethics, because it has fuller social implications, morals being the customs of a society *at a given time*. In this respect the Hindu behaves in accordance with dharma, which varies from one jati to another. Thus one may eat meat and another be vegetarian. According to the *Bhagavad Gita* this may exist between varnas. As we have already seen, Prince Arjuna, a Kshatriya, is required to fight – that is his dharma – but he has no wish to do so for a number of reasons. He seems eager to behave like a Brahmin, who should not pollute himself with the shedding of blood. His charioteer, who turns out to be the Supreme Deity, Krishna, rebukes him, telling him that it is 'better to do one's own dharma badly than another's dharma well'.

Caste

The very fact that the *Gita* deals with the issue of performing caste duty is an indication that, even 2000 years ago, the system had its critics. These numbered Buddhists, Jains and Charvakas. It is therefore possible to argue that caste was an ethical issue long before the Arya Samaj, Gandhi and the man who framed modern India's constitution, Ambhedkar, criticized caste discrimination and the India Constitution outlawed it. It also provided for the scheduled classes, previously called 'untouchables', to be treated with positive discrimination in certain areas such as education.

Untouchability is another ethical issue that arises out of caste. Untouchables were men and women who were outside the Hindu varna structure and who were in a state of permanent pollution because of their birth and occupation. The Indian Constitution made this practice, which Gandhi had described as 'a crime against humanity', illegal, and positive discrimination in the areas of employment and education was introduced; but oppression nonetheless continues. Cases are difficult to prove, and belief in purity and pollution is not going to be eradicated by parliamentary legislation. It must be admitted that much of the oppression of *dalits*, or 'the oppressed', as they call themselves now, instead of Gandhi's paternalist name of *Harijan*, 'children of God' (which can also mean 'love child' or 'bastard'), is usually socially and politically motivated, with religion serving, as so often, as a pretext to justify inhumanity.

Women

This is another area of ethics that has become important recently, though Hinduism has seen their status change dramatically more than once in its long history. By considering this in some detail we may achieve some perspective on the tradition. It is simplistic to imagine Hinduism as a religion that has always been the same. This is far from true.

Scholars tend to divide their studies of the place of women in Hinduism into three historical periods. These are: from ancient times to about the third century BCE; a long middle period from then until the 19th century, when little appeared to change; and modern times.

There is some evidence that in the vedic era women received sacred thread initiation, upanayana, and thereafter studied the *Vedas* with a Guru. In fact, the *Brihadaranyaka Upanishad* contains an account of a woman philosopher, Gargi Vacaknavi, questioning the famous teacher Yajnavalkya, who according to some traditions was the originator of the doctrines of Yoga. Though this is only one example, it is sufficient to affirm that such things did happen. For good measure, however, it may be pointed out that Yajnavalkya also instructed his own first wife, Maitreyi, in the nature of the soul, according to the same *Upanishad*, which also teaches the ritual for securing a scholarly daughter. There is evidence too that girls could offer sacrifices, that sons were not an absolute necessity for this purpose, and that women need not marry but might become ascetics in pursuit of moksha. In the heterodox movements of Buddhism and Jainism women played important roles. There was, however, a trend in the opposite direction. In the *Mahabharata*, which belongs to this early period, the sage Dirghatamas ordained that no woman should remain unmarried. Kuni, a celibate, was told that she could not go to heaven unless she married, despite all her other qualities. She persuaded the sage Shringavat to marry her, and stayed with him for one night so meeting the requirement successfully. The *Atharva Veda* provides details of the rituals for securing a son rather than a daughter.

From this evidence it can be seen that women had a positive role in the tradition that became Hinduism, but that there was also a tension, perhaps related to its differing Aryan and Dravidian strands. The attitude towards woman was ambivalent. She was to be honoured like Lakshmi, whose tears could move a tyrant, but the *Rig-Veda* also said that she was fickle and unstable, and the *Mahabharata* portrayed her as a temptress. By the time of the Laws of Manu, somewhere about 300 CE, this ambivalence was being resolved to the detriment of women. Manu states that women should always be protected: by their fathers, then by their husbands, and finally, if necessary, by their sons. It also lays down that they must obey these guardians.

The story of the middle period is that of the suppression of women, though there are a few examples to the contrary. When the great ninth-century philosopher Shankara debated with Mandanamishra, the latter's wife acted as umpire. However, the status of women had fallen so dramatically that even nunneries had gone out of vogue in Buddhism by the fourth century CE. In Hinduism child marriages were becoming more the norm, and with them came neglect of a girl's education; and the thread ceremony became only a formality, instead of initiation into education with a Guru. In fact it was acceptable to class girls with Shudras, as having no thread of their own, their status depending on their husband.

One factor more than any other seems to have affected the place of woman in the Hindu tradition: the concept of ritual pollution. According to this teaching women are periodically impure, mainly because of menstruation. Contact with her rendered food impure, as well as the people she might accidentally brush against. Even today, there are Gurus who will not allow the glance of a woman to fall on them, those in the Swami Narayan movement, for example. Women must turn their backs on the approach of a Guru to avoid this happening.

The coming of Islam, and with it the seclusion of women, including those who were members of Hindu families, only further diminished their status. In modern times there have been changes. Hindu reformers such as Ram Mohan Roy and the Guru Swaminarayan opposed female infanticide and the practice of sati, which was outlawed by the British in response to Hindu pressure in 1829. The Brahmo Samaj, a reform movement founded by Ram Mohan Roy, built some girls' schools – though the emphasis was upon education for domesticity rather than for a career. The Arya Samaj, a later movement, encouraged the provision of a full curriculum rather than mere domestic training. It also opposed child marriage, and argued that the modern status of women did not reflect their position in the *Vedas*. It allowed female participation in the vedic fire ceremony, *havan*. Professor D. K. Karve (1857–1961) married a widow in 1893 after the death of his first wife. This was something for which the Brahmo Samaj had successfully campaigned, but for a well-known Brahmin actually to do it was more effective than any legislation. Divorce became legal only with the Hindu Marriage Act of 1955.

Hindu feminists refer back to the early period of Hinduism, to argue that they are merely seeking the status they once had. They are also reinterpreting such stories as that of Rama and Sita, emphasizing their role as women of moral courage. However, Brahmins teach that only boys can be initiated through the thread ceremony, and perform the funeral rites and annual memorial ceremonies for the dead. A son is still preferred to a daughter. The strong economic reasons for this are not always appreciated. Sons remain with their parents. They provide the only security against old age in a society where pensions are rare. Daughters leave home to join their husbands. Girl beggars continue to thank the giver by saying, 'May you be blessed with sons'; there is still a long way for the Hindu woman to go before the ideals she claims were reality in the vedic period become reality today. Dowry deaths, where a young married woman dies mysteriously in the home of her in-laws because the dowry was not large enough or had not been paid in full, indicate the inferior status of women compared to men, as does the need of the Indian Parliament to restrict the use of amniocentesis and ultrasound for determining the sex of a foetus in 1994. So great has the rate of abortions of girl babies become in recent years that legislative action has become necessary.

This mention of parliamentary legislation to outlaw discrimination against dalits and women serves a purpose, reminding us of an overarching issue of principle. There are Hindus who strongly believe that the Indian government has no right to interfere in such matters; they are religious matters and, they claim, governments have no right to pronounce upon them.

Medical ethics

Medical eithcs do not necessarily have the same priorities in India as they do in the West. For most Hindus, the question of when to turn off a life-support machine is unreal; so is receiving an organ transplant, but numbers of poorer people have been persuaded – and paid – to part with a kidney to meet Western demands. Birth control is widely accepted in theory and often adopted in practice. India has reduced its level of births considerably, but it must be remembered that in a country where only a minority of professional people enjoy pensions, the parents' guarantee of a bearable old age lies in having as many sons as possible to care for them. Indian stamps and roadside posters depicting a mother and a father with a son and daughter carry the slogan 'A Happy Family is a Two-Child Family'. It takes courage to accept this teaching in practice, especially when one of the children will end up in another family supporting its old people!

Abortion is legal and accepted by Hindus as a method of ending unwanted pregnancies, and therefore of birth control. The danger of using it to reduce the chances of having a daughter has been mentioned already. Suicide has never been considered wrong in Hindu society. It was often seen to be an act of religious merit, the final austerity. But it is not approved of as a way of escaping from suffering. Mercy-killing is not acceptable, but the use of opium to remove pain is likely to cause death eventually.

Drugs

Most Hindus regard the use of drugs such as speed or crack as wrong, but there has always been a tradition of some Hindu groups using hallucinogenic drugs to enhance spiritual awareness. Cannabis has often been used for this purpose. Hashish is made into a cigarette or sometimes chewed, as is ganja. Bhang is a drink made from its leaves.

Alcohol

Alcohol is regarded as acceptable. The *Rig Veda* refers to *soma*, a special intoxicating drink. The plant from which it was made is no longer known. Alcohol and its manufacture is regarded as polluting, but the ban on alcohol in some Indian states is motivated by social concern and has no religious basis.

Food and fasting

Vegetarianism is not the whole story. Not all Hindus are vegetarian. Some eat mutton, but it is very rare to find one who will eat the meat of a cow. Members of the Prajapati caste, Gujarati artisans, eat meat, but will ask for vegetarian food on aeroplanes to avoid the possibility of being given beef. They might adopt the same strategy when visiting non-Hindu friends or at school. There are also vegetarians who will avoid such things as onions and garlic. Sometimes red foods are not eaten – beetroot, carrots, red water melon and red wine – because red is the colour of blood. Such groups as ISKCON, or the devotees of Satya Sai Baba, are vegetarian. This may be because meat is thought to arouse the passions of sex and anger, and perhaps because the breath which utters the sacred mantras from the *Veda* should not be contaminated.

Occasionally Hindus will fast completely, for example at the birth festivals of Rama and Krishna. Usually only certain foods are avoided at the times of a fast (*vrat*, or *barat* in Punjabi). These include preparations using rice, wheat, millet and pulses, but every rule has its exceptions. When special prayers were being offered to Shirdi Sai Baba, a woman might eat a mixture of lentils, rice and spinach, and nothing else. Permitted foods include milk, peanuts, fresh fruit, dates, almonds, sago, yoghurt, sweet potatoes, coconuts and clarified butter (ghee). The high protein level of many vegetarian or fasting foods means that health is not threatened in any way by diet. Concern is often more in the minds of older people in the West who are brought up to believe that meat is an essential part of diet, than a reality. Some Hindus, when they came to countries like Britain, accepted the idea, but many of them reverted to their Indian food traditions with no ill effects! Vrats are associated with certain groups; on Thursdays with Sai Baba, on Fridays with followers of Santoshi, for example. A special Punjabi fast is Karva Chaut, which is celebrated about 11 days before Divali. Married Sikh as well as Hindu wives, and sometimes their daughters, observe it for the welfare of their husbands, and will fast completely from dawn until the moon is sighted in the evening. It may be an exaggeration to say that Hindu women are always fasting, but they do so frequently.

Purity-conscious Hindus will carry food in tiffin boxes when they make a journey or go to the office, rather than risk eating food in a canteen or buffet. Of course, many Indians do this simply as a health precaution, or because they prefer their own food.

Wealth and work

Asceticism has been mentioned many times. Despite its importance there is as much a place for wealth, *artha*, as there is for leisure, *kama*. These are proper pursuits in life (see pages 92, 168). They should be kept in check, however, and not allowed to dominate life. The very existence of the fourth stage of life is a reminder that wealth, especially, has limited worth. It should also be properly acquired, by honest and appropriate work. Traditionally, a Brahmin could not be a surgeon, doctor, or soldier, as these occupations involve contact with blood: but today they are to be found in most forms of employment, though the low status of being a butcher (as well as handling carcasses) would deter them from selling meat.

As the Indian army is made up of volunteers, it is difficult to know how important an issue pacifism is for most Hindus, and whether purity and the avoidance of pollution, or the awareness of God's presence in everyone, as with Gandhi, might be the motive. (Most Ayurvedic doctors are Brahmins.) It is likely that Hindus who are very concerned about ritual purity bathe and put on clean clothes as soon as they return home if they work in conditions that might cause pollution, as most do in cities.

Prejudice

Prejudice is often seen to be one of the most difficult evils to eradicate in modern India. The varna system (see Chapter 06) seemed to justify and perpetuate it, especially as it developed over the centuries. *Varna* means colour and still one comes across marriage advertisements that state that a woman has a light complexion, or that a man seeks a bride who has a pale skin. In cities, advancement may be possible if a migrant can conceal the family name, which often denotes a person's caste. After all, India has had a prime minister and several cabinet ministers who came from one of the scheduled or *dalit* castes, but many more cases are documented of suicide because, despite a good honours degree or similar qualification, a person finds it impossible to break out of restrictions imposed by tradition. Dalits may come into their own at election time, because they are numerous enough to affect the vote in most constituencies, but they are not usually well enough organized to be fully effective. Once the MP has been elected, however, election promises may easily be forgotten. Those who face prejudice and discrimination because of caste or gender can only hope for redress when leaders arise who can harness their latent power. Since Mahatma Gandhi, no one has been able to unite the 'teeming masses' of India, to use his phrase.

Care for the needy

This must be mentioned for three reasons. Firstly, Westerners often think that only Mother Teresa cares for India's poor. In fact, there are many Hindus who care for the exploited and disadvantaged. Secondly, stories persist of Hindus who will not help the crippled and poor because their lot is the consequence of karma, and to go against it is to attempt to thwart God's will, and must result in dire consequences. We have to admit that there have always been people who create a peculiar theology which absolves them from helping others. They are usually the better off! In fact, care for the needy is a meritorious act which can bring karmic benefits to the one who performs it.

Against the notion of interfering with karma there is the strong teaching of social responsibility which is found in Hinduism. One must care for one's extended family and for one's *biradari*, or caste group. Those Hindus who employ servants often act towards them with paternal concern. In the West, servants are now memories of a bygone age, whereas in India, schoolteachers may employ servants, at least part-time, even though they will never be rich enough to own a car! Wages are low; technology is expensive; a motor scooter is the finest mode of transport that teachers and doctors may hope to own, although more are now joining the car-owning classes. To provide work for the poor by employing them, as washermen and women, as ironers of clothes, to clean the house, to garden, is an act of social responsibility in a country where there is no unemployment pay or welfare benefit. Not to give them work would be an act of meanness, and Hindus should be people of a generous spirit. Often, having a servant means caring for a family, and including them in the family to some degree. The parents work directly; and their children are helped to receive an education. When someone falls sick, any doctor's bills are paid by the employer. Traditionally, Hindus have believed that there are five great wrongs which they should not commit:

- killing a learned Brahmin, for this is an attempt to sustain ignorance against wisdom and knowledge
- drinking alcohol, especially spirits, for this clouds the mind
- stealing gold
- having disrespect for one's Guru and his wife
- permitting wilful abortion.

In the past these acts denoted a lack of moral and physical goodness, and threatened the fabric of society. Now that life is more complex, and perhaps less religious, these traditions are no longer observed. Some Hindus note a decline in society as a whole and blame neglect of traditional values for it.

15

Hinduism since 1757

In this chapter you will learn:

- about the influence of Islam and European Christianity on Hinduism
- about the work of Ram Mohan Roy, Swami Narayan's work, Ramakrishna, Annie Besant, Rabindranath Tagore, Ambedkar and Satya Sai Baba
- about the Arya Samaj
- about Hindu society reformed from within.

Influence of Islam and European Christianity

On 20 May 1498, Vasco da Gama sailed into the harbour of Calicut, thus opening up a route for European trade with the East not dependent upon Muslim countries. Europeans established trading posts in India, but it was not until 1757, when the British under Sir Robert Clive defeated the French and their allies, that the prospect of European colonization became a reality. Britain replaced the Mughal Empire, and ruled India until 1947.

During this time Hinduism developed considerably, partly, no doubt, because of this European presence. Islam had affected Hinduism in earlier centuries, as we have seen (p. 150), but by 1757 it was a spent force, even though the Mughal Empire was to survive for another century. The last Mughal was asked to intervene in an argument between two men that was taking place below him, just outside the walls of the Red Fort. He is reputed to have replied, 'My power does not stretch that far'. When Clive won the Battle of Plassey in 1757, things were not really so different.

The 1757 picture given by scholars is one of a stagnant Hinduism. It had survived the Islamization policies of Emperor Auranzeb (effectively emperor from 1658 to 1707) and his immediate predecessors, but had not been challenged intellectually. The European Enlightenment occurred at about the same time as European colonization of India. The Enlightenment Europeans, mainly French but British too, brought scepticism and sometimes critical hostility to India. They openly attacked the heathenism that they encountered in the caste system and the treatment of women, especially *sati*, infanticide and the seclusion of widows. The truth of the view, which many held, that religion imprisoned the human spirit, seemed borne out there even more than in Europe. They were not the first to criticize the disregard of human rights, of course. The Buddha and the Sikh Gurus were amongst Indians who had earlier voiced their disapproval. What the Europeans brought was power to effect change, (especially as India became colonized), and European education, which many liberal Hindus found attractive. In this respect their attitude contrasted appreciably with that of Muslims who, for the most part, retained their allegiance to Persia, and so ruled themselves out of employment by the East India Company and any significant part in the development of British India during the 19th century.

Ram Mohan Roy was the first Hindu of note to respond to European influence, but it should be stated that his early education and employment had already brought him into contact with the monotheism and anti-caste beliefs of Islam. He was a Bengali Brahmin living in the part of India that was the centre of East India Company activity and of British rule, until the time of King Emperor George V.

Ram Mohan Roy (1772 or 1774–1833)

Ram Mohan Roy was born into a brahmin family which had a long history of service in the Muslim government of Bengal, and later in the East India Company. His religious background was one of devotion to the Hindu bhakti teacher Chaitanya (see page 150). At school in Patna he learned Persian and became aware of the teachings of the Sufi mystics of Islam. He may also have encountered Muslim rationalist teachings. He served the British in the Bengal Civil Service. He was clearly a precocious young man, for at the age of 16 he wrote his first tract, a Persian critique of what he described as the idolatrous system of the Hindus. It caused a temporary rift with his family, and raises the question as to whether Roy is actually to be regarded as a Hindu. The answer is that he was definitely not an orthodox Brahmin in the strictest sense of the word. If he had been, he would have had no social or employment contact with non-Hindus, whose very presence would pollute him. His writings on Christianity show that he did not accept the Trinity or the vicarious suffering of Jesus for the sins of humanity. If labels are needed, he was between a free-thinking Hindu and a Unitarian. In fact, he established a Vedanta College in Calcutta in 1816 for the 'propagation and defence of Hindu unitarianism'. In 1823 the Unitarian Society of London published *The Precepts of Jesus: A Guide to Peace and Happiness*, which had appeared in India in 1820. During the controversy that it caused with Christian missionaries at Serampore, he persuaded one of them, the Reverend William Adam, a Baptist, to become a Unitarian! Social reform was also a great importance to Roy. He had seen his sister-in-law commit sati on her husband's funeral pyre, and this intensified his already strong opposition to the custom. It was his influence that led to the British government, always reluctant to interfere in Indian religious affairs, declaring sati illegal. He also supported the education of women and was against the practice of child marriages.

To describe Ram Mohan Roy as the founder of modern Hinduism, which is a popular assertion, must depend upon a number of factors, including each individual's standpoint. He certainly seems to have awakened many Hindus from a period of intellectual stagnation. His own critique of the religion may predate his knowledge of Christianity, but in anticipating its attacks on what it considered to be idol worship, and what he called its fanciful mythology, as well as Hindu ethics, especially regarding the treatment of women, he demonstrated the persistent ability of Hinduism to criticize and reform itself from within. It may be that his response deflected intellectual Hindus from the path of conversion to Christianity. He may have done little to alleviate the position of people of low caste, but he did attack the exploitation of them by Brahmins, and the way in which they were often denied access to their spiritual heritage because of the attitudes of the Brahmin priests. It might be claimed that the movement which Roy founded, the Brahma Samaj, produced men who were eventually to take up the cause of the oppressed classes.

The eclectic nature of modern Hinduism owes much to Roy. It can be argued that his openness to other views is characteristic of the religion, and with this comes the ability to find responses within the rich diversity of Hinduism itself. Certainly, in his readiness to study the Sufis and Christianity, he pioneered the approach which many other Hindus were to follow, especially Ramakrishna, also a Bengali Brahmin. Roy died in Britain, worn out by tours of England and France, during which he had impressed society tremendously. In this he might be said to have anticipated the influence of Vivekananda, Ramakrishna's disciple, 70 years later.

The purpose of Ram Mohan Roy's visit to Europe was partly to give evidence about the state of India to a British government committee. There can be no doubt that he was a patriot, not an Indian who unquestioningly accepted Western ways and ideas. In his opposition to the British government's establishment of a Sanskrit college, and his support instead for one which was science-based, he was showing the way ahead for India as he understood it. The 'quit India' movement lay many years into the future. It would be unfair to side with later Hindu nationalists who criticized his co-operation with Britain, though it might be correct to say that in that sense of nationalism he was certainly not a founder of the freedom movement. At a time when much of India was still outside British control, and the

Mughal Empire had not yet been overthrown, the prospect of independence scarcely existed. It was a concept which India might be said to have forgotten. Hinduism is a religion with no original founder and is splendidly diverse. To describe Ram Mohan Roy as founder of any kind in this context may be to ignore these considerations. However, he was the person who seems to have awakened Hinduism from its slumbers, and replaced stagnation with a vibrancy that continued throughout the 19th century to the present day.

The Brahma Samaj

In 1828 Ram Mohan Roy founded the Brahma Sabha, which became the Brahma Samaj (also spelt Brahmo Samaj) in 1830. It met every Sunday evening and encouraged worship of the Eternal, Immutable Being, using approved passages from the *Vedas* and *Upanishads,* and sermons and hymns composed by Roy himself. The services began with Sanskrit verses read by Brahmins in a separate room from the rest of the congregation. Its membership always tended to be high caste and intellectual. It attempted to purify Hinduism from what it considered to be the same kinds of excesses as those which the Arya Samaj later decried. However, its approach was rationalist and, after Roy's death, increasingly eclectic, using Muslim and Christian material in its liturgies. These features did not help it when Indian politics and Hinduism assumed a nationalistic tendency in the late 19th century. The Brahmo Samaj still exists, but the influence it exerts upon Hindu thought and life is minimal.

The Arya Samaj

A very different society is the Arya Samaj. It is dedicated to the restoration of pure vedic religion, and to the insight of one man, Dayananda Saraswati, more than any others.

Dayananda Saraswati was born in Gujarat in 1824 into a Shaivaite Brahmin family. At the age of 14, during a night-time vigil, he saw a mouse enter the building, sniff round the murti, and eat the food that had been offered to it. When other devotees awoke he told them of his experience. They informed him, quite correctly, that the murti was not the visible presence of God but only a symbol of deity. However, the experience had its effect; he could no longer accept the idea of image worship.

He began to question other aspects of this tradition, and set off to live the life of a sadhu. He learned yoga and found a Guru, Virjananda Saraswati, who asked him to vow to reform Hinduism of its impurities: image worship, belief in *avatars* (the doctrine of divine incarnation), and the ideas contained in the *Puranas*, the myths which provide a basis for popular Hinduism. His views alarmed orthodox Brahmins, who debated them with him at Varanasi (also called Banares and Kashi). Though defeated he remained undeterred, and in 1875 founded the Arya Samaj, which he led until his death in 1883.

Dayananda summed up his teaching, which became Arya Samaj doctrine, as follows:

> I hold that alone to be acceptable which is worthy of being believed by all men in all ages. I do not entertain the least idea of founding a new religion or sect. My sole aim is to believe in truth and help others to believe in it, to reject falsehood and to help others in doing the same.

The key to understanding his thought and impact lies in his belief that the *Vedas* are not only the oldest scripture, but that they contain the eternal truths which all humanity should accept. These are that there is one God, who is the primary source of all true knowledge; that God is All-Truth, All-Knowledge, All-Beatitude, Incorporeal, Almighty, Just, Merciful, Unbeggoten, Infinite, Unchangeable, Without Beginning, Incomparable, the Support and Cause of all, All-Pervading, Omniscient, Imperishable, Immortal, Exempt from Fear, Eternal, Holy, the Cause of the Universe, the One to whom alone worship is due. The *Vedas* are the books of true knowledge, which every Arya should read, or hear being read, to teach them and preach them to others.

This is a paraphrase of the first three principles of the Arya Samaj. The other seven tend to reinforce them, with one additional thread running through most of them, namely an insistence upon the treatment of all other human beings with love and justice in accordance with their merits. The most important consequences of this teaching were the rejection of caste and eventually of discrimination against women, accompanied by programmes of social reform, the establishment of schools and colleges so that the poor and socially disadvantaged could obtain an education, and, above all, the assertion that the criterion of truth was the *Vedas* as they interpreted them. This brought them into conflict with the Sikhs in Punjab where, for a time, a Sikh-Arya alliance against the Christian missionaries seemed a possibility. More importantly, it led to a strong Arya reaction against the missionaries, and a counter-claim to their assertion that Jesus and the Bible were the expression of divine truth. Arya missionaries went around the villages persuading people to take part in a *shuddhi*, or purificatory thread ceremony. They were particularly successful in winning people of low caste and in developing a pride in the Hindu heritage. From just under 4000 in 1881, their numbers grew to over a million in 1931. The movement was strongly critical of the Bramha Samaj. The *Arya Magazine* of May 1882 summed up its opposition as follows:

> They declaimed the observance of Durga Puja festival as unfit to be reformed, and began to exchange presents at Christmas, to which they saw no objection. They thus saw all evil in everything national, and all good in everything European.

Quite simply, the Aryas thought the Brahmas despised the Hindu heritage, which they claimed to be the foundation of all learning and culture worldwide, derived from the world's oldest civilization. It is likely that the 'Quit India' movement would have developed sooner or later without the Arya Samaj. However, the argument can be made that the Brahma Samaj might have encouraged India to remain a British territory; the Arya Samaj could never be happy with the relationship. The Arya Samaj continues its educational work especially through Dayanand Anglo-vedic (DAV) schools and colleges and its members often display a pride in Hinduism that is tinged with criticism and suspicion of the West and the Christian religion as well as a strong social conscience, which results in them working among the poor.

Swami Narayan (Sahajanand) (1781–1830)

Swami Narayan was another person who established a movement that came to have considerable influence in India and beyond, although the person most famously associated with it was a man born Ghanashyam Hariprasad Pande. He was initiated into the Narayan order, which traced its teachings to the philosopher Ramanuja. Upon initiation he was given the name Sahajanand. Sahajanand was born in Uttar Pradesh in 1781. When his parents died 11 years later, he renounced the world and became a wandering student, eventually settling in Dwarka in Gujarat. Through him the Swami Narayan movement became well known, and in recent times it has enjoyed a strong following, first among East African Gujaratis, and more recently in Britain and other countries to which they migrated, especially when Uganda expelled its Asian population in 1972. Gujaratis form the largest Hindu ethnic group in the UK.

Sahajanand encouraged the building of hospitals and care for the poor. He joined in the opposition to sati, which resulted in it being outlawed, and condemned infanticide. He also supported the right of young widows to remarry should they wish to do so. Nevertheless, the satsang has strict rules for the separation of the sexes. There are separate women's meetings, but in mixed gatherings women must observe from the back, and should turn their back on leaders of the community (*acharyas*) whenever they encounter them. The reason for this stringency is an acceptance of ritual pollution.

Swami Narayan told the Anglican Bishop Heber, when they met, that there would be no caste in the hereafter, but accepted its existence, and built into his teachings such things as the prohibition of taking food or water from people of lower caste. These people are divided into two groups: Sat Shudras, who are traditionally part of Hinduism, and Shudras, those who used to be called untouchables but now refer to themselves as dalits. Sat Shudras may enter the movement and become ascetics; in fact the third successor to Sahajanand was of the tailor jati – Pragji Bhakta, who died in 1897.

The satsang accepts the truth of all religions, encourages vegetarianism and is pacifist. It requires high moral standards from members, and their discipline has often led to them becoming trusted and successful businessmen like the Jains. Wealth, however, should lead to generosity; it has no intrinsic value and is regarded as a great threat to spiritual development. Sahajanand taught that blessing came from the distribution of wealth. The movement remains very largely Gujarati in membership and culture. What will happen as the children of Western members cease to have access to the language remains to be seen.

Sri Ramakrishna (1834–1886)

Sri Ramakrishna was a poor Bengali Brahmin. He believed that God is present in every religion, and may be found through any of them. He taught that, 'A truly religious man should think that other religions are also paths leading to the truth'. This has become one of the principles of modern Hinduism. He also maintained, 'Every man should follow his own religion. A Christian should follow Christianity, a Muslim should follow Islam, and so on. For Hindus the ancient path, the path of the Aryan Rishis, is the best'. The most famous and influential of this followers was Narendra Nath Datta, better known as Swami Vivekananda (1863–1902). It was he whose attendance at the Chicago Parliament of Religions in 1893 first introduced many Westerners to the spiritual riches of the East – so much so that some of them questioned the propriety of sending missionaries to India!

Sri Ramakrishna was not at all political in his motivation, nor was he antagonistic to Christianity, though he was active at the same time as Dayananda Sarasvati. He himself founded no society, but his disciples established the Ramakrishna Mission, which has developed his syncretism (a blend of ideas from several religions), and is therefore influenced to some extent by Christianity. However, it is eclectic in its approach, and has chosen only to accept the liberal aspects of Christian teaching. As with Ram Mohan Roy decades earlier, its interpretation is one which has upset many Christians for its neglect of the salvationist work of Jesus' death and resurrection. A typically Hindu viewpoint, they valued the light which Jesus brought to humankind, but found the idea of victory over evil through participating in his death unattractive, if not offensive.

Annie Besant (1847–1933)

Annie Besant was neither Indian nor Hindu, but went to India after meeting Madame Blavatsky the Theosophist in 1889. She founded the Madras Hindu association in 1904 'to promote Hindu social and religious advancement on national lines, in harmony with the spirit of Hindu civilization'. She was President of the Indian National congress from 1917–1923. Her place in these pages serves as an additional indication of the cross-fertilization between Europe and India which was taking hold towards the end of the nineteenth century.

Rabindranath Tagore (1861–1941)

'I am a singer of songs and am ever attracted by the strains that come from the House of Songs,' is one of his famous sayings. He too was a Bengali Brahmin. Awarded the Nobel Prize for literature in 1913, his emphasis on the Divine Love and his denunciation of nationalism as 'organized selfishness' made him attractive to the liberal intelligentsia of the West at the time of the founding of the League of Nations. With Nehru and Gandhi (whom he may have been the first to address as 'Mahatma'), he personified India in the West. Perhaps he was more popular than Gandhi, since he did not see colonialism as responsible for India's ills, or independence as the solution to them. He looked instead to education, setting up Shanti Niketan (Abode of Peace), at Bolpur near Calcutta. The college has no temple, to emphasize the role of all religions in the quest for peace.

> Be not ashamed my brothers, to stand before the proud and the powerful
> With your white robe of simpleness.
> Let your crown be of humility, your freedom the freedom of your soul.
> Build God's throne daily upon the ample barrenness of your poverty.
> And know that what is huge is not great and pride is not everlasting.

Tagore, Ramakrishna, and Vivekanada, are men who emerged from their undoubtedly Hindu backgrounds to testify to something that transcended all religions and provided India with its secular ideal of respect for all religions, without according any one of them a position of privilege.

Bhimrao Ranji Ambedkar (1891–1956)

A story of Ambedkar's childhood tells how he and his brother were going to visit their father, who was a soldier. They were given a lift on a cart, but in the course of conversation the driver came to know that they belonged to the Mahar jati, by occupation collectors of the carcasses of animals, a highly polluting activity. He raised one end of the vehicle and threw them into the road. The boys were thirsty but no one would give them water or allow them near water tanks or wells.

This was apparently Ambedkar's introduction to caste, and discrimination on grounds of untouchability. Although he had to overcome many difficulties, the boy went to high school, where a Brahmin teacher named Ambedkar gave him encouragement. Ambedkar decided to change his name from the family name of Ambavadekar to that of his teacher, though his hopes that his would shield him against discrimination were mistaken. He went to Elphinstone High School in Bombay, took his degree, was employed by the Maharaja of Baroda and was sent to the USA, where he gained a doctorate.

When he returned to India in 1917 he discovered that even the Maharaja's patronage meant nothing in the office. No one would work with him or give him water, and he could find nowhere to live. Further education in England was still followed by discrimination back home. He led campaigns to win untouchables the right to water supplies, and took part in the Round Table Conferences with the British, which discussed a constitution for India. He won a large reservation of seats for untouchables in the proposed parliament. When India became independent, Ambedkar, as Law Minister, was largely responsible for enacting India's constitution. However, he was never convinced that caste discrimination could actually be overcome and finally decided to convert to Buddhism. This he chose in preference to Christianity and Islam, because he saw it as an Indian religion having cultural affinities with Hinduism, even though it had long been extinct in the subcontinent. Sikhism was presumably not considered because it was, erroneously, thought to be a form of Hinduism and was known to accept untouchability. His followers, 600,000 members of what by then were known as the secluded classes, converted with him shortly before he died.

Satya Sai Baba (1926–)

Well known, perhaps more outside India than within it, is Sai Baba. His picture may be seen in many *mandirs*, and in a large number of homes. He is instantly recognizable by his Afro-style haircut and broad smile. His birthplace was in Andra Pradesh; his name was Satyanarayan Raju. In 1940 he declared himself to be the reincarnation of Sai Baba of Shirdi, who died in 1918. Sometimes pictures of this elderly, long-haired, rather stereotypical ascetic may also be found in homes. In 1963, Sai

Baba affirmed that he was the incarnation of Shiva-Shakti, the divine creative power in both male and female form. God is beyond form (*nirguna*) according to the Baba's teaching. Appearances are merely illusion (*maya*) and unreal. The widely attested miracles popularly associated with the Guru are signs of paranormal powers (*siddhis*). Love and God are one, so worship consists of singing devotional songs (*bhajans*) and serving the community at large (*seva*). Bal Vikas classes are organized for children (*Bal*) to help them blossom (*vikas*) into moral and spiritual beings through living according to the values of peace, non-violence, truth, right conduct and love. The satsang's programme of Education in Human Values has been implemented in schools in India with Government support. In 1984 and 1985, with the Inner London Education Authority, (now defunct), the Sai Council in Great Britain organized courses for teachers on moral education in a multi-ethnic society. The movement attracts members from all ethnic and religious groups.

Hinduism, as we see, continues to evolve. Conservative orthodoxy lives on, as the recent growth of the Bharatiya Janata Party demonstrates. Its appeal to Hindus, associated with a spirit of nationalism, questions many assumptions about the eclectic, tolerant nature of the religion. New expressions of Hinduism arise, for example the cult of Santoshi Mata, a little known deity (the daughter of Ganesha) until a film transformed her into a popular goddess overnight.

The presence of Hindus worldwide, and respect for the sanatana dharma which Mahatma Gandhi and other modern Hindus created, have meant that the West's interest in Eastern spirituality continues. What impact meditation and attachment to a Guru will have upon Christianity, as it struggles against materialism, remains to be seen – as does the manner in which Hindus themselves cope with the materialism which is challenging the traditional values of Indian society.

Some of these matters are taken up in Chapter 17.

16 Mohandas Karamchand Gandhi

In this chapter you will learn:
- how Gandhi's politics were influenced by Hindu ethics
- about the influence of the *Upanishads* and the *Bhagavad Gita* on Gandhi
- about Gandhi's life of work in the service of others
- what the result of Gandhi's beliefs were
- about Gandhi and Hinduism today and the right wing Hindu influence in Indian politics.

To devote a whole chapter of this book to one Hindu might seem rather excessive. The reason will hopefully become clear as the story of Gandhi and his religious thought unfolds. It lies in his ability to criticize Hinduism from within, a common feature of the religion through the ages. He was a major figure of the 20th century, to the extent that the centenary of his birth was commemorated in 1969 by almost every country in the world when special stamps were issued. In India he is probably best remembered now for his contribution to the Independence Struggle (in this Richard Attenborough got it right. In the 1980s Attenborough directed a film, *Gandhi*, which brought this great Indian to the attention of many people who had never heard of him. His spirituality emerged implicitly but the film emphasized his political role). Almost every Indian town has a street named after him, and most towns of any size boast a statue. His samadhi in Delhi, a square plinth of black marble, is a place where all visiting dignitaries must pay their respects. In London's Tavistock Square, there is a beautiful and emotive statue where marigolds can still be seen, placed in his honour.

If it was Ram Mohan Roy and the Brahma Samaj who introduced Western philosophers and rationalists to Indian thought, it was Gandhi who captured the popular imagination. Of course, not everyone took to this 'half-naked faqir', as the war-time British Prime Minister Winston Churchill described him, but when he visited England in 1931 he gained the affection and respect of people ranging from Quakers to mill-workers. The press found him to be 'good copy'. He told one of them, 'You people wear plus-fours, mine are minus-fours'. When, wearing his usual loin cloth, shawl, dollar watch, and sandals, he went to tea at Buckingham Palace, he said afterwards that, 'The king had enough on for both of us'.

Mohandas Karamchand Gandhi, popularly known as 'Bapu', was born at Porbandar in Gujarat on 2 October, 1869. His family was of the Bania jati, belonging to the Vaishya varna. When he came to England at the age of 18 to train as a lawyer, he was already married and the father of a son. The early years of this marriage were not happy and convinced him of the folly of the custom of child marriages. He was called to the bar in 1891. In 1893 he went to South Africa, to take up a court case on behalf of a Muslim merchant. It was there that he first experienced discrimination, at Maritzburg. Although he possessed a first-class ticket he was forcibly ejected from the railway carriage because a white man objected to sharing it with a 'coolie'. This event led to his embarking upon a lifelong struggle against discrimination and oppression, which is how he came to view British colonialism, though at first he collaborated with the British and saw merit in their government.

He was assassinated in Delhi on 30 January 1948.

Gandhi's politics influenced by Hindu ethics

Underlying Gandhi's life of action was a deep spirituality. He might be described as the perfect *karmayogin* of the *Bhagavad Gita*; a man devoted to the service of Rama, his family's ishtadevata, rather than Krishna, and who expressed his love in desireless action on behalf, especially, of the weak members of society. It was with the name 'Rama' on his lips that he died. His so-called Talisman read:

> Recall in the face of the poorest and most helpless person whom you may have seen and ask yourself if the step you contemplate is going to be of any use to him, will he gain anything by it? Will it restore him to control over his life and destiny? In other words, will it lead to swaraj, self-rule, for the hungry and also spiritually starved of our countrymen?

> Then you will find your doubts and yourself melting away.

It is not too difficult to see that this teaching emanates from the first verse of the *Isa Upanishad*, his favourite Hindu text:

> All this, whatsoever moves on earth, is pervaded by the Lord. When you have surrendered this, then you may enjoy. Do not covet the wealth of anyone.

Gandhi was not a natural ascetic, and was always opposed to those who followed the path of self-denial to the point of refusing help to those in need. Such asceticism was merely selfish. This was only one way in which by his example he demonstrated that the life of action, and not the path of inaction, was the preferred way of Hinduism; he thus implicitly criticized the tradition which made so much of the fourth stage of life, that of sannyas.

His whole method of teaching was practical. The story is told of a young American who walked with him at six o'clock in the morning, hoping for wise words, only to find that Gandhi said nothing, but bent down constantly to remove night soil from the path. 'Will you teach me?' asked the young man. 'I have been teaching you; perhaps you were not listening', was Gandhi's reply. C. F. Andrews, a Christian missionary from England and his close friend, described him as 'A saint of action rather than contemplation'.

The main literary influences upon Gandhi, who was a widely-read man, were John Ruskin's *Unto this Last*, *The Kingdom of God*, by Leo Tolstoy (with whom he corresponded), the Sermon on the Mount from the Gospel of St Matthew in the New Testament, the *Bhagavad Gita* and *Upanishads*, and especially, from his own tradition, the *Ramayana*. Though he demanded that the British should quit India and objected to the work of Christian missionaries, he was more representatively Hindu in his eclecticism than the Arya Samaj and the many nationalists who rejected the thought of the West as well as its political presence.

It was, however, interaction with people that affected him more than reading. Perhaps the most important of these were a Jain, Raychandbhai, who was the nearest he had to a Guru, and his wife Kasturbai, who he married when they were both 13 years old. His treatment of Kasturbai, especially in his younger years, was often inconsiderate. He forced his ideas of poverty and the acceptance of untouchables almost violently upon this woman from a very traditional, pollution-rejecting society. Her loyalty and common sense won her his respect and made him a more tolerant person. When she died in 1944 he was bereft, and on the 22nd of each month until his death (she died on 22 February), a memorial service was held, at which there were special prayers and a recitation of the *Gita*.

An important teaching that Gandhi used to considerable practical effect was the doctrine of *ahimsa*, non-violence, This, fasting, and asceticism were practices drawn from the Jainism of Raychandbhai, though in each case he modified them and gave them an interpretation of his own. The Jain tends to see the avoidance of pollution as the major reason for not harming other living beings; for Gandhi it became a reverence for life, which respected his opponents to an extent that might annoy them, but sometimes also won them over to his views. Jains also believe in the many-sidedness of reality, *anekantavada*, the belief that we only have a fragmentary knowledge of truth. This led Gandhi to believe that we have no right to impose the fragment that we possess upon others, or believe it to be the complete truth. Jain asceticism might in fact be directed at individual spiritual perfection, but Gandhi justified it socially as the way one should live in a country of poor people, on the grounds firstly that fasting was energy-creating, and secondly that with so much to do, time spent on food and clothing would be better used in serving the great causes of independence and social welfare. Here we see Gandhi, as so often, taking established traditions and reinterpreting or developing them.

Gandhi was deeply religious but not a mystic, though he was very much aware of the inner voice of God. He wrote:

> The time when I learned to recognize this voice was, I may say, the time when I started praying regularly. That is, it was about 1906.

Later he described the experience in some detail. It was:

> Like a voice from afar and yet quite near. It was as unmistakeable as some human voice, definitely speaking to me and irresistible. I was not dreaming at the time I heard the voice. The hearing of the voice was preceded by a terrific struggle within me. Suddenly the voice came upon me. I listened, made certain it was the voice, and the struggle ceased. I was calm . . . not the unanimous verdict of the whole world against me could shake me from the belief that what I heard was the voice of God.

Each day he held a morning and evening prayer meeting, first at his ashram in Sabarmati, then at Wardha. The ashram hymnal, *bhajanavali*, included *Rock of ages*, *Abide with me*, *Who would true valour see*, and his favourite Christian hymn, *Lead, kindly light*. The emphasis of some Christian thought on the 'blood of the lamb', or the 'power of the blood', offended him as a vegetarian and believer in ahimsa (although *When I survey the wondrous cross* was also a favourite hymn). God was gracious, compassionate and protecting. This was his experience; its theological basis lay in the *Ramayana*, in which Rama, his ishtadevata, seeks his wife and dutifully cares for his people. From this comes the concept of *lokasamgraha*: the welfare of all, not merely a concern for the inhabitants of Rama's kingdom but for the whole of humankind, and a belief that everyone must share that concern. Lokasamgraha is also the basis of Ramrajya, the kingdom of righteousness on earth, which again is a universal concept not confined to Hinduism or India.

In mandirs, especially those in which Rama is particularly revered, Hanuman stands in a position to give darshan before anyone else because of the devoted service which he rendered to the king. Gandhi expressed his own devotion to Rama thus:

> Hanuman tore open his heart and showed there was nothing there but Ramanama. I have nothing of the power of Hanuman to tear open my heart, but if any of you feel inclined to do it, I assure you that you will find there nothing but love for Rama, whom I see face to face in the starving millions of India.

God and dharma were inseparably linked, and both were combined with moksha. Religion and politics could not therefore be divided. Dharma and moksha were social, not individual concepts. Or *samajik*, to use Gandhi's expression. In the *Gita Krishna*, God is a friend (*bandhu*) who comes to Arjuna in his time of distress. This should be remembered when we read that for Gandhi, 'Truth is God'. Truth is no impersonal absolute, nor a substitute for God. Truth clarifies what God meant when he used the term. It is also a source of power; hence his use of the word *satyagraha*, truth force. Once he explained it thus:

> Its root meaning is holding onto truth, hence truth-force. I have also called it love-force or soul-force.

An observer of many of his actions, Madeleine Slade, Mirabhen, wrote:

> With Bapu (an affectionate name that meant far more to Gandhi than the term Mahatma, which he disliked), it is his 'life and acts (from the most important to the smallest) that speak more than words (that are more eloquent than words)'.

One example of many must suffice. On one occasion he was walking from village to village in East Bengal to console the victims of communal rioting when he came across a child who needed an enema. Eventually he managed to obtain one, and walked back to the village to administer it to the sick child.

To be assured that he was acting out of true motives was essential. In his early days at the bar he learned a lesson that he never forgot. His elder brother Laxmidas had antagonized the British political agent in Porbandar, a man who could secure him the prime ministership of the small native state; Mohan (Gandhi) had met the man in London. Naturally his brother expected assistance. Gandhi responded in the only way that an Indian family could understand, even though he was uncomfortable at the thought of interceding. The agent told him that if Laxmidas has a complaint he should seek redress through the proper channels. When Gandhi obstinately persisted in his protest the agent ordered his peon to eject him. Gandhi had failed. When he came to analyze his failure, he decided that the reason was that he had not been acting from a position of truth. He knew in his heart that he had been trying to defend untruth, so there had never been any possibility of success. In case there is a temptation still to see heartless principle at work in the name of truth, two other phrases might be quoted; 'out of truth emerge love and tenderness'; and, the seeker after truth should have a heart 'tender as a lotus'. This truth led Gandhi to refuse to drink cows' milk when he saw how cows were treated, and above all made him reject the idea of untouchability, the most inhuman aspect of Hindu society.

It is difficult, if not impossible, to fit Gandhi into any of the philosophical schools of Hindu philosophy but some scholars might regard him as an *advaitist*, for his belief in an ultimate unity between God and the universe. He wrote:

> I subscribe to the belief or the philosophy that all life is in essence one and that humans are working consciously or unconsciously towards the realisation of that identity. The belief requires a living faith in a living God who is the ultimate arbiter of our fate.

Here the Western reader, brought up on tales of Eastern fatalism (be it in the form of karma or kismet), should realize that this is a belief expressed by, 'He's got the whole world in his hands', or the prayer, 'Thy will be done'. Gandhi's God was effective, not merely an intellectual concept.

Elsewhere he wrote:

> Man's ultimate aim is the realization of God, and all his activities, social, political and religious have to be guided by the ultimate aim of the vision of God. The immediate service of all human beings becomes a necessary part of the endeavour, simply because the only way to find God is to see him in his creation and be one with it. This can only be done by service for all. I am part and parcel of the whole, and I cannot find him apart from the rest of humanity.

The search for salvation or liberation can be selfish, claimed Gandhi; hence his criticism of the sannyasin who left society, including his family, to pursue his own spiritual journey. Buddhist teachers and Swami Vivekananda had expressed the view that no one would obtain moksha until the last one had achieved liberation. Gandhi shared the view that:

> He is a true Vaishnava (devotee of Vishnu) who feels the suffering of others as his own suffering.

These are opening words of his favourite hymn, composed by Narsinh Mehta. It has sometimes been claimed, that far from desiring moksha, Gandhi's wish was to be reborn an untouchable.

The consequences of Gandhi's beliefs

The Mahatma's aims and methods were based on his beliefs. The concept of ahimsa convinced him that those who used outward force became caught up in the bondage of violence. His captors often found, during his 2089 days in Indian, and 249 in South African prisons, that it was they not he who was the prisoner. Some accused him of deceitful manipulation, of playing on their weaknesses, but often he won over his opponents through the use of *satyagraha*, the convincing truth of his arguments.

Less evident, but just as real, questions on caste and the position of women were influenced by his belief in the presence of God in all human beings. On caste he wrote:

> Caste has nothing to do with religion. It is harmful both to spiritual and national growth.

and also:

> The varnashrama of the shastras is today non-existent in practice. The present caste system is the very antithesis of varnashramadharma. The sooner public opinion abolishes it the better.

On aerograms today his words can often be found: 'Untouchability is a crime against humanity', but it nevertheless persists, and caste is still a potent force in Hindu life, although in theory most Hindus agree with the constitution, which outlaws caste discrimination. Gandhi's witness is an important inspiration to those who are still working to allieviate its effects.

The need for their work continues. Not long ago the British press carried a report of a Hindu dalit girl who had gained a degree but could find no better employment than that of her mother: washing eating utensils and scrubbing floors. These words of the Mahatma's are still frequently unheeded in practice:

> Men should learn to give place to women, and a community or country in which women are not honoured cannot be considered as civilized. Marriage must cease to be a matter of arrangement made by parents for money. The system is ultimately connected with caste. So long as choice is restricted to a few hundred young men or women of a particular caste, the system will persist, no matter what is said against it. The girls or boys or their parents will have to break the bonds of caste if the evil is to be eradicated. All this means education of a character that will revolutionize the mentality of the youth of the nation.

The dowry system (though illegal now) and dowry deaths show how great the gap between law and practice is, and how strong traditions are which are not only still found in Hinduism, but are present among Indian Christians and Muslims, as well as Sikhs.

Religious pluralism was another belief with practical consequences. Gandhi combined personal commitment with an openness to other faiths, as we have seen. In practice this meant that his friends and influences ranged across the spiritual traditions but also, when communal violence arose in the run-up to partition and independence, he was to be found visiting troubled areas and threatening to fast to the death until harmony between Hindu and Muslim was restored. His entreaty, 'Let each keep his own religion and become better within it', did not mean building barriers but bridging divisions.

Gandhi and Hinduism today

It is in the area of religion that the teaching of the Mahatma might best be remembered and revived. At present there is a resurgence of Hindu nationalism, accompanied by a suspicion of Islam and Christianity as alien to India and threatening to Hindu values. Even moderate Hindus may be heard to say that they have been too tolerant to the minority religions. There has been a recent rise in militant Hinduism, seen in the growth of the Bharatiya Janata Party (BJP), which won considerable support in the 1991 elections. Much of the religious support of this political party comes from the Rashtriya Swayamsevak Sangh (RSS), an organization which was founded in opposition to the pluralistic stance of Nehru and Gandhi who advocated, successfully, the establishment of a secular state (that is, one in which all religions are given equal respect, and none is given a position of advantage). The RSS wanted a Hindu state. One of its supporters was the man who assassinated Gandhi in 1948. The recent Muslim-Hindu tensions, which came to a head during the Ayodhya temple-mosque dispute, demonstrate a threat to the tolerant secularism effected by the Mahatma, and are causing Indians, especially Hindus, to discuss the relevance of his teaching for today. The Jain concept of ahimsa greatly influenced Gandhi, who renounced violence and became a pacifist. Satyagraha (truth-force), a word which he coined in South Africa where he first employed the method of non-violent opposition – relying instead on the moral force of the truth of one's argument – was the form that Gandhi's pacifism took. Its relevance to the crises facing Hinduism and other religions in India today is yet to be explored. Perhaps it can only be an effective instrument in the hands of a person of the Mahatma's moral stature. The importance of Gandhi in the context of inter-religious tension, not only between Hindus and Muslims but also in the Hindu-Sikh situation in the Punjab, and in occasional allegations that Christians and Muslims are not truly Indian, lies in the fact that he provided an alternative to sectarian violence.

Mahatma Gandhi is universally revered in public in India, but is sometimes considered to be a figure of the past. This is largely because of his attitude towards Western technology and products. Each day he spent a period of time at his spinning wheel, less to produce thread than to affirm his belief in traditional Indian ways. He preached the gospel of *swadeshi*, the use of only Indian-produced cloth and other raw materials. The majority of Indians, like most people of countries that were once European colonies and are now recovering economically, look to the West and its technology for solutions to their economic difficulties. There are now supposedly detached observers, mostly Western, who doubt that what India needs is a technological revolution, but Indian politicians are suspicious of this being the latest Western scheme for keeping power in the hands of Europe and America. Gandhi's importance in this respect is doubtful. India is unlikely to return to its pre-industrial past. It might, however, listen to his view that the land of the villages should be given to the peasants, rather than amassed as the possession of a few rich landowners.

Gandhi is a reminder, as Ram Mohan Roy and Dayananda Saraswati were before him, that Hinduism possesses the ability to criticize and reform itself from within. As the religion moves in a more nationalistic and militant direction, there are many other Hindus who wish to maintain the secular principles of the Indian Constitution, and who believe that it is time to turn again to the teachings and practices of the Mahatma.

17
some aspects of Hinduism today

In this chapter you will learn:
- some aspects of Hinduism today
- about the Hindu diaspora.

Hinduism is now a world religion, not only in terms of its widespread distribution but also in its impact upon ideas and its ability to attract people of different cultures.

It is not usually considered to be a missionary religion but can be in some of its forms. Movements are at work among the tribal people in India, attempting to bring them into Hinduism, and the Arya Samaj continues to attempt to win Hindus to its particular ways of thinking. Best known in the West, however, is ISKCON, the International Society for Krishna Consciousness, better recognized by its popular name of the Haré Krishna movement. Once it was merely regarded as a hippie cult of the sixties. Now, despite the misgivings of some ultra-orthodox Hindus in India, it is an accepted form of Hinduism. When, in the 1980s, a temple was opened on the island of Inish Rath in Northern Ireland, the ceremony was attended by Indian-born Hindus from many parts of the UK and the Irish Republic. During the Bhakti Vedanta Manor dispute of the 1990s the majority of Britain's Hindus supported ISKCON. Its attractively produced literature is to be found in many mandirs and homes, and has made a large contribution to the religious nurturing of British-born Hindus. The Haré Krishna movement's origins can be traced to 15th century Bengal, with the appearance of a spiritual teacher and social reformer named Chaitanya. He was a devotee of Krishna (in fact, many Hindus regard him as an avatar of that deity). Following a doctrine taught by the 13th-century philosopher Nimbarka, known as dualistic non-dualism, he believed that God was both the same as, and yet different from, individual souls. Chaitanya travelled widely in northern India and encouraged devotion to Krishna, especially expressed through *kirtan*, the chanting of devotional songs, though only eight of his own verses have survived. He died in 1534, and the movement he initiated continued, though the popularity it enjoyed in his lifetime was not sustained. We may pass over the story of the movement (which is well told by Kim Knott in *My Sweet Lord*, Aquarian Press, 1986) to the year 1933. In that year a man named Abhay Charan De was initiated into the Gaudiya Vaisnava Mission, as it was now called, and given the name Prabhupada. His Guru, Bhaktisiddhanta Sarasvati, had a vision of the message of Chaitanya reaching the English-speaking world beyond Bengal and India and, two weeks before his death in 1936, he entrusted the work to his disciple. Prabhupada responded by publishing a magazine in English, *Back to Godhead*, and preparing a commentary on the *Bhagavad Gita*. In 1959 he left his family to take the vows of a sannyasin and, in 1965, he set sail for the United States. He eventually attracted some young people and students, and in September 1966 initiated his first disciples and conducted the marriage ceremony of two initiates. Soon afterwards he announced, much to their consternation, 'We are going to chant in Washington Square Park'. Such an act was unheard of, and could only provoke ridicule or even hostility, but since then it has become one of the normal sights that greet visitors, work people and shoppers in many countries. In August 1968, three married couples came to England. Before very long they had achieved one of their important aims: meeting the Beatles. The *Haré Krishna Mantra* was issued as a single in August 1969 with devotees appearing on *Top of the Pops*. Seventy thousand copies of the single were sold on the first day. For a large number of Britons this was the first time they had heard of the movement. At the time of writing, ISKCON passes unnoticed by most of the British public. Its kirtan-singing processions now attract little attention. The Rathayatra celebrations of the birth of Krishna, marked by processions in London, and other major cities on either side of the Atlantic, no longer feature on national television; despite attracting thousands of Hindus, the anti-cult press pays little notice. There has been a legal battle relating to an approach road to Bhaktivedanta Manor, the donation of George Harrison, and this has attracted most media attention in the mid-1990s. ISKCON is no longer winning devotees in great numbers (most movements gained dozens or hundreds of adherents, rather than thousands, anyway, despite press allegations and parental anxieties; and the drop-out rate of converts in the first two years is about two out of three). The appeal of novelty has gone, to be replaced by a respected, non-suspected, mission, whose literature and educational services are widely used within the Hindu community and in UK schools, and greatly valued. Many students of religion would argue that one kind of impact, ephemeral and limited, has been replaced by another that is more sustained and effective, and one for which British Hindus are extremely grateful. Others might speak in terms of failure, if the aim was to capture the hearts and minds of Westerners in great numbers. One of the distinctive features of ISKCON is its demand for clear commitment to a lifestyle that requires chastity, the rejection of alcohol and tobacco as well as drugs, and vegetarianism. This kind of severe commitment may no longer be what people are seeking at the end of the century.

No movement or established religion, such as Islam, has yet succeeded in replacing Christianity in the West, despite its decline in appeal and membership. The vacuum may be being filled to some extent by movements offering techniques to aid spiritual development, rather than demanding membership of an organization. In these less formal ways, Hinduism is having an impact upon the non-Hindu world. The most important of these are meditation and yoga. These disciplines have been made popular by teachers such as the Guru Maharishi Mahesh Yogi and Swami Abhishiktananda.

Guru Maharishi Mahesh Yogi's fame was linked with the Beatles, but since the breakup of the group he has continued to have a following. His teaching of Transcendental Meditation (TM) is based upon Vedanta, but he claims quite justifiably that it can be used independently of Hindu philosophy. TM courses are on offer in many British cities. In the 1992 general election and the 1994 European elections the Natural Law Party, based upon his teachings, contested every constituency in Britain. It won several thousand votes but no seats. It did, however, win the right to make a party political broadcast on radio and television, due to the number of candidates it put up, and copies of its manifesto were sent to every voter. The presence of Hindu-influenced meditation centres in the West is often seen as an indication of traditional religion's inability to meet spiritual needs. Once they were dismissed as a passing phase that young people went through, but they have persisted. Yoga classes are to be found advertised in the programmes of most adult education institutions. Sometimes the emphasis is on bodily keep-fit exercises. As noted earlier, yoga for health falls short of the true purpose of the practice if its aims are only physical. Yoga is the arresting of all mental activity. It aims at nothing short of emptying the mind. This void has been found threatening by some Christians, who fear that the mind will be filled by evil, and who have consequently denounced yoga. Abhishiktananda, however, has declared that the void is not actually wanted for its own sake but that once the mind is emptied and the mental processes stopped, the deep power of light, which normally lies hidden and inactive within everyone, rises up and shines forth by itself. The Quakers speak of this: of God in everyone, and the inner light. Christian practitioners of yoga believe that their meditation is enabling them to respond to the presence of God.

Of course, yoga is not the path for everyone. Hindu spiritual masters stress that the most suitable way depends on the temperament and calling of the individual. Here again, Hinduism may have something to offer to Christians. It is clear that diversity is as much a characteristic of their religion as it is of Hinduism, but for many centuries attempts have been made to promote uniformity as the norm. It may be that an understanding of Hinduism may enable Christians to rediscover a diversity of which its scholars too are again becoming aware. However, Hinduism does not exist to serve other religions, and one of the important attractions of yoga is that, unlike prayer, which presupposes the existence of a deity, it need not be attached to any religious belief. Perhaps this is one of the reasons why it is popular in the West. Another may be that it does not require commitment to a set of doctrines, or a lifestyle, as most new religious movements do.

We have briefly mentioned Swami Abhishiktananda. He was born Henri Le Saux in a town in Britanny in 1910, and died in India in 1973. He became a priest and a member of the Order of Saint Benedict, and served in the French army until its defeat in 1940. In 1947 he went to India, and with another Frenchman, a priest from Lyons named Jules Monchanin, set up a Christian ashram in 1950, at a place called Shantivanam. This was the year in which Sri Ramana Maharshi died. Le Saux had not known the famous sage long, but had been deeply impressed by his spirituality. In the vedic chanting of the teacher's followers he became aware of 'a call which pierced through everything' and of these experiences he wrote 'their hold on me was already too strong for it ever to be possible for me to disown them'. In keeping with Indian tradition Le Saux took a new name, Abhishiktananda (Bliss of the Anointed One). Shantivanam is north of Madras. Abhishiktananda came increasingly to feel that his ashram should be in the north, near the Himalayas and Ganges. In 1968 he moved north, leaving his original ashram to Bede Griffiths. There he lived until his death in 1973. Abhishiktananda went to India believing that taking sannyas would enable him to witness effectively as a Christian to Hindus. By the time Ramana Maharshi died, he was unable to state that Christianity was the only authentic way of coming to God, and he moved beyond believing that Christianity was the fulfilment of Hinduism. For him the *Upanishads* were true, and the Bible was true. As he wrote to one of his sisters, his primary concern was 'to pass on the honey which I gather in the Hindu world, and vice versa, however dislocating it may be at times'. As God became more and more 'a cosmic mystery' and 'the cosmic Christ' identical with Ishvara and the Purusha (archetypal human being) of the *Upanishads*, he found it increasingly difficult to express his beliefs and experiences in words. He might be called a Christian advaitist. A film of his life was shown on TV in 1994.

James Stuart wrote *Swami Abhishiktananda: His Life told through his Letters* (Indian SPCK, Delhi, 1989), which readers wishing to learn more about this man may find helpful. Bede Griffiths is the other name that springs to mind when we think of Hindu influence upon Christian belief and practice. He died in 1993 at Shantivanam (The Forest of Peace), the ashram given to him by Abhishiktananda and his companion Jules Monchanin, Swami Panama Arubi Anandam. He too was a Benedictine, and his ashram was authentically Christian, based on the rule of that monastic order. However, he dressed like a sannyasin and incorporated Hindu symbols into his worship, for example using sandal paste placed between the eyes at morning prayer to signify consecration, kumkum at midday as a symbol of illumination, and ash in the evening for purification. This was not, however a form of syncretism. It was the use of the symbolic language of the land in which he was living, just as many Western practices, and the vestments worn by priests, belonged originally to the European world into which the religion spread. He once set out his aim saying, 'We try to live within the Christian contemplative tradition, but following the customs and way of life of India. In other words in a way which is totally Indian and totally Christian'. (Notice he did not use the word Hindu.) Perhaps he should be described as a Hindu-influenced Christian who remained far more rooted in the Christian tradition than Swami Abishiktananda.

There are a host of other ways in which Western interest in Hinduism is noticeable, ranging from cuisine to music. It must be admitted that most people who enjoy Indian food do not consider the concepts that underlie it; most, in fact, cannot distinguish between a Bengali Muslim-run restaurant and one owned by Hindus. Nevertheless, the growth of vegetarianism since the end of the 1970s has often been associated with Hindu ideas about bodily health. Likewise, the significance of concerts devoted to Indian dance and music, the nine-hour performance of the *Mahabharata* on television, and the influence of Indian music upon Western composers may be difficult to estimate, but (at least) it seems to point to an intellectual attitude far different from that of Lord Macaulay who, in his famous minute of 1834, claimed that one shelf of European literature was worth more than all the books produced by the East!

Tolerance and respect are the aims of British governments, and to this end they have recently recognized the developments that have been taking place in Religious Education in schools. It is a compulsory subject from which teachers and pupils may withdraw only if they make formal written application to do so. Few do. A Department of Education Circular of January 1994 requires that all the major religious traditions found in Britain today to be taught to children. Hinduism is one of these religions. One might argue that the United Kingdom is the only country in the world where every child should learn about Hinduism as well as Buddhism, Christianity, Islam, Judaism and Sikhism. The purpose of Religious Education is to understand. Whether study will have some kind of affective outcome, or only a cognitive one, time alone will tell.

A significant group committed to interreligious dialogue is the Brahma Kumaris, as was evident in 1993, the Year of Interreligious Dialogue and Co-operation, being the centenary of the Chicago Parliament of Religions mentioned above. They organized a special pilgrimage to Mount Abu. Global Co-operation House in London is also an important interreligious focus in Britain. Similar centres exist in other countries. Brahma Kumaris accept that they are a movement that has Hindu origins. The movement began in the 1930s in Hyderabad in Sind. From there, after persecution, they moved to Karachi and finally to Mount Abu in Rajasthan, the site of their present headquarters. Their lifestyle is vegetarian, and celibate, and smoking and alcohol are also forbidden.

'Meditation is both the journey and destination, revealing the secrets of consciousness, the treasures of the soul and the power to be more alert and effective in our interaction with each other and with our precious world', to quote one of their pamphlets. They are active in the United Nations through the Global Co-operation for a Better World Movement. Its literature states that it is active in 55 countries, and an independent estimate gives its membership as about 250,000. Hindu influences are to be found in the Indian membership and clothing of many of the movement's members; in the belief that we are living at the end of the Kali Yug, the fourth Hindu era or kalpa, which will be followed by a new Golden Age; and the belief that human beings are souls rather than bodies, who will attain mental union with God: soul consciousness. The movement is probably unique in being woman-led. It works energetically to improve individuals, and create a world based on peace. This global concern could make an impact in another form: concern for the environment. Hindus have always taught the unity of life; humankind and its environment are one. Another international movement is the Ramakrishna Mission. It may not have enjoyed the success that its visionary founder hoped for (see page 178), but through its centres, and such monks as Swami Bhavyananda, who died in England in 1993, it shared in the work of such organizations as the World Congress of Faiths and the Interfaith Network, UK, reminding people of faith, and of the Hindu teaching of many paths leading to one goal.

Sir Sarvepali Radhakrishnan (1888–1975), Spalding Professor of Eastern Religions and Ethics at Oxford and President of India 1962–1967, was another intellectual who brought up an awareness of the profundity of Hinduism to the rest of the world. Between his Oxford career and the presidency he represented India at the United Nations.

Perhaps the summary of direct or indirect Hindu contributions to Western life and thought may have offset the image still presented by the media of the kinds of activities and lifestyles associated with such people as Bhagvan Rajneesh, whose loving meditation and 'orange people' (as his most fervent devotees were called because of their dress), made news headlines in the 1970s. When he died in 1992 his movement had been largely discredited.

The Hindu Diaspora

Since the 1830s at least, Hindus have migrated, and are now to be found worldwide. At first they went to the Caribbean to work on plantations, when the newly freed slaves refused to work for their former owners. They went especially to Trinidad and to the country now known as Guyana. This explains the long line of cricketers of Indian origin who have played for the West Indies, including one captain, Rohan Kanhai. They also migrated to the south Pacific, Mauritius, and East and South Africa. A second wave of migration took place after the Second World War, especially to Britain and North America.

The effect upon the countries where they settled has been slight, compared with the influence of intellectuals and personalities like Vivekananda and Gandhi. This is because the majority of Hindus who settled in these countries were economic migrants, who had often to accept employment in menial occupations. Their children and grandchildren are now moving into the professions, but still their contributions are likely to be economic rather than cultural. They have come to countries with deeply established cultures and, unlike the British in India, they have not come in as powerful rulers able to determine educational and other developments. As a rule, then, we have to talk about the effect of migration upon the Hindu communities. Here we will concentrate on Britain, home to the largest population of Hindus outside India. It is impossible to do more than guess at its size, as British censuses include no religious questions, but a figure of about 360,000 has been suggested by Dr Kim Knott of Leeds University.

The main influx of Hindus to the UK occurred in the 1950s and 60s, in response to appeals for workers that even Irish migrants could not meet, though they were then and still are the largest ethnic minority in Britain. These Hindus came mainly from Gujarat, Punjab and East Africa, though most parts of India are now represented in Britain's population as well as the Caribbean. The total may now be almost 400,000, nearly two-thirds of whom are British-born. It is not easy for new migrants to gain entry to Britain, even though they may be relatives, perhaps ageing parents of Hindus already in the country.

Migrants came from areas with a tradition of migration. Those from East Africa, as well as Sikhs and Muslims, were the descendants of people who had gone there in the 1890s to provide the newly-developing parts of the British Empire with its commercial and skilled artisan class. They built its railways and created businesses in the new cities, and they left when former colonies became independent and began programmes of africanization. Many stayed on in such countries as Kenya, but President Idi Amin expelled almost all of them from Uganda. The Ugandans were unable to bring with them most of their possessions, but other East Africans were, and they provided some of the wealth and many of the leadership skills that strengthened communities already in Britain. It is often argued that the growth in mandirs following their arrival was more than coincidental. The migrants went to regions and occupations where labour was needed; to the Midlands, Yorkshire, Lancashire, London; and to the textile mills, not to the declining coal or shipbuilding industries. Often, Gujaratis would settle in one part of a city and Punjabis in another; though they might share the same Hindu faith they spoke completely different languages. Kim Knott has skilfully mapped the settlement of Hindus in Leeds in *Hinduism in Leeds* (Leeds University, Department of Theology and Religious Studies, 1986).

Extremely strict orthodox Hindus would never cross the *Kala Pani*, as they call the oceans around India. Those who migrated were, therefore, somewhat more liberal in their attitudes to the kinds of work they would do, to purity and pollution, and to social mixing between castes. It is to be noted, however, that management committees of mandirs are often led by Hindus, though whether it is for caste reasons or because they happen to be the best-educatd members of the community it is difficult to assess; and marriages are usually still arranged, with caste as an important consideration.

Features of traditional Hinduism are not always evident in mandirs. Food will be vegetarian, but it has been known for visitors to be invited into the kitchen to see it being prepared. (They should not assume that a family they visit will share this attitude.) Despite what has been mentioned earlier, the president may not be a Brahmin, and women *can* be found in leadership positions. In fact, mandirs are instruments for the development of a new concept of Hinduism, based on a community of believers and unity of belief. We have frequently suggested that in India there are Hindus and Hinduisms; it might be said that a new Hinduism is emerging, as differences give way to an emphasis on certain basic essentials and unity. Worship has often to be regularized and limited in timing because of the availability of people to conduct it. Increasing affluence has enabled mandirs to employ priests on a full-time basis, but many still officiate only on Sundays, or in the evenings, when members are free from their daily occupations.

Passing on the culture is a conscious process as it has never needed to be in India, where the extended family and the village nurture children in the parental and social aspects of their dharma. Grandparents are missing, parents have little time to tell stories to their children, or to do the puja, which children would observe and into which they would gradually be absorbed. Classes in Gujarati, Hindi, or Punjabi are held in mandirs or schools hired at weekends; dance and music classes are also given. We have noted the positive contribution of ISKCON in providing literature in English which Hindu children can use and show teachers at school, certain that they will present a good image to teachers who might be inclined to comment adversely on the quality of some publications produced in India. Attention has also been drawn to the potential for enabling children to learn about Hinduism in Religious Education lessons in school, and so develop self-esteem. But it has to be said, reluctantly, that the education system of Diaspora countries is more often a threat to Hindu, Muslim, Sikh, and Jewish children; for apart from Religious Education, (in those countries which have such a subject in the curriculum, and in those schools which take it seriously in the UK), the rest of the curriculum places little or no value on the language, history, music, literature, or ethics of the cultures that they bring to school. Members of the second generation can be found who have deserted the parental tradition, being taught by implication that it is of no worth outside India, a land to which they will never return. This is not the whole story, though it may be typical of many British-born Hindus. Racism is forcing many of them to return to the tradition, as they have been told effectively that they are not British. Others, for positive reasons, are growing up within their culture, attending the mandir, observing fasts and festivals, and developing their personal spirituality, as well as being members of Britain's fast food society! Robert Jackson and Eleanor Nesbitt have documented this in detail in respect of Coventry in *Hindu Children in Britain* (Trentham Books, 1993).

Meanwhile, in India, there are of course changes taking place in Hinduism. To quantify them is difficult, as it is with social, political or religious developments anywhere in the world. The media may claim that 'everyone is agog', waiting for news of the World Cup, or that the latest political crisis, or incident concerning a royal, or presidential scandal is what everyone is talking about over coffee. We all know it not to be true. Similarly, Hindu life in Varanasi, or one of India's thousands of villages, may be unaffected by some of the issues that we now discuss. When Mahatma Gandhi was assassinated by Nathuram Godse in 1948, India-watchers were reminded that the peculiarly Indian secular ideal of a state, in which all religions should be respected equally and none given privileged status, was not shared by everyone. The dominance of the Congress Party suggested that factionalism was not very important, but in 1970 the Bharatiya Janata Party (BJP) was formed. It was a coalition of several Hindu sectarian and nationalist groups, including the Rashtriya Swayamsevak Sangh, (RSS), who felt that secularism espoused by the Nehru dynasty and Congress governments had gone too far. The dominant Hindu population, numbering about 80 per cent, was suffering neglect at the hands of various minority groups, especially the Muslims. In 1991 they almost won the general election. Disputes surrounding a mosque at Ayodhya, standing on the site of a former mandir where Lord Rama was born, have been the focus of agitation and communal violence during the 1990s, and this has enabled the BJP to maintain its criticism of the central government for inaction and implicit favouring of the Muslim minority.

Until recently, communal disturbances might have been kept local; now a new factor has to be dealt with by Indian governments who exercised careful and strict control on radio and television, namely the ability of satellite television to broadcast pictures worldwide. Mrs Indira Gandhi, Nehru's daughter was a great exploiter of the media. She made black-and-white television sets available at low prices, so that most villages could possess one. The evening news seldom contained fewer than six clips of her activities each day, and none of her opponents – unless it was to their discredit. The newspapers remained free of censorship, often at much cost to owners and journalists, but, of course, comparatively few people could afford a newspaper. Now CNN can beam pictures into homes and villages that have invested in satellite dishes to pick up sport and films. When the Ayodhya temple/mosque dispute made international news, coverage was seen in most of India, and communal rioting was more widespread and better coordinated than in former times.

The impact of international television upon Indian life cannot yet be gauged, but for a long time the Indian film industry has exerted a strong influence, not only in India. In the late 1980s, mandirs and gurdwaras in Britain lost worshippers when Hindi films were scheduled for soon after noon on Sundays. Children complained if activities prevented them from being home for the start of the film. The 94-episode Hindi *Mahabharata* film, with English subtitles, proved so popular that a weekly repeat was provided. Videos have now led to viewing times being less restricted, life in mandirs and gurdwaras has reverted to normal. How these broadcasts are providing an incentive for children to learn their parental tongue would be an interesting subject for research. Children of course may be satisfied with subtitles!

Vijay Sharma's *Jai Santoshi Ma* is a film about a Hindu goddess who, a Brahmin once pointed out very sharply and dismissively, 'is not vedic'! The story is of Santoshi Mata, goddess of contentment, daughter of Ganesha and his wife Riddhi-Siddhi, and therefore the granddaughter of Shiva and his shakti. This places her within the Hindu pantheon, but not in the aloof position of her more established classical counterparts. Her popularity seems to be related to her ability to understand and respond to the kinds of modern problems and needs that women have. Devotees perform *vrata* every Friday. The vow consists of fasting throughout the day, and making a simple and inexpensive offering of one-and-a-quarter *annas'* worth of *gur*, raw sugar, and *cana*, chick peas. As the *anna* ceased to be legal currency in 1957, this indicates that devotion to the goddess predates that year. (Such apparently minor details are important, for the history of devotion to the goddess is not easily discovered). Members have claimed that she was worshipped in what is now Pakistan before partition, and was brought into India by Hindu refugees. At Hardwar, when an enquiry was made about the age of the mandir there the reply came, 'It is very old'. (An inscription dates it to 1964!) Material gifts are not what the goddess wants. She desires only affection. The kinds of boons that are sought are things like washing machines ('It is no good asking Parvati or Ambaji for such things, they wouldn't know what I was asking for', was what one woman said.) A husband's promotion is another petition. When the request has been answered, a special meal must be prepared and fed to a group of eight boys. The film *Jai Santoshi Ma* describes Santoshi enduring and overcoming the cruelty of her three sisters-in-law, Parvati, Lakshmi and Brahmani (not part of the original myth). This is a trial that many brides have had to face. Eventually she wins through, and the three women, with their consorts, Shiva, Vishnu and Brahma, make obeisance to her. Perhaps part of her popularity lies in her successful anti-establishment rebellion.

Of a very different sort is the story of Roop Kanwar, who attracted international attention in September 1987 when she committed sati on the funeral pyre of the man she married nine months earlier. She was 18 years old. This was said to be the 40th act of its kind since independence. During the previous 100 years only four deaths by this method had been recorded. Why Roop Kanwar achieved more fame or notoriety than other women it is difficult to say. Her youth may have had something to do with it; for us it may be enough to note that defenders of her action, mostly but not exclusively men, came forward, and that people flocked to her village in Rajasthan to revere and

'Oppressed of Indian' turn on Gandhi

John Rettie in New Delhi

For for the first time since Mahatma Gandhi's assassination 46 years ago, his role as the revered and saintly 'father of the nation' is being challenged by leaders of the people he called Harijans or Children of God – the Untouchables.

Now calling themselves Dalits – the Oppressed – the leaders of the Bahujan Samaj Party (BSP), which was swept to power in the northern state of Uttar Pradesh last year, have denounced Gandhi as 'the biggest enemy of Dalits'.

The upper castes who dominate the media, the bureaucracy and the armed forces have reacted with outrage. But conscious of the new-found voting power of the Dalits, India's Brahmin prime minister, P. V. Narasimha Rao, went to Bombay yesterday to unveil a statue of their hero, the late Dr Babasaheb Ambedkar.

'Ambedkar carried out the daunting task of demanding rights for the lowest people, but the still more daunting task of implementing his ideals remains,' Mr Rao said. 'Only when caste discrimination stops and political parties stop getting mileage out of these divisions can we say his dream has come true.'

Mr Rao was not the only one to cash in on the 103rd anniversary of the birth of Ambedkar, the Untouchable who beat the system by going to the United States and Britain, becoming a brilliant lawyer and drafting India's constitution.

The leaders of many states and political parties attended public meetings, to be seen garlanding his statues or unveiling new ones.

The day emphasized what last November's elections had shown – that Dalits are at last demanding their own rights.

Gandhi, whose trader caste is a sub-group of Vaishya, third on the overall scale, grew up as an orthodox Hindu, although he opposed the denigration of Untouchables. For much of his life he believed in caste as an orderly system of doing one's duty and 'following one's father's calling' which could protect India from the greed and venality of the West. But as a result of his long dispute with Ambedkar, he gradually accepted that the rigid caste system was unjust, and he even advocated inter-caste marriage.

To modern Dalit leaders this change was too little and too late.

'Our society is still dominated by upper castes who are *chelas* (disciples) of Gandhi,' said Ms Mayawait, deputy leader of the BSP.

'These people treat Gandhi as their god. I don't.'

She accused him of 'gestures smacking of tokenism' when he helped Untouchables to clean latrines and shared meals with them – practices which caste Hindus regard as intolerably polluting.

'There is a new awakening among the Dalit masses who realize that they were misled all these years,' she declared. 'This awakening is bound to result in them becoming more assertive in demanding their rights. If they don't get them, they'll fight.'

The veteran socialist historian, sociologist and one-time MP Madhu Limaye said the BSP was making a serious blunder. The Dalits' situation was still bad, although, with reserved positions for them in parliament, the bureaucracy and the forces, 'it is much better than in my youth'.

'Mayawati and others are causing great harm to the Dalits because they'll lose the sympathy of millions of Dalits who respect Gandhi,' he said.

While Gandhi has certainly been idolised in the past, even by Dalits, the independent country he forged has done little for the overwhelming majority of Dalits.

The BSP is the engine of their impatience, but whether it can be the vehicle that will solve their problems, is another matter. Mr Limaye thinks not. He accused the BSP leader, Kanshi Ram, of dismissing questions about his economic policies by saying: 'Just give us power, the rest will follow.'

'A party with no policy for production and creating jobs has no future," Mr Limaye declared. "It may not last for more than three years.'

worship her. For many she had become a goddess, and the site of her death a place of pilgrimage. She certainly attained a position of respect and importance in the home of her in-laws, which she had not enjoyed during her brief life with them. We mention this incident to remind ourselves that the old traditions of Hinduism still have those who would justify them. Sati has been illegal for over a century and a half, and the vast majority of Hindus would agree with those Hindus who worked for its abolition in the 1820s, but some can still assemble a theological argument to justify it.

Caste oppression also has its supporters, who argue that the order established in the *Vedas* cannot be changed. They are not being oppressive; they assert that the so-called liberals are flouting dharma. The result of disregarding cosmic law (rta) must be catastrophic. Dalits, meanwhile, continue to struggle to win the rights which the Constitution gave them. They have formed their own political party, the Bahujan Samaj Party, and lost patience with other groups who, they claim, offer only words. Even Mahatma Gandhi has become an object of scorn, as the previous article illustrates.

The Dalit issue is one which will not be resolved quickly. The BSP may be the latest attempt to exert pressure on the government; it is unlikely to be the last. Perhaps another Gandhi or Ambedkar is needed. Individuals, not parties, seem to have most effect in India.

The Hindu Mahasabha

Hinduism has no central authority. The great assembly, the Hindu Mahasabha, which comprises many sectarian groups and ascetic orders, is its nearest equivalent. It will meet at certain times when large numbers of Hindus are together, for example at the *Kumbha mela*, a festival held at the confluence of the rivers Ganges and Jumna at Allahabad every 12 years. Some 15 million people have been known to take part in this five-day festival. Indeed, it is estimated that over 17 million took part in the January 1995 gathering. Almost by definition, the members of the Mahasabha are orthodox and conservative. They are unlikely to respond positively to the demands of women or dalits, or become involved in any other social and political issues. Were they to do so, and to agree, it is uncertain what practical impact they could have.

The future of Hinduism is at least as difficult to predict as that of any other religion. We will therefore not attempt it!

Hindu population in the world

1 Australia – Some Hindus
2 Bangladesh – Hindu minority
3 Bhutan – Hindu minority
4 Burma – Hindu minority
5 Canada – Some Hindus
6 Fiji – 40% Hindu
7 Germany – Some Hindus
8 Guyana – Some Hindus
9 India – 83% Hindu
10 Indonesia – 11% Hindu and Buddhist
11 Kuwait – 5% Hindu and Christian
12 Malaysia – Small Hindu minority
13 Mauritius – 51% Hindu (31% Christian; 17% Muslim)
14 Nepal – 90% Hindu
15 New Zealand – Some Hindus
16 Singapore – Hindu minority
17 South Africa – Hindu minority
18 Sri Lanka – Hindu minority
19 Surinam – 28% Hindu
20 Trinidad and Tobago – 25% Hindu
21 UK – Hindu minority 500,000
22 USA – Some Hindus

Some Hindus live in Kenya, Tanzania and Uganda.

global Hinduism

In this chapter you will learn:
- about Hinduism in a world context
- about Hinduism in relation to other faiths.

It is over 100 years since Swami Vivekananda drew the attention of liberal religious people to the Hindu tradition in 1893. Since then Hindus have migrated to many parts of the world, especially to countries linked to India through the British Empire and Commonwealth. The results of contacts with Hindus by members of other faith will constitute the bulk of this chapter. The diaspora locations of Hindus are given elsewhere (see end of Chapter 17).

Everything has not always been felicitous, certainly in the United Kingdom, and it is perhaps as well to begin with the downside. All too often there is a pretence that this does not exist.

Problems and prejudices

In his famous Minute Macauley, (1834) asserted that one shelf of European literature was worth more than the totality of the literature of the East. This sense of Western superiority has persisted even into the 21st century. It has often been accompanied by colour prejudice. There are patients who would wail long and in pain rather than see a doctor from the subcontinent. The same people, however, unless the trouble is abdominal, will happily go home to a curry, Britain's favourite dish!

Interfaith challenges

Missionary societies prospered on money collected to alleviate the spiritual plight of 'little brown babies overseas' whose eternal prospects were bleak unless they came to Jesus. This is still the belief of some if not many evangelical Christians who will not attend interfaith gatherings and are certainly opposed to anything that might be described as interfaith worship. Some will not enter a mandir. One girl who did on a school visit wrote: 'The people were lovely and friendly. We had a wonderful time, but it made me very sad to think that they were praying and singing so sincerely but God was not listening to them because they were not worshipping in Jesus' name'.

It is still possible to hear Hindus described as idol-worshippers and polytheists, though not long ago a former missionary wrote a book entitled, *What is Idolatry?* (Roger Hooker; British Council of Churches; 1986: ISBN 0-85169-122-6), in which he challenged many Christian assumptions and misunderstandings, laying to rest, for many evangelicals this particular notion. Still difficulties persist in using appropriate language; sometimes we are not happy to take on board new words when there already seem to be ones that adequately express our meaning. Thus we may find 'idol' being used by some, those who are more sensitive using 'statue', while the even more sophisticated may prefer 'icon'. There is a need to add 'murti' or 'rupa' to the language. Neither is included in the *Oxford English Dictionary* of 1998. The same must be said of 'mandir' for which 'temple' is frequently used and sometimes even 'Hindu church'. It must be admitted that sometimes Hindus are themselves the culprits, employing 'church' or 'idol' in an attempt to be helpful to British students, or visitors to their places of worship.

Caste

Other prejudices are related to caste. polytheism and women. The first of these is real enough, of course, but often it is described in lurid terms more to do with Victorian England than today and with no recognition or admission of discrimination being a global phenomenon. Birth, accent, skin colour and gender can affect the way a person is treated in Britain. This, of course, is not a defence of the caste system, just a plea that self-criticism might accompany the readiness to criticize others.

Polytheism

The second feature of Hinduism that might be described as common knowledge and a subject of Christian opposition is polytheism. That Hindus worship many gods is still a popularly held concept, not helped by the tendency of some activists in the interfaith movement to talk about the three monotheistic religions. When challenged they may rephrase their comments and refer to the three *great* monotheistic faiths, so justifying the exclusion of Sikhism, or the three *abrahamic* religions, thereby justifying their choice. (There seems to be no awareness that Islam regards Christianity as polytheistic, as do many Jews!) We have dealt with the Hindu views of God elsewhere, here we would simply remind readers that one of Hinduism's features is its willingness to express the unity and diversity of divinity pictorially whilst the three abrahamic faiths choose the verbal path, the 99 names of God, for example, or the words of the Christian hymn:

Immortal, invisible God, only wise,
In light inaccessible hid from our eyes,
Most blessèd, most glorious, the ancient of days,
Almighty victorious, thy great name we praise.

Equality for women

Finally, stories are still transmitted that describe the role of
women in Hindu society as mere chattels. Again there is little
readiness to accept that women in the West have only gone part
of the way to winning an equality with men that is expressed in
some passages of the New Testament. It is easily forgotten that
India had a women Prime Minister earlier than the United
Kingdom and that there is much evidence that women do not
receive equal pay for equal work in either country. Should the
reader argue that we are leaving religion behind and making
social comparisons, a Hindu might point to the Roman Catholic
attitude to the ordination of women into the priesthood and the
continued opposition of some Anglicans. They might argue that
notions of ritual impurity apply in both faiths when it comes to
the status of women.

Violence

A further concern of Christians is the treatment that some
Indian members of the faith have received recently. Most
influential was the murder, in 1999, of an Australian missionary,
the Reverend Graham Staines, who had worked among leprosy
sufferers for 20 years. He and his two sons were burnt to death
while sleeping in their jeep. They had been attending an
evangelical rally. Mr. Staines's widow decided to remain in
India, continuing their work. A year later, in May 2000, a large
number of youths entered a girls' hostel run by Christian
missionaries in a village in Nashik district. Property was
damaged but the girls, though scared, were physically
unharmed. Blame for these and other disturbances aimed at
Christians, has been focused on the Vishnu Hindu Parishad
movement, and the Rashtriya Sevak Sangh. Both of these
organizations have links with the governing BJP party.

Hindutva

At this point we must introduce the concept of Hindutva. It means 'Hindu-ness' and was coined by V. D. Savarkar in 1923. He was opposed to Gandhian ideas of harmonious co-existence between Hindus and Muslims and favoured an exclusive Hinduism. India was the land of the Hindus and foreign religions, Christianity and Islam, if they were to remain in India must recognize the place of the dominant religion and desist from all missionary activities. Existing Indian Christians and Muslims might practice their religion, but they must not attempt to spread it. While it is possible to trace Hinduism back through the Arya Samaj to the Aryans the supporters of Hindutva are unwilling to accept the idea of an Aryan invasion of India. The Aryans were indigenous to the land. The teaching that there are many paths to the one goal of moksha favoured by Ramakrishna, was at best secondary to the view that India is the Holy Land and the religion of Hinduism the one from which all others emanated. Hindu nationalism is founded on Hindutva theology. The Rashtriya Sevak Sangh was founded two years later, in 1925, by K. B. Hedgewar, originally as a right wing, non-political national cultural revival movement.

In 1999 Hindu hostility to Christians was further aroused by the actions of Southern Baptist Christians in the USA. They issued a pamphlet that described India as '900 million people lost in the darkness of Hinduism'. The Hindus of Bombay (Mumbai), were, 'slaves bound by fear and tradition to false gods and goddesses'. Calcutta was under the rule of Satan 'through Kali and other gods and goddesses of Hinduism'. This was published to coincide with the festival of Diwali in 1999. A week later the Pope vistited India and was well received. Large crowds turned out to welcome him, witnesses to a Hinduism that is accepting and respectful of all forms of spirituality. Since 2000 there has been little Hindu-Christian tension but there is an awareness of the need to work hard to recreate the earlier atmosphere of tolerance. Christians and Muslims can still be made to feel that they are members of foreign religions and Hindus may encounter aggressive evangelism.

The positive side

There is an upside. Some aspects may seem trivial but in a situation where the Western world continues to be convinced of its superiority and that it has nothing to learn from Hinduism, almost anything may be welcomed. For example, in the major towns and cities of Britain Hindu restaurants are beginning to flourish, especially among the nation's growing vegetarian population, though most Britons may still be unaware that Indian restaurants are, for the most part, Muslim owned. School meals usually include vegetarian dishes. Government publications are increasingly to be found in Indian languages. The term 'host community' is employed less and less as Hindus and others are acknowledged to be citizens, not guests who will one day go home! Religious Education, a compulsory subject in the schools of England and Wales, is required to include Hinduism in syllabuses intended to introduce pupils to the six major faiths found in Britain today. There is an Interfaith Network, founded in 1987, which includes over 80 groups in its membership, many of which are Hindu. In 1993 it published the first Directory of Faith Organizations with essays on all of them and the address and other details of places of worship. The third edition appeared in 2001. While a clergyman may attract headlines in the press by refusing permission for the church hall to be used for yoga classes, he will now be an exception rather than the rule. Yoga, including meditation, is a popular exercise on the curriculum of many institutions. The path taken by Bede Griffith years ago is now congenial to many seekers after spirituality. Meanwhile those who cannot make his journey spiritually or geographically experience the Hinduism exemplified by Vivekananda and Gandhi, one concerned with universal values, social justice and human rights, respect for all, ecology – where else might one come across the book for younger children entitled *The Earth our mother?* This global Hinduism is adding its insights to those of members of other faith or none that take these issues seriously.

Internationally, 'Hinduism' is to be found on the Internet, (see pages 223–4). Oxford University, UK, established a Chair in Sanskrit in 1832 and now Hinduism may be studied at first degree level in many universities worldwide. Which has been the greater influence, the so-called 'hippie' interest in Indian spirituality in the 1960s or the presence of a Hindu diaspora is difficult to judge. It is, however, significant that the increasing liberalism of Western societies during the last half century, coinciding with the migration of Hindus, Sikhs, Jains and Muslims, has led to more interfaith activity, of the kind mentioned above, than there was in earlier times, even though members of these faiths have lived in many large cities for over a century. Christians, it has to be said, have been the initiators and promoters of religious dialogue, for several reasons. One is their majority status; a second is that immigrants, with a few exceptions, are primarily concerned with such necessities as setting up their homes and finding employment. Thirdly, it has to be admitted that dialogue is a minority activity. Many Hindus, as also Sikhs and Muslims, have been surprised when the society that sent missionaries to evangelize them, is now eager to visit their places of worship and learn about their beliefs and practices! Jews, who have been members of the British community and have lived in Britain since their readmission by Oliver Cromwell in 1655, are even more amazed that people who ignored them or caricatured them, (Fagin comes readily to mind), now have many Christian members in the Council of Christians and Jews.

Dialogue is still a minority interest. The young sometimes feel no need for it. They have an open attitude. Those who are involved in matters spiritual and religious may take a 'live and let live' attitude. Evangelicals may seek the conversion of other faith members to Christianity. Generally speaking, the forms of dialogue that exist are Christian and all other faiths, or Christian, Jew and Muslim, the three abrahamic traditions. Only in completely inter-religious meetings do faiths other than Christian have much conversation with Hindus.

The death of George Harrison, late in 2001, resulted in a revival of interest in a Hindu lifestyle, and once again his bhakti composition, 'My sweet Lord' found its way into the charts of popular music. For about 20 years Hindu bhajans have been performed at the BBC Promenade Concerts. What was once a minority interest of music lovers familiar with compositions by Delius and Holst have entered the music repertoires of the young.

Diaspora Hinduism is itself being affected by the major community in which it lives. Mandirs have been established which serve as community centres. In India this is unnecessary. Services are congregational, though many individuals and families come for puja daily. (In Leicester, UK, the William Carey Memorial Baptist Church is now one of that city's 50 mandirs!). Often these reflect the regional representations to be found in the locality but they combine to celebrate major festivals and to take part in interfaith activities. Most Hindus are content to have their children taught in mainstream schools; there is little desire for the creation of Hindu faith schools.

Concerns about mixed marriages are to be found in every community, but less so among Hindus than Jews or Muslims.

Finally, almost unknowingly, elements of Hinduism are creeping into religious life in general. It is becoming customary, in prayers for peace to find used the famous Hindu prayers,

> From the unreal lead us to the real
> From darkness lead us to the light
> From death lead us to immortality.
> Peace. Peace. Peace.
>
> (*Brihad Aranyaka Upanishad*: 1:3:28)

taking it further

Further reading

The Indian Way   John M. Koller, Macmillan, 1982.
A study of philosophy.
Hinduism   David R. Kinsley, Prentice Hall, New Jersey, 1982.
Hindu Children in Britain   Robert Jackson and Eleanor
Nesbitt, Trentham Books, 1993. An examination of their
religious nurturing and development.
My Sweet Lord (The Haré Krishna Movement)   Kim Knott,
Aquarian Press, 1986.
Gods, Demons and Others   R. K. Narayan, Heinemann,
1964. Narayan is one of the world's greatest short story
writers. Most of them, and his novels, give humorous and
authentic insights into the Hindu way of life.
Seasons of Splendour   Madhur Jaffrey, Pavilion Books, 1985,
and Penguin paperback (less well illustrated). The festivals
and their foods fascinatingly told.
Gandhi: An autobiography   Jonathan Cape, 1949, with many
reprints. Also published as *Gandhi: my experiments with truth*.
We Are Hindus   Hemant Kanitkar, St Andrew's Press, 1987.
The Indestructible Soul   Geoffrey Parrinder, Allen and
Unwin, 1973.
The Hindu Scriptures   Hemant Kanitkar, Heinemann, 1994.
A beautifully illustrated survey of the variety of Hindu
sacred texts.
Hindu Festivals and Sacraments   Hemant Kanitkar, privately
published. Available from HSK Bookshop, 46–48
Loughborough Road, Leicester LE4 5LD
Religions in the UK, A Multifaith Directory   University of
Derby, 1993. Lists most mandirs and Hindu organizations
(and the same for other groups). Invaluable. Every library
should have one. Persuade yours!

Hinduism in Leeds Kim Knott, Leeds University. Detailed and advanced but a good next step for readers interested to learn about a particular community so that they can then begin exploring their own.

Meeting Hindusim W. Owen Cole, Longman, Harlow, 1987.

Skills in Religious Studies (3 vols.) Fageant, J. & Mercier, S. C., Heinemann, Oxford, 1990. 3 vols.

Approaches to Hinduism Jackson, R. & Killingley, D., John Murray, London, 1988.

Upanayana Ritual and Hindu Identity in Essex, Kanitkar, H. A., in Rohit Barot, ed., *Religion and Ethnicity: Minorities and Social Change in the Metropolis*, Kok Pharos Pub. House, Kampen, 1993 (pp. 110–22).

Hinduism Kanitkar, V. P. (Hemant), Stanley Thornes, Cheltenham, 1989 (reprinted 1993, 1994).

Hinduism Penny, S., Heinemann, Oxford, 1988.

An Introduction to Hinduism Gavin Flood, Cambridge University Press, 1996. ISBN – 0521 438780

Websites

http://www.hindunet.org/ *The Hindu Universe – Hindu Resource Center.* Largest Hindu and Hinduism site on the net. Contains comprehensive introduction to Hindu dharma, complete text of 85 books, several scriptures, listing of Hindu temples around the world, newsgroup archives, information on Hindu culture, etc.

http://www.hinduism-today.com/ *Hinduism Today* magazine, affirming Sanatana Dharma and recording the modern history of a billion-strong global religion in renaissance.

http://www.punjabi.net/Faith/Hinduism Punjabi virtual community.

http://www.amesefc.org/hindu.html Hinduism website.

http://ccat.sas.upenn.edu/~jfuller/rels163.html Hinduism syllabus – Introduction to Hinduism at the University of Pennsylvania.

http://www.hindu.org/ The Directory of Hindu Resources Online – a massive Hindu resources website dedicated to Hindu solidarity, culture and the dissemination of the vast and timeless knowledge of Sanatana Dharma to all the people of the world.

glossary

Agni The Lord of Fire.

akara Shape or form.

Antarala The space between the assembly hall and the inner shrine in a temple.

Ardha-Mandap A porch at the front of a temple.

artha One of the four aims of life.

Arya Noble.

asceticism The practice of rigorous self-discipline, fasting, meditation and prayer.

Ashrama A stage in life, e.g. student stage, householder stage, etc.

Atharva-Veda The fourth Veda.

Atman The animating energy in any living creature, usually referred to as the Soul.

Aum The sacred syllable (also spelt Om) – it is believed to contain the sound of all Reality.

Avatar An incarnation of God. (The avatars of Vishnu are more widely worshipped than those of Shiva.)

Bhagavad-Gita An important and popular Hindu religious book.

brahmacharya The student stage in life.

Brahman The Supreme Spirit in Hinduism.

brahmanas Religious texts composed for the guidance of priests in the performance of sacrifices.

Brahma The Creator aspect of Brahman in the Hindu Trimurti.

Brahma-Sutras Holy books in concise verse containing Hindu philosophy.

Brahmin A member of the first group in the social divisions called varna.

caste An occupational group within the larger varna divisions.

darshan Viewing an image in a temple.

deity   A name for a God or a Goddess.

deva   A Sanskrit word for God.

devata   A minor deity.

devi   A Sanskrit word for Goddess.

dharma   Religious or moral duty of a Hindu based on his/her age, education, occupation and social position.

Dharma-Shastra   A book containing the customary law relating to social conduct.

Dhoti   A cotton garment, five metres long and one metre wide, worn to cover the lower part of the body.

Ganga   Indian name for the river Ganges.

Garbha-Griha   The innermost room in a Hindu temple where the image of a deity is installed, the holiest part of a temple.

Gayatri   A hymn from the Rig-Veda praising the Sun God.

Gopuram   The tallest structure above the main gateway in a south Indian temple.

Grihastha   A householder; the second stage in life.

havan   A sacrifice where offerings are made to the sacred fire.

Indus   A holy river whose Hindu name is *Sindhu*.

ishta-Devata   A personal deity worshipped by a Hindu (see *Ishwara*).

Ishwara   A personal deity worshipped by a Hindu.

jati   Indian word for caste, signifying one's social position, which is determined by occupation.

jnana   Philosophical knowledge of God, man and man's position in the world.

kama   Enjoyment of the good things in life; the third aim in life.

karma   The total effect of one's actions. (The word also means action.)

Kshatriya   A member of the second group in the varna division.

kum-kum   Red powder used in a puja; it is also used as a tilak on the forehead.

Mandala   A religious diagram used in a special puja or meditation.

Mandap   The assembly hall in a temple.

mangala sootra   The marriage necklace of a Hindu woman.

mantra   A sacred formula, always in Sanskrit.

moksha   Liberation of the soul from successive births and deaths.

Murti   An image of a deity in a temple.

namaskar   Indian word for greeting.

Om   The sacred syllable (see Aum).

Pinda   A ball of cooked rice offered to the spirits of departed ancestors at the time of shraddha.

prasad A blessed offering distributed among the worshippers at the end of a puja.

puja A common form of Hindu worship.

Puranas Ancient Hindu myths and legends.

Rig-Veda the first of the four ancient holy books.

sacred thread A loop of three or five strands of strong cotton thread used in the initiation ceremony.

Sama-Veda The third *Veda*, an ancient holy book.

samsara The cycle of successive births, deaths and rebirths.

Samskara A life-cycle ritual performed at important stages during a person's life, to purify the body and the spirit.

sanatana-dharma The ancient or eternal way of life.

sannyasi A person who gives up his name, family ties and most of his possessions, and devotes his life to meditation in order to attain liberation (moksha).

Sanskrit An ancient language of India.

satya Truth.

satyagraha 'The insistence upon truth', a method of non-co-operation used by Mahatma Gandhi.

Shikhara The tallest structure above the image in a north Indian temple.

shraddha The annual rites of offering pinda to the spirits of the deceased ancestors. (The first 'a' is sounded as 'a' in car.)

Shruti A holy book believed to have been 'revealed' by God to wise men, and therefore 'heard' by them.

Shudra An artisan, a member of the fourth group in the varna division.

Smriti A holy book, composed by wise men from 'remembered tradition'.

Upanishad A book of Hindu philosophy.

Vaishya A member of the third group in the varna division.

Vanaprastha The retirement stage in life.

varna A social category (The four varnas are Brahmin, Kshatriya, Vaishya and Shudra.).

Vedanta A system of philosophy composed at the end of the vedic period.

Vimana The inner sanctuary in a temple (see Garbha-Griha).

Yajur-Veda The second *Veda*; an ancient holy book of the Aryans concerned with the performance of sacrifice.

Yama The Spirit of Death.

Yamuna A holy river in north India, also spelt Jumna.

yatra A pilgrimage; the word also means a procession.

yoga A system of philosophy combining physical exercises and meditation.

index